Demystifying
SYNDROMES II

CLINICAL AND EDUCATIONAL
IMPLICATIONS OF COMMON
SYNDROMES ASSOCIATED WITH
PERSONS WITH INTELLECTUAL
DISABILITIES

Editors
Shelley L. Watson
Dorothy M. Griffiths

Copyright © 2016 NADD Press

NADD An association for persons with developmental disabilities and mental health needs.

NATIONAL ASSOCIATION FOR THE DUALLY DIAGNOSED

132 Fair Street
Kingston, New York 12401

All rights reserved

No part of this book may be reproduced, stored in a retrieval system or transmitted in any form by means of electronic, mechanical, photocopy, recording or otherwise, without written permission of NADD, 132 Fair Street, Kingston, New York, 12401

LCCN: 2015961055

ISBN: 978-1-57256-140-3

Printed in the United States of America

PREFACE

This book represents a revision of a 2004 edition called *Demystifying Syndromes*. *Demystifying Syndromes II* was developed to be a practical summary of some of the common syndromes related to developmental disability. The book was designed for:

i. current professionals working in the field;
ii. community college or university students who are studying developmental disabilities; and
iii. parents, family members, and/or other interested persons who wish to learn more about this area.

The editors have selected some common and some lesser known syndromes that are associated with persons with developmental disabilities and coexisting mental or behavioral challenges, specifically fragile X syndrome, Down syndrome, Williams syndrome, Smith-Magenis syndrome, autism spectrum disorder, 22q deletion syndrome, Smith-Lemli-Opitz syndrome, and Angelman syndrome. However new to this edition is a chapter that addresses the importance of understanding syndromes for families and various professionals. Most of the syndromes have known genetic markers for the development of the syndrome. The objective was to demonstrate how and why support and treatment can be individualized by recognizing the differential realities of persons, with various syndromes, who are all labeled as having a developmental disability.

The book was intended to provide a holistic understanding of the biopsychosocial implications of the various syndromes for the lives of persons with developmental disabilities. So often the public, and particularly families seeking information, rely on the internet as their sole source of information. Although many internet sites are accurate and informative, others are not. This book was, therefore, written by individuals who work with persons with the syndromes on a daily basis and whose knowledge is grounded in both research and practice.

The chapters in the book will provide the reader with an informative and accurate description of each disability, written by individuals with an integrated understanding of how the physical, psychiatric, or biochemical influences may interact with the psychological factors (learning approaches, communication, skills) of the individual, and with the social-environmental aspects (supports, adaptations, and vulnerabilities). The authors have not merely focused on the challenges presented by the syndrome but the strengths and resiliency that each present; as Chapter 1 highlights an advantage of diagnosis is identifying the strengths or advantages of the specific syndrome. Moreover, as much as we have discussed the mental health needs related to the various syndromes, we have attempted to also discuss issues of mental wellness, as well as proactive and preventative intervention strategies. Simple, non-technical language was used as much as possible; however, given the medical complexity of many of the conditions, the appropriate medical terms have also been used so that the reader is able to explore these areas further. In some cases, such as chapter 1, a glossary of terms has been included.

Content of Each Chapter

The chapters have been written by noted professionals working in the field of developmental disability. Although each chapter was written by a different author or group of authors, there was a common outline for each chapter. All the authors were asked to address the syndrome in terms of how it affects the learning and functioning of the person and what can be done to enhance the functioning and development of the person. Resources have been provided to assist the reader to explore the syndromes further.

This book was not designed to be everything one needs to know about persons with a specific syndrome or the genetics of developmental disabilities. The book was developed as a practical guide for current professionals in the field, students in college or university studying developmental disabilities, and parents, family members or other caregivers who wish to learn more about syndromes.

Regardless of the incredible skill that different disciplines bring to the field of developmental disability, this field is rapidly changing and many faceted. As such it is hoped that the book will provide a readable update on some of the research and implications of an area of research and understanding that is literally being uncovered every day. This quote from Dykens, Hodapp, and Finucane (2000) puts some perspective on this newest shift:

> No one can simultaneously know everything about all aspects of behavior and about all aspects of what is called "the new genetics".... Both personal and disciplinary limits to knowledge suggest caution, even humility. (p. 21)

Chapter 1 provides an introduction to the topic of syndromes and the importance of understanding the influence of syndromes on the biomedical, psychological, and social experience of the individual.

Chapters 2-9 provide in-depth descriptions of eight syndromes associated with developmental disabilities and behavioral/emotional challenges. These are fragile X syndrome (Chapter 2), Down syndrome (Chapter 3), Williams syndrome (Chapter 4), Smith-Magenis syndrome (Chapter 5), autism spectrum disorders (Chapter 6), 22 Q deletion syndrome (Chapter 7), Angelman syndrome (Chapter 8), and Smith-Lemli-Opitz syndrome (Chapter 9).

Chapter 10 has been added in this edition to provide the reader with the perspectives of family and various professionals as to why syndrome identification is important and how it changed their perspective and interactions/interventions based on this knowledge. This concluding chapter features the words of family members, speaking to why syndromic identification was important for their family.

The editors are indebted to the authors who have taken time from their busy clinical practices to share their ideas, insights and research on this important topic.

Editors Shelley L. Watson & Dorothy M. Griffiths

Reference

Dykens, E. M., Hodapp, R. M., & Finucane, B. M. (2000). *Genetics and intellectual disability syndromes: A new look at behavior and interventions.* Baltimore, MD: Paul H. Brookes.

TABLE OF CONTENTS

CHAPTER 1
Demystifying Syndromes Associated with Developmental Disabilities ...1
Shelley L. Watson, Dorothy M. Griffiths, & Anne S. Bassett

CHAPTER 2
Fragile X Syndrome 37
Marcia Braden & Brenda Finucane

CHAPTER 3
Down Syndrome 61
Robert Pary

CHAPTER 4
Williams Syndrome 79
Brenda Finucane

CHAPTER 5
Smith-Magenis Syndrome.. 95
Elliott W. Simon, Barbara Haas-Givler, & Mary Schuster

CHAPTER 6
Autism Spectrum Disorder 115
Sandra Fisman

CHAPTER 7
22 Q Deletion Syndrome 159
Chelsea Lowther, Erik Boot, Kerry Boyd, & Anne S. Bassett

CHAPTER 8
Angelman Syndrome..179
Jane Summers

CHAPTER 9
Smith-Lemli-Opitz Syndrome 209
Malgorzata J. M. Nowaczyk & Elaine Tierney

CHAPTER 10
When Syndromes Demystify: Family and Professional Perspectives 227
Kerry Boyd, Deborah Richards, Courtney Bishop & Shelley L. Watson

APPENDIX 237

AUTHORS 245

CHAPTER 1

Demystifying Syndromes Associated with Developmental Disabilities

Shelley L. Watson, Dorothy M. Griffiths, & Anne S. Bassett

Why does the man with moderate developmental disability who lives in Welland, Ontario, Canada look, act, and talk almost identically to a man in Denver, Colorado, USA?

Why is it when clinicians hear about certain physical features or behavior patterns in persons with developmental disabilities, they start to make associations and begin to ask questions about other features and behaviors that no one has yet disclosed?

Why does the aging mother of a middle-aged woman with developmental disabilities (and her clinicians) find renewed hope in hearing for the first time about a genetic cause for her daughter's lifetime of medical and psychiatric disorders?

This chapter explores some of the common syndromes associated with developmental disabilities and their importance for better understanding, supporting, and caring for individuals with complex needs. The chapter will outline the main reasons to identify syndromes and summarize the genetic testing that is now the standard of care. Using case examples, we will demonstrate the value of syndromic evaluation and advances in genetic diagnosis that promise to help individuals, caregivers, and clinicians alike.

Introduction

Two young boys were overheard talking at the primary school one day. They were pointing and talking loudly about three boys with exceptionalities. The teacher lingered, curious to know if they were in some way planning to tease or bully these young boys with exceptionalities. (To her delight, she found this was her mistaken bias). Instead what the boys were saying was even more amazing to her. They were arguing as to whether the three boys were brothers. The one boy was absolutely sure they were not because they all had different last names, but the other boy was convinced they were brothers because they looked and acted so much alike. By the end they decided they must be cousins, because sometimes cousins look alike. Actually the boys were unrelated at all except through a chromosomal variation that creates Down syndrome.

Down syndrome is the one syndrome that most people in the general population can identify. Because it is the most common chromosomal syndrome and usually has a readily recognizable pattern of physical features, the general population has become experienced in identifying individuals who have Down syndrome. In the mind of the general public, persons with Down syndrome are, for the most part, the typical images of persons with developmental disability. We see people with Down syndrome as actors on television, models in magazines, and visually portrayed in publicity photos for agencies who serve persons with special needs. See Table 1 for a description of some of the characteristics common to persons with Down syndrome.

Although Down syndrome is a common syndrome and many of the associated characteristics of a medical, cognitive or behavioral nature are known to most clinicians and many of the general public, there are several other syndromes that affect developmental functioning that are perhaps not as common or noticeably visible. The general population may not be able to identify the individuals with some of the syndromes as persons with developmental disabilities by sight, but they may know there is something unique about the person. Clinicians, too, unless they have experienced working with many individuals with a particular syndrome, may have difficulty identifying what might be the cause of this person's special cluster of characteristics.

How Syndromes Develop

There is no single gene responsible for intellectual or developmental disability. In fact, most individuals with developmental disability do not have a clinically recognizable syndrome like Down syndrome. The causes are thought to involve one or more of the following: genetic, prenatal, perinatal, and/or postnatal influences. There is some evidence that specific genes and certain environmental factors (e.g., maternal infection like rubella alone or together with genetic factors) cause developmental disability. Since the first edition of this book, published in 2004, there have been remarkable advances in our understanding of genetics that are particularly relevant both to our understanding of specific syndromes and of developmental disability in general.

Genes affect brain development in many ways (how the brain is formed in the fetus and in the early years of life, production of brain chemicals and regulatory processes that enable the brain's nerve cells to function). Genes—the factors that largely

Table 1:
Down Syndrome

Incidence: 1 out of every 700-1,000 live births
Etiology: Extra copy of chromosome 21
How to test: Amniocentesis, chromosome studies

Physical Characteristics

Characteristic facial appearance:
- Small head with flat-looking face
- Small ears and mouth Protruding tongue
- Upward slant to eyes, with epicanthal folds at inner corners
- Broad neck

Short stature Hypotonia

Increased mobility of joints

Small or undeveloped middle bone of the 5th finger

Single crease across center of palm

Brushfield spots (white spots in iris)

Lack of Moro reflex

Behavioral Characteristics

Often amiable personality, a facility for imitation

Obstinacy, keen sense of the ridiculous, and excellent memory

Alzheimer's disease

14-40% of people with Down syndrome show behavioral symptoms of Alzheimer's, usually after age 45

Depression (please see Chapter 3 for discussion)

Common Medical Vulnerabilities

Congenital heart defects- 50%

Hearing loss (ear infections)- 66-89%

Ophthalmic conditions (strabismus)- 60%

Gastrointestinal- 5%

Hypothyroidism- 50-90%

Dental (crowding, periodontitis)- 60-100%

Orthopedic (atlantoaxial subluxation)- 15%

Obesity- 50-60%

Skin conditions (dry skin, eczema)- 50%

Seizure disorder- 6-13%

Risk of seizures increases with age Males are generally sterile

Fertility rate in females is low

Women with Down syndrome may be at an increased risk for post- menopausal health disorders, such as breast cancer, depression, and osteoporosis

Alzheimer's disease

After age 30, nearly all people with Down syndrome show the plaques and tangles characteristic of Alzheimer neuropathology, although there is not a direct correlation between plaques and tangles and the severity of Alzheimer's

Preventative strategies

Regular cardiac, hearing, vision, and thyroid exams

Neck radiography after 3 years Preventative dental care Weight management

Cognitive Implications

Strengths

Clear developmental trajectory

Visual memory strengths

Sequential processing intact

Can learn sequential tasks well

Weaknesses

Lower IQ scores as develop across childhood/ adolescence

Developmental rate slows throughout childhood

Average IQ is 55

Strategies

Manual signs easier to acquire-bridge to verbal language

Acquisition of communication as early as possible

Break tasks into small steps (traditional tasks analysis works well)

Inclusive setting (sociability)

determine physical and behavioral traits—are organized on chromosomes in the human genome. Chromosomes contain DNA, which is a "blueprint for how the body develops and functions from conception to death" (Dykens, Hodapp, & Finucane, 2000, p. 28). There are 22 pairs of chromosomes, numbered 1 to 22, called autosomes, and 1 pair of sex chromosomes (XX for female, XY for male). Across these 23 pairs of chromosomes that make up the human genome, there are about 21,000 genes that code for proteins. Proteins form the actual structure of the cells that make up our bodies and make them work throughout life. Genes are like the "recipe" or blueprint for proteins. Other parts of the DNA in the genome are involved in regulating genes and other functions we are just beginning to understand.

Since the 1950's we have known that large chromosomal structural changes are associated with developmental delay. These large structural changes can be seen under the microscope, such as the extra chromosome 21 that causes Down syndrome. Chromosomal microarray testing now allows us to detect much smaller structural genetic changes, called copy number variations (CNVs). Several of these CNVs are clinically important causes of developmental delay (Miller et al., 2010).

If we consider the human genome as a book (like the "Book of Life"), then the DNA coding sequence can be considered to be the letters that form words. There are only four letters (nucleotides) in the DNA code. The arrangement of these letters in the genes is the code or the recipe for the proteins that are in all of the cells in our body. This recipe is important from conception, all through development and throughout life. Changes in the recipe can take the form of sequence changes (and even just one letter of the code can make a difference).

Another kind of change is in the structure of the DNA that makes up the normal 23 pairs of chromosomes. These changes in DNA structure are like whole paragraphs, or even chapters, of the DNA code that can be missing or can be duplicated (i.e., have extra copies). DNA changes, in sequence (individual letters) or in structure (paragraphs), can involve genes or other DNA regions where there are no genes. Any of these genetic changes can either be inherited from a parent or can be a new change (i.e., neither parent has the genetic change). New (spontaneous or "*de novo*") changes can occur when either the egg or the sperm is being made (i.e., before the egg and sperm come together at conception). New genetic changes can also occur after conception (e.g., as for many forms of cancer).

Genetic changes in DNA can have diverse expressions or associated features in different people, even between people who are related to each other in the same family. Expression can be physical or involve brain functions and thus be observable as cognitive, emotional, and/or behavioral changes. Changes to the brain or other bodily organs can be observable at birth or can arise later in life. Therefore, it is likely that even when there is a major genetic change, other factors can modify expression. Furthermore, we now have a better understanding of the multiple genetic changes that are associated with developmental delay. So, the same genetic change can have several different outcomes, and the same outcome (observable condition) can have many different genetic causes. This variation is normal in nature. Research into developmental disabilities is leading the way to understanding this diversity; understanding genetic syndromes is a key first step mirroring the progress in human genetics.

Syndromes can develop in many ways:

- *Cytogenetic syndromes* are the result of a difference in the number or structure of the chromosomes that typically are visible under the microscope with a standard karyotype (e.g., Down syndrome, Klinefelter syndrome, Turner syndrome, Cri-du-chat (5p-) syndrome); these usually disrupt many genes and result in a developmental disability.

- *Genomic disorders* (e.g., 22q11.2 deletion syndrome, Smith-Magenis syndrome, Williams syndrome, Prader-Willi syndrome, Angelman syndrome, and more recently identified conditions like 15q13.3 deletion syndrome) are usually associated with structural changes in the chromosomes that are too small to be seen under the microscope. These structural changes, often disrupting several genes, can now be readily identified through standard, high resolution techniques (e.g., genome-wide chromosomal microarray) available at most clinical laboratories.

- A change in the DNA sequence for a single gene causes other genetic conditions that are associated with developmental disability (e.g., Smith-Lemli-Opitz syndrome, PKU, Fragile X). Some genetic disorders result from a new mutation (nonfamilial), while others are familial and inherited (e.g., Fragile X syndrome), although expression is often variable within a family. In either case, genetic testing targeted to the individual condition is available to confirm the diagnosis.

- Examples of typical patterns of inheritance or transmission of a genetic change can include:

    1. *Autosomal dominant inheritance* where the genetic change has, on average, a 50% chance of being passed from one generation to another and may, therefore, be observed across several generations, though not always with the same expression;

    2. *Autosomal recessive inheritance* where the genetic change has a 25% chance of being observed in offspring, and the disease condition is usually only observed within a single generation because it depends on a genetic change being present in the same gene in both parents; and

    3. *X-linked recessive inheritance* where the genetic change is present on the X chromosome and males have a 50% chance of inheriting the affected X chromosome from their mother; usually only males in a family appear affected because they have only one X chromosome, whereas females have a compensating X chromosome.

- Most disorders, even those previously considered "single gene" disorders, are the result of some combination of genetic predisposition and other (sometimes environmental, e.g., diet in PKU) factors. This is sometimes called a "multifactorial" pattern, which means that one will often not observe disorders clustering in families in a predictable manner, as previously thought to be the case for simple single-gene disorders.

- Advances in genetic techniques such as genome-wide chromosomal microarray have revolutionized genetic diagnosis for individuals with developmental disabilities, such that these have now become the standard first-line recommended test for anyone with an intellectual or developmental disability (Miller et al., 2010). For those with a negative (normal) karyotype result, microarray can provide an answer in about one of five persons with developmental disabilities.

- Next generation sequencing, using even higher resolution methods, will further revolutionize clinical genetic diagnosis for individuals with an intellectual or developmental disability. This approach to genetic testing will include many with recognizable patterns of inheritance and those with new genetic changes.

- Many developmental conditions, previously thought to be completely separate from developmental disability, including autism spectrum disorder, epilepsy, schizophrenia, and major congenital anomalies, are now known to share many of the same genetic causes (Bassett, Scherer, & Brzustowicz, 2010).

Table 2 outlines tests that are most typically used to identify genetic syndromes.

Advances in Genetic Diagnosis

People who work with individuals with developmental disabilities are often amazed at the complex medical, psychological, social, and behavioral features present. In recent decades there has been an ever-increasing interest in syndrome identification and genetic diagnosis. As part of ongoing advances spurred by the Human Genome Project, scientists have developed technologies that are helping to identify what genetic changes are responsible for various aspects of disturbances of human development and human diseases. As part of these efforts, there has been improved understanding of clinically recognizable human syndromes. In addition, these advanced techniques have enabled the recognition of syndromes (e.g., recurrent genomic disorders that share the same genetic change). Genomic disorders associated with copy number changes (deletions or duplications), although individually rare, collectively account for a significant minority of individuals with intellectual disabilities. They are recurrent in unrelated families due to the increased likelihood of new genetic changes arising related to the presence of segmental duplications (highly similar DNA sequences) in the human genome that flank the regions that are thus more prone to deletion or duplication (Bassett et al., 2010). See Table 3 for a list of the most common microdeletion and microduplication syndromes associated with developmental disability. Individuals with developmental delays associated with dysmorphic features, major congenital anomalies, or epilepsy may be particularly likely to have such pathogenic copy number variants and these may be new or inherited genetic changes (Bassett et al., 2010; Lowther et al., 2015; Mulle et al., 2014). Resources for these recurrent genomic disorders are updated regularly on well-established websites, including Genetics Home Reference (www.ghr.nlm.nih.gov) and Gene Reviews (www.ncbi.nlm.nih.gov/books/NBK116).

Table 2:
Types of clinical tests commonly used to diagnose syndromes

Laboratory diagnostics	How is it done?	Examples of syndromes that can be identified
Genome-wide microarray	Standard blood, amniotic fluid, or other tissue sample sent to a clinical lab for genome-wide analysis of changes in DNA copy number (structural changes)	22q11.2 deletion syndrome, Williams syndrome, Smith-Magenis syndrome, Prader-Willi syndrome, Angelman syndrome, Wolf-Hirschhorn syndrome, 15q13.3 microdeletion syndrome, in addition to those identifiable by *karyotype such as Down, Klinefelter, Turner, XXX syndromes, and many others, all would be identifiable with this one test.
DNA mutation and/or methylation analysis	Standard blood, amniotic fluid, or other tissue sample sent to a clinical lab for targeted analysis to detect known genetic changes in DNA sequence or in DNA methylation pattern associated with a specified condition	Fragile X syndrome, Smith-Lemli-Opitz syndrome, PKU, Rett syndrome; certain forms of Angelman and Prader-Willi syndromes require methylation and/or mutation analysis

*Although standard karyotype would still be adequate for Down syndrome, Klinefelter syndrome, Turner Syndrome, and Cri-du-chat (5p-) syndrome, and remains essential to detect balanced translocations, the standard of care now for genetic diagnosis in intellectual and developmental disabilities is genome-wide microarray (Miller et al., 2010). Targeted methods such as FISH (fluorescence in situ hybridization), available since the early to mid 1990s, require a clinical index of suspicion to specify the chromosomal probe location to be used (e.g., TUPLE1 for 22q11.2 deletion syndrome). FISH will miss atypical deletions not overlapped by the specific probe used, and is often inadequate for detecting pathogenic duplications. Genome-wide microarray will detect typical and atypical pathogenic copy number losses and gains (i.e., deletions and duplications). Detection is efficient for changes that are submicroscopic and are under the resolution of karyotypic detection (e.g., < 10 Mb), as well as those that are very large and thus usually detectable on standard karyotype. All clinical genetic testing is performed at a clinical laboratory that maintains strict standards and quality controls (e.g., CLIA certification).

Table 3:
The most common microdeletion and microduplication syndromes associated with intellectual disability, from highest to lowest prevalence estimates for clinical populations

Microdeletion syndrome	Syndrome name and OMIM number (where applicable)	Reciprocal microduplication syndrome and OMIM number
1 in 167 to 1 in 1000 patients		
22q11.2 deletion	22q11.2 deletion syndrome[a] #188400/192430	22q11.2 duplication syndrome #608363
16p11.2 deletion	#611913	#614671
1q21.1 deletion	#612474	#612475
15q13.3 deletion (BP4-BP5)	#612001	None
7q11.23 deletion	Williams-Beuren (#194050)	7q11.23 duplication (#609757)
15q11-q13 deletion	Angelman/Prader-Willi[b] (#105830/176270)	15q11-q13 duplication (#608636)
16p12.1 deletion	#136570	None
17q21.31 deletion	#610443	#613533
17p11.2 deletion	Smith-Magenis (#182290)	Potocki-Lupski (#610883)
Fewer than 1 in 1000 patients		
8p23.1 deletion	#179613	#179613
5q35 deletion	Sotos (#117550)	
3q29 deletion	#609425	#611936
10q23 deletion	#612242	
17q11.2 deletion	Neurofibromatosis type 1 (#162200)	

Table 3 is adapted from Table 2 in Moreno-De-Luca et al., (2013). The prevalence estimates are based on those for each microdeletion/microduplication syndrome identified among 31,516 cases with developmental delay/intellectual disability submitted for clinical microarray testing [Moreno-De-Luca, 2013]. [a]The 22q11.2 deletion syndrome has had other names, including DiGeorge and velocardiofacial syndromes, but the current convention is to use the more consistent and accurate name, 22q11.2 deletion syndrome (22qDS). [b]The 15q11-q13 region contains an imprinting (methylation) region, therefore the expression of the microdeletion depends on whether the maternal or paternal region is deleted. Deletion of the maternal and paternal region leads to Angelman syndrome and Prader-Willi syndrome, respectively. OMIM; Online Mendelian Inheritance in Man (www.omim.org) is a comprehensive and continuously updated database of human genetic and genomic disorders. Molecular and clinical details on each microdeletion/microduplication syndrome can be searched by identification number (where applicable). BP; breakpoint, per conventional numbering system in the region specified.

As of 2014, up to 62% of individuals with severe intellectual disability where both parents are unaffected can be provided with a genetic diagnosis using the highest resolution techniques available, called next generation sequencing (Gilissen et al., 2014). For intellectual disability of any severity level, a genetic cause can now be identified in approximately 50% of individuals (Kaufman, Ayub, & Vincent, 2010; Roach et al., 2006; Schwartz & Neri, 2012), which includes familiar chromosomal abnormalities such as Down syndrome, inherited conditions such as Fragile X, and the addition of about 15% to 20% more when standard genome-wide microarray methods are used to detect pathogenic copy number changes (Miller et al., 2010; Nicholl et al., 2014). These proportions are likely to rise as further advances in genetic technology are made (Palmer et al., 2014). Approximately 400 genes are estimated to be involved in contributing to developmental disability (Oortveld et al., 2013); however, there remains much to be discovered with respect to the remaining 50% of cases with unexplained intellectual disability.

Typical Syndrome Clinical Recognition

Case Example 1

> One of the authors was conducting a sexuality consultation where a counselor in attendance asked her about a new and unusual case she had just begun. The man, Tim Kingsley, was sticking objects in his rectum and urethra. This problem had been going on for many years and had been treated in many different ways, most of them punitive and restrictive. The previous agency that served him had assumed that the orifice stuffing was a sexual problem and had treated this issue by preventing Mr. Kingsley from engaging in this behavior through clothing restraints. He was required to wear jean overalls, secured from being open, all his waking hours. The counselor from the new agency that was supporting him was not comfortable with that approach and wanted to explore alternative options. The author was curious as to the motivation or function for this behavior. Was it sexual? Was it a medical problem? She presented this case to the consultant and the consultant started asking questions about Mr. Kingsley.
>
> Does he seem to hug himself (like he is cold)?
>
> YES, she said with some reluctance.
>
> Does he put things in his ears or nose?
>
> YES AND HE IS ALWAYS PICKING HIS NOSE
>
> Any other self-injury?
>
> HE PICKS AT HIS HANDS AND PULLS OUT HIS NAILS
>
> What is his voice like?
>
> HOARSE
>
> How does he sleep?
>
> VERY POORLY

Does he have vision or hearing problems?

YES TO BOTH

Are there any problems with his urinary or fecal incontinence?

YES

Do you ever notice there is a problem with his hands and feet?

YES, HE LIKES TO GET THEM RUBBED AND WILL TRY RUBBING THEM UP AGAINST OTHERS

Does his upper lip look like a cupid's bow?

At this point she pulled out a picture of him and said OH MY YES. The woman looked at the consultant and asked "Why these questions?"

The consultant's questions stemmed from associations made with other similar individuals who had been presented to her with orifice stuffing or digging. They too showed this cluster of behaviors. The consultant's mind wandered back to a brilliant course on Genetics and Developmental Disabilities that she had taken with two of the authors of this book, Brenda Finucane and Elliot Simon, at the International Dual Diagnosis Certificate Programme in 2001. The consultant wondered "Could it be that this person has Smith-Magenis syndrome?" This cluster of behavior and challenges are synchronous to what she remembered about that syndrome. A summary of these characteristics is described in Table 4.

Not being a medical doctor or a geneticist, the consultant suggested that the counselor present this cluster of behaviors, with a copy of a chapter on Smith-Magenis syndrome, to her local physician and seek his advice on whether genetic testing was warranted. He agreed and the family consented.

The counselor had never heard of this syndrome; neither had the general practitioner. That was not surprising because the syndrome was not identified until the 1980s and typically goes undiagnosed especially in adults for whom family members have long since stopped asking *"Why?"*

Today, every individual regardless of his or her age deserves a genome-wide microarray, which would include all individuals with previous negative testing results using low resolution methods such as karyotype and/or only targeted testing such as FISH for Williams syndrome or mutational testing for Fragile X. Standard array CGH testing for Case Example 1 would detect the deletion on chromosome 17 associated with Smith-Magenis syndrome, even without the astute counselor's clinical observations.

Table 4:
Smith-Magenis Syndrome*

Incidence: 1 in 25,000
Etiology: Deletion of chromosome 17p11.2 region How to test: Chromosomal Microarray Analysis (CMA) and in some cases, FISH

Physical Characteristics

Flat mid-face Flat head shape

Broad nasal bridge

Upper lip shaped like a "cupid's bow"

Fair hair and complexion

Hypotonia

Missing secondary lower bicuspids

Lurching gait

Thin appearance to lower legs

Dry skin on hand and feet

Short in stature

Short fingers Ear anomalies

Deep, hoarse voice Strabismus Nearsightedness

Behavioral Characteristics

Engaging, endearing, full of personality, a sense of humor

Appreciate attention, and appears to crave one- to-one interactions and may often compete with others for attention; eager to please

Perseveration- repeatedly asking the same questions

Onychotillomania (picking at/pulling at fingernails and toenails) and polyembolokoilamania (orifice stuffing) are common. In females there may be vaginal stuffing, which may appear like an indicator of sexual abuse, but actually form of self-injury

Self-injurious behaviors- hand biting (most common); head banging (many outgrow this); skin picking

Sleep disturbances- frequent awakenings at night; deficient REM sleep; early wake-up; narcolepsy- like episodes during day; abnormal melatonin metabolism

Poor impulse control- aggressive hugging, prolonged tantrums, outbursts

Do not adjust well to changes in routine

Hugging- aggressive (rib-crushing; indiscriminate hugging of others)

Self-hugging- almost like a tic "spasmodic upper body squeezing tic thing, with facial grimacing". This is involuntary and appears when excited (less common with age)

Tactile defensiveness

Typically difficult times include transitions from activities and changes in routine; therefore, try to prepare the individual for such changes

Medical Vulnerabilities

Sleep abnormalities- aberrant levels of melatonin, disturbed biological clock and circadian rhythm

Some have poor vision (extreme near- sightedness, detached retina)

Hearing impairments

Teeth large pulp chambers and low levels of enamel; therefore, get lots of cavities

Peripheral neuropathy (numbness/ tingles in fingers and toes)

Scoliosis

Chest abnormalities (pes cavus or pes planus)

Chronic ear infections- lead to conductive hearing loss and speech problems

25% have cardiac problems

Heightened risk of hypothyroidism

Seizures

Urinary tract anomalies

Cognitive Implications
Strengths

Long-term memory for places, people, and things

Letter/word recognition

Simultaneous processing skills

Weaknesses

Moderate to mild range of intellectual disability

Weaknesses in sequential processing and visual short-term memory

Strategies

Structured classroom with consistent well defined limits

Close student: staff ratio

Reinforcers and motivators

Care providers need to be:

Emotionally neutral in response to challenges to avoid power struggles

Comfortable with close proximity

Consistent approach among staff; frequent staff meeting

*Characteristics are not in order of prevalence or incidence and may not be present in all individuals at all ages.

The Importance of Syndrome Identification

Why is it valuable to identify the syndrome responsible for the disability?

This is a question people often ask when we suggest genetic testing, and it is an important line of inquiry. Individuals with developmental disabilities have already been subjected to a host of neuropsychological and medical tests. Clearly additional testing should have some benefit to the individual if this avenue is to be pursued. Some professionals and family members alike think that genetic testing merely brings a new label to what is already known. They do not feel that a new label can add much to the support or treatment the person may receive; labeling traditionally meant identification of people by intelligence classifications that were not helpful and often harmful. Others argue that so many of the causes of developmental disability are still unknown so there is little to be gained by undergoing testing, which may be time consuming, expensive, and inconclusive.

It is important before proceeding with any syndromic testing that a clinician clarifies the benefits of diagnosis. Making a genetic diagnosis to identify a syndrome is no longer a costly or challenging venture in most cases. In fact, most genetic testing in Canada is covered by provincial health care plans (e.g., genome-wide microarray are covered everywhere for individuals with ID, consistent with current clinical practical guidelines [Miller et al., 2010]). Despite these advances, some physicians may not be as comfortable as Mr. Kingsley's doctor in ordering or facilitating genetic testing or may be concerned about how to fully understand the results and/or the subsequent follow-up with the patient and family. Consultation with a medical genetics specialist may be necessary to assist with this process. Some individuals with developmental disabilities who are competent to understand the benefits may not want to have the simple blood test. Rarely, families may be reluctant to pursue testing because they do not want to know the root cause of the intellectual disability, or they may feel testing may lead to further disappointment with negative results or lead to blame. For some families, the idea of genetic testing engenders anticipation of a "cause" that may threaten to create greater guilt or blame than they may be already feeling. For other families, there may be a belief that nothing is to be gained by knowing the cause of their family member's disability. These feelings must of course be respected. As will be discussed in Chapter 10, each family must make its own decision regarding genetic or chromosomal testing.

In the above case of Tim Kingsley, both the physician and the counselor asked the consultant a very important question:

"What will this do for Tim if we get a diagnosis of this syndrome?"

Interestingly enough, in his case the family did not ask that question; they still really wanted to know and understand why their son was unique in the manner that he was. They had searched for an answer for so long but had given up. Would this be the answer for them or would it once again be a fruitless effort at understanding Tim's behavior?

Demysifying Syndromes Associated with Developmental Disabilites

Knowing the syndrome can provide important information regarding why certain individuals behave the way they do and what can be done to assist them. Specific genotypes (i.e., genetic make-up) produce behavioral phenotypes (i.e., characteristic behavioral patterns); understanding the experiences and needs of each unique individual with a disability *can* be enhanced greatly by knowing the syndrome that caused their disability. With the syndrome identification comes a cluster of cognitive and social strengths and challenges, medical issues, and behaviors. Chromosomal and genetic testing can lead to identification of a syndrome that has a behavioral phenotype or a recognizable pattern of behavior. People who have similar genetic causes of their developmental disability present with similar behavioral phenotypes, which are a cluster of motor, cognitive, linguistic, and/or social aspects that are associated with a particular biological syndrome (Flint & Yule, 1994). Some of these phenotypes are unusual and unique to the syndrome. Dykens et al. (2000) provides several examples, including the extreme self-injury associated with Lesch-Nyhan syndrome, the high level language abilities coupled with lower overall intelligence level and poor visual spatial functioning associated with Williams syndrome, the hand wringing of Rett syndrome, the cat cry during infancy with cri-du-chat syndrome, the self hugging and stuffing of objects into body orifices related to Smith-Magenis syndrome, or the food fixation and hyperphagia associated with Prader-Willi syndrome.

Because the behaviors associated with many syndromes can be very confusing and difficult for families and other care providers or teachers, the identification of the syndrome, coupled with appropriate counseling regarding the syndrome, can be extremely helpful for those supporting the individual. The identification of the behavioral phenotype allows family and others to know what to expect (the trajectory of the syndrome) and how to develop realistic and knowledgeable strategies for supporting the child throughout the lifespan. The behavioral phenotype is not necessarily static; it can change and become more or less prominent at different times through the life. For example the child with Rett syndrome may show no visible signs of a disability until the second year of life. Rett syndrome virtually remains undiagnosed in early years because of the apparent lack of early symptomatology; however, once skill deterioration begins, families become frantic to search for an explanation for the devastating change in their child's development (See Table 5 for a description of Rett syndrome).

Families and service providers should know about the possible benefits of receiving a genetic diagnosis so that they can make an informed decision. The authors have identified eight benefits of syndromic identification, which are listed in Table 6. Each of these benefits will be elaborated below, using examples of various syndromes to illustrate the points.

Table 5:
Rett Syndrome

Incidence: Primarily in females
1 in 10,000 female births
Etiology: Mutations in the MECP2 gene on the X chromosome
How to test: Molecular analysis of the MECP2 gene

Physical Characteristics

Wide-based gait, similar to Angelman syndrome

Poor circulation – cold hands and feet

High metabolic rate

Scoliosis

Very expressive eyes

Normal head size at birth, but slowed growth between 5 months and 4 years

Hypotrophic (underdeveloped) small feet

Behavioral Characteristics

Period of regression, withdrawal (normal progress from 6 to 18 months)

Loss of acquired hand and speech skills by age 1-2 years

Onset of stereotypies – hand wringing or washing, hand mouthing

Lifelong stereotypies – often unable to use hands

Self-injury – 40-50%

Common Medical Vulnerabilities

Seizures

Hyperventilation

Central breathing dysfunction

Sleep disturbance – 70%

Scoliosis

Constipation

Strategies

Pharmacological, especially for seizures

Careful monitoring of scoliosis

Cognitive Implications
Strength

Very expressive eyes

Weaknesses

Severe to profound intellectual disability

Severe, impaired expressive and receptive language develop between 1-4 years

Strategies

Communication board

Table 6:
Benefits of Syndromic Identification

1. Syndrome identification can lead to increased support for families, caregivers, and the individual.
2. Diagnosis of a syndrome not only allows the challenges presented by the syndrome to be identified, but also the strengths and advantages associated with the syndrome to be recognized and promoted.
3. Identification of a syndrome can provide invaluable information regarding the individual's learning challenges and may provide collective knowledge that can lead to educational adaptations.
4. There can be medical prognostic advantages and anticipatory care that can be effected once there is identification of a syndrome
5. The information can lead to knowledge about mental health risks or resilience of the individual.
6. Identification of a syndrome can lead to communication within clinical and medical disciplines and across disciplines to develop greater understanding and more effective treatment strategies. It may lead to not only clinical and medical collaboration, but to research that can enhance the field and the lives of countless individuals.
7. The nature of the human experience is an interaction of biomedical, psychological, and social factors. There are many biopsychosocial implications of identifying the syndromes that individuals possess.
8. Genetic information allows families to make informed decisions about reproductive choices.

Syndrome identification can lead to increased support for families, caregivers, and the individual.

Identification of the syndrome that leads to the specific behavioral phenotype in the individual can be extremely helpful for families at many levels. First, there is the obvious understanding that can come with the knowledge of how their family member came to have their unique special need and how the syndrome relates to the biological, social, and psychological profile the person presents.

Second, families often experience considerable guilt or self-doubt that they may have done something wrong to cause the disability (Watson, 2008). Understanding the nature of the development of a syndrome can in many ways relieve that guilt. In her research, one of the authors remembers one mother saying, "So it was not that cold I had when I was pregnant that caused my son's disability." She was so relieved to know that she was not responsible for her son's challenges.

Third, and perhaps the most valuable reason for appropriate diagnosis for a family, is the opportunity that identification provides to connect this family with other families who have a member with the same syndrome. With the invention of the Internet, families all over the world can easily share stories, information, strategies, and supports with each other. This type of support can be especially valuable for families with young children who are learning about the complexity of their family member. Similarly, teachers and care providers can share information that can enhance their interactions with the child. Likewise, of special benefit is that the individuals themselves often enjoy being part of an identifiable peer group. It is very heartening for individuals with Williams syndrome to be able to get together and share their stories of their unique talents, or to see the joy when a group of persons with Down syndrome note that they think they should rename their syndrome to Up syndrome because there is nothing negative about them.

Diagnosis of a syndrome not only allows the challenges presented by the syndrome to be identified, but also the strengths and advantages associated with the syndrome to be recognized and promoted.

Case Example 2

> At a plenary session at the annual conference of NADD (as association that serves persons with mental health needs and developmental disabilities-dual diagnosis), a woman was introduced by her father to the hundreds of conference attendees. She took the stage and began to sing a series of songs in perfect pitch. She sang both classical and popular music with equal ease. Her presentation was confident; she was comfortable in this public appearance, and tremendously talented. What might have been surprising to many was that this woman had Williams syndrome and had an intellectual disability.

We often think of persons with developmental disabilities as a compilation of challenges and deficits, yet many of the syndromes also present with skill and ability strengths and in some cases remarkable abilities. Persons with Williams syndrome provide a perfect example of these strengths (See Table 7). Their sociability and musical talents are often amazing and can be developed to provide the individual with enormous pleasure and development.

Table 7:
Williams Syndrome

Incidence: 1 in 20,000 live births
Etiology: Microdeletion of chromosome 7q11.23
How to test: If diagnosis is clinically suspected, targeted FISH analysis of 7q11.23; chromosomal microarray analysis done for other reasons will also identify 7q11.23 microdeletion

Physical Characteristics

Characteristic face: Short, upturned nose Long philtrum
Broad forehead with bitemporal narrowing
Full cheeks
Puffiness under the eyes
Prominent earlobes
Starburst pattern in iris
Hoarse voice Hyperextensible ,joints

Behavioral Characteristics
Sociability
High rates of anxiety/fears/ phobias
Friendly demeanor- no stranger anxiety
Hyperacusis/ hypersensitivity to sound- increased interest in music
Difficulty making or keeping friends
Vulnerable to exploitation

Strategies
Minimize distractions (Ritalin)
Sound sensitivity management
Be attuned to obsessions- set boundaries
Social skills training Anxiety/phobia management Comfort/reassure/ move on
Cognitive behavior therapy- systematic desensitization

Common Medical Vulnerabilities
Infantile hypercalcemia
Supravalvular aortic sclerosis
Other cardiac problems
Hypertension
Peptic ulcers, diverticulitis
Constipation, abdominal pain
Otitis Media
Premature aging of the skin
Tendency to develop hernias, urinary tract infections, and bladder diverticulae
Strabismus

Strategies
Primary care provider should follow published health care guidelines for people with WS

Cognitive Implications
Strengths Verbal abilities and expressive language
Facial recognition
Weaknesses
Mild to moderate ID
Major impairments in visuospatial tasks
Strategies
Verbally-presented instruction in addition to visual materials
Occupational therapy for visuospatial deficits

So often when we think of a person having a syndrome related to a developmental disability, we think of the limitations or challenges that the syndrome may present for the person. However, so many of the syndromes also have associated strengths that are overlooked. These strengths can serve as resiliency factors for the mental wellbeing of the individual and may enable the person to live a more positive life. The individual may demonstrate skills, talents or abilities that distinguish him or her with areas of strength that, if capitalized on by the individual, can bring great satisfaction and achievement, as in the case above.

Some examples of strengths include:

- perfect musical pitch, sociability, and kind spirit of persons with Williams syndrome;

- mental health resilience, adaptive daily functioning, and social skills of persons with Down Syndrome;

- energy, sociability and helping nature of persons with Prader-Willi syndrome; and
- happy personality of persons with Angelman syndrome.

Intervention strategies were historically reactive to an individual's behavior, meaning that individuals were provided appropriate intervention, if and only if they presented with challenges. The reactive strategies were typically of a punitive or aversive nature. However, in recent decades there has been a movement in the field towards strategies that are more proactive, preventative, and incorporate positive supports and interventions. Understanding the challenges and strengths of an individual can lead to the development of an intervention plan that is positive and preventative.

Positive support and intervention for persons with a developmental disability refers to:

- the addition of events, reinforcements, and activities to the environment and interactions;
- promotion of the development and maintenance of functional behavior serving to bring the individual natural positive rewards; and
- allowing the individual to escape from and avoid situations that bring internal distress and discomfort (Griffiths, Gardner, & Nugent, 1998).

By understanding the nature of the syndrome, it is more likely that environments and interactions can be developed that will bring the individual greater natural rewards and avoid situations that may predictably bring distress. Just as different individuals in the general population may learn best using different approaches and modalities, research has shown that persons who experience different syndromes have identifiable ways in which their learning can be enhanced.

Oliver Sacks, in his amazing book *An Anthropologist on Mars* (1995) cites a quote from Vygotsky, one of the classic learning theorists, who suggested many years ago that:

> A handicapped child represents a qualitatively different, unique type of development... [if a child with a disability] achieves the same level of development as a normal child, then the child... achieves this in another way, by another course, by other means; and for the pedagogue, it is particularly important to know the uniqueness of the course along which he must lead the child. This uniqueness transforms the minus of the handicap into the plus of compensation. (p. xvii)

Research has shown:

- Long-term memory for places, people, and things, letter/word recognition, simultaneous processing skills, expressive language development higher than would be predicted based on overall level of cognitive functioning in persons with Smith-Magenis syndrome;
- Persons with Williams syndrome have great verbal expressive skills and an aptitude in facial recognition;

- Persons with Angelman syndrome demonstrate strength in receptive language;
- Persons with Down syndrome have strong visual memory skills and abilities in sequential processing and tasks;
- Excellent long-term memory, verbal skills, a repertoire of acquired knowledge, and expressive and receptive vocabularies are strengths of persons with Fragile X syndrome.

It is evident that syndromes not only come with some challenges but strengths that can be used in educational and social settings to maximize a person's potential for happiness and success. All of these strengths are the unique paths by which the disability can be transformed, as Vygotsky (1993) suggests, into a very positive compensation strategy. Rather than focusing on the aspects of life that the person may not be able to achieve or may not wish to explore, enhance and explore those areas where the person gains pleasure and derives success. These abilities can be developed to promote personal competencies and self-esteem and as compensating features for other challenges. These strengths and approaches can also assist in greater learning and less personal frustration.

Identification of a syndrome can provide invaluable information regarding the individual's unique learning challenges that may provide collective knowledge that can lead to adaptations.

The brain is remarkably adaptive to the needs of the individual and the unique diversity of the brain development (Luria, 1966). Clinicians who understand the learning strengths and challenges of an individual can develop strategies to allow for adaptations. Individuals do not all learn in the same manner. Some people learn best through auditory stimuli (hearing), some through visual processing (seeing), and others need things modeled for them. The brain is remarkably adaptable and creates new organization and order to allow the person to compensate; however, learning strategies need to be developed to ensure that the individual is able to learn in the best modality that suits his or her learning style.

Case Example 3

Roger LaPierre was referred for an assessment following his placement in a new integrated work program that was associated with a large factory. Mr. LaPierre and seven of his colleagues worked in an enclave of a large factory. He has excellent long-term memory, as well as good expressive and receptive verbal language relative to his overall abilities, but he appeared to be extremely shy and anxious. The staff member that operated the program thought he would do well in an integrated setting. His job consisted of working on an assembly line. He and the individual across from him on the line would be working together on their piece of the assembly. The assembly task involved rotating and attaching several pieces to make a whole. The task consisted of a moderate degree of sustained attention. The staff member knew that some people had problems with the task and so she explained the job to him several times. She felt confident that he would be able to do the task because of his good verbal skills; he was able to repeat the instruction phrases. However, an hour or so following the training session he became very aroused and anxious. He seemed anxious and aroused during the training. It appeared as if the noise from the factory was causing him some discomfort, but he did not react immediately. However, about an hour after the training session he began to bite his wrists to the point where he drew blood. When the staff member intervened to try to get him to attend and look at her so she could discuss his distress, he became verbally aggressive. The staff was stunned. What brought this on? They looked at the environment and could not see what triggered this behavior.

Many individuals with developmental disabilities would have coped well with this setting. It was highly structured and the assembly task was one that other persons in the program had mastered easily with instruction. However for Mr. LaPierre, this environment was a culmination of a variety of environmental and social triggers to which he was particularly vulnerable because of the nature of his syndrome. Mr. LaPierre had Fragile X syndrome, which is described in Table 8.

In examining this table, it can be seen how the environment in which he was placed was a critical influence on triggering this behavioral event. First, the environment was noisy and over-stimulating. Second, the nature of the task required that he a) sit across from another individual, hence forcing eye contact, which for him is very aversive and b) use both sequential processing skills (i.e., following several steps) as well as visual spatial perceptual organizing skills (i.e., rotating the object). These types of processing are both challenges for him. Third, the instructor's method of teaching was based on auditory verbal instruction, rather than imitation. For individuals with Fragile X syndrome, there should be less emphasis placed on auditory short-term memory, while emphasis on visual integration and contextual learning is important (Dykens & Hodapp, 1997). Fourth, once M. Lapierre was over-aroused, the instructor's efforts would require him to look at her so she could calm him down; because of Mr. Lapierre's Fragile X syndrome, his aversion for eye contact would result in the opposite effect than she desired.

If the instructor had known about Mr. LaPierre's syndrome and what his sensitivities and challenges were, this situation need not have occurred. As was discussed earlier, had Mr. LaPierre been diagnosed with Down syndrome, he might have thrived in this environment, as individuals with Down syndrome do well at sequential tasks (Dykens et al., 2000). Often persons with developmental disabilities experience this type of disharmony in their programming, and often they are "blamed" for the failure. In reality, it is an inappropriate matching that has resulted from a lack of knowledge about the individuals that are being supported; syndromic identification provides many pieces of that knowledge base necessary for setting people up for experiencing success, not failure.

Table 8:
Fragile X Syndrome
Incidence: 1 in 4000 males and 1 in 8000 females
Most common hereditary cause of intellectual disabilities in all populations Etiology: X-linked inheritance with trinucleotide repeat expansion
How to test: DNA analysis of FMR1 gene

Physical Characteristics	Behavioral Characteristics	Common Medical Vulnerabilities	Cognitivec Implications
Macrocephaly Large ears	Speech pattern- short bursts, repetitive phrases	Mitral valve prolapse-	**Strengths**
Long, narrow face Macroorchidism Low muscle tone	Imitation skills with inflection Delayed emotional reactions Stalling-avoidance Overreaction to minor events Attention deficits	Seizures	Excellent long-term memory
Hyperextensible joints		Strabismus	Verbal skills
Flat feet	Verbal vs. physical aggression		Repertoire of acquired knowledge
Soft skin	Gaze aversion (not just poor eye contact)- starts at age 2		Expressive and receptive vocabularies
	Hyperarousal is often the root of anxiety (eye contact, overstimulation); this is demonstrated by self-injury (hand, wrist-biting); mouthing objects and clothes; hand flapping		**Weaknesses**
			Auditory-verbal short-term memory
			Visual-perceptual short-term memory
	Strategies		Sequential processing Sustaining attention Integrating information
	Be aware of anxiety triggers:		Certain visual-spatial and perceptual organization tasks
	Forced eye contact		**Strategies**
	Personal space		
	Tactile defensiveness		Teach task to another student; child with Fragile X will observe and learn task
	Emotional tone of peers and staff		
	Changes in routine		Respond well to structure and routine
	Auditory stimuli		
	Changes in environment		

Learning style has been the focus of much of the behavioral phenotype literature and syndromic learning style should be considered when teaching new skills as well as for addressing problematic behaviors (Simon, Haas-Givler, & Finucane, 2014). Some specific learning strategies for particular syndromes are as follows:

- Structure and routine, as well as enough preparation when transitioning from one task to the next, for individuals with Fragile X syndrome

- Seating individuals with Down syndrome and Smith-Magenis syndrome near the front of the class, due to their prevalent vision and hearing losses

- Because of their affinity for music, using music for teaching math concepts to individuals with Williams syndrome

- Modeling behaviors for individuals with Smith-Magenis and Fragile X syndromes

- Individuals with Down, Williams, cri-du-chat, and Fragile X syndromes learn well when auditory information is paired with visuals (e.g., textual, pictorial cues)
- Using water-related activities to teach individuals with Angelman syndrome
- Building on receptive language strengths for individuals with cri-du-chat syndrome
- Repetitive tasks are recommended for individuals with Prader-Willi syndrome in order to transfer information to long-term memory
- Emphasizing simultaneous processing for individuals with Smith-Magenis syndrome through video presentation of the whole skill
- Alternative communication boards are recommended for individuals with Rett and Angelman syndromes, as well as any child who has limited verbal abilities; sign language has been shown to be effective for many individuals with Smith-Magenis and 22q11.2 deletion syndromes; augmentative communication strategies that require less fine motor dexterity are recommended for individuals with cri-du-chat syndrome
- Students with Rubinstein-Taybi syndrome respond better to small group work or individual activities, rather than large or loud group activities

There can be medical prognostic features to the identification of a syndrome.

In general, research has shown that different syndromes are associated with potential medical challenges and risks. By knowing these possible medical features, physicians can be routinely testing for high-risk medical situations that are associated with these conditions and perform preventative and proactive medical care. Additionally, the medical information provides direction for pharmacological or other interventions related to some associated challenges.

One of the most remarkable outcomes from identification of a genetic condition is knowledge regarding phenylketonuria, often called PKU. Developmental disability is caused when these children fail to metabolize the amino acid phenylalanine. However, diagnosis followed by a specialized diet can alleviate the effects of the genetic disorder leaving only subtle cognitive and attention problems, where otherwise severe/profound developmental challenges would have occurred (Channon, Goodman, Zlotowitz, Mockler, & Lee, 2007; Waisbren et al., 2000).

Specific genetic syndromes may also affect the individual's sexual development and fertility (Watson, Richards, Miodrag, & Fedoroff, 2012). Individuals with specific syndromes can also display inappropriate sexual behavior resulting from vulnerabilities presented by their genetic makeup. These challenges may be distinctive to a particular syndrome (e.g., extreme self-injury in Lesch-Nyhan syndrome or polyembolokoilamania in individuals with Smith-Magenis syndrome) or more general (e.g., inhibited sexual desire; Watson et al., 2012). Many genetic syndromes are associated with hormonal issues, resulting in sexually related bodily changes. Individuals with Prader-Willi syndrome, for example, have low gonadotropic hormones (Schulze, Mogensen, Himborg-Petersen, Graem, & Brondum-Lielsen, 2001), which often results in hypogonadism and decreased production of testosterone. The genetic syndrome may lead to changes in structure (anatomy) and function (physiology) of the individual, such as possible cryptorchidism, precocious or delayed puberty, menstrual issues, and fertility concerns. Please see Watson et al. (2012) for more detailed information about the sexuality effects of Down, Williams, and Fragile X syndromes.

Knowledge of the nature and trajectory of the syndrome allows care providers to be *proactive* in their approach. Medical challenges are commonly associated with various syndromes, for example:

- Persons with 22q11.2 deletion, Angelman, Rett, Fragile X and Smith-Magenis syndromes are more susceptible to scoliosis;
- Persons with Down, Smith Magenis, Smith-Lemli-Opitz, Fragile X, and 22q11.2 deletion syndromes often experience heart defects;
- Sleep disorders are common in persons with Rett, Angelman, and Smith-Magenis syndromes and, in the latter case, melatonin has been shown to be of great value in many individuals;
- Persons with Smith-Magenis syndrome have heightened risk of hypothyroidism, ear infections, and experience peripheral neuropathy;
- Seizures are more likely in persons with Rett, 22q11.2 deletion, Smith-Magenis, Angelman, and Fragile X syndromes,
- Individuals with Williams and Smith-Magenis syndromes are vulnerable to urinary tract infections
- Women with Down syndrome may be at greater risk of post menopausal heath disorders such as osteoporosis and breast cancer;
- Hirschsprung's disease is common in Smith-Lemli-Opitz syndrome, and
- Hearing loss is common in persons with Down, 22q11.2 deletion, Smith-Magenis, and Smith-Lemli-Opitz syndromes. (See more on Smith-Lemli-Opitz syndrome in Table 9).

Table 9:
Smith-Lemli-Opitz Syndrome

Incidence: 1 in 40,000 live births
Etiology: Autosomal recessive disorder of cholesterol metabolism How to test: 7 dehydrocholesterol analysis

Physical Characteristics	Behavioral Characteristics	Common Medical Vulnerabilities	Common Medical Vulnerabilities
Epicanthal folds	Feeding problems as babies	Low blood cholesterol level	**Strengths**
Ptosis Microcephaly Small jaw	Poor growth, failure to thrive	Photosensitivity	Acquisition of good language and adaptive skills is common
Small upturned nose	Behavioral difficulties or Autistic features	Cardiac defect	
2nd and 3rd toe syndactyly (>95%)	Severe sleep disturbance	Pyloric stenosis	**Weaknesses**
Short thumbs Postaxial polydactyly Cleft palate Hypotonia		Constipation	Intellectual disability
		Hearing loss	Expressive language disorder
Genital malformations from hypospadias to female genitalia in boys		Frequent ear infections	**Strategies**
		Gastroesophageal reflux	Speech therapy
		Food allergies	Audiology
		Strategies	
		Dietary therapy, aimed at correcting cholesterol deficiency	
		Surgical treatment of pyloric stenosis	
		Feeding tube placement	
		Hearing tests are important due to risk of hearing loss	
		Dietician consultation	
		Nutritional support	

Back to Mr. Kingsley:

Because of Mr. Kingsley's Smith-Magenis syndrome, he should have regular hearing, dental and vision checks (near-sightedness and risk of detached retina). There should be increased medical awareness of the risk of cardiac problems, hypothyroidism, chest abnormalities, scoliosis, seizures, and chronic ear infections.

However, specific to his presenting challenges, we can also learn some valuable information: Mr. Kingsley was noted for "frottage" (rubbing himself up against others). Reports in his file showed that this had been considered a problem in the past because he would always try to rub his feet up against staff and other residents. He had been on several behavioral programs to stop this behavior but the effects were always short lived. Knowledge that Mr. Kingsley had Smith-Magenis syndrome and probably was experiencing peripheral neuropathy (numbness and tingling in the fingers and toes) provided valuable information that would produce both a more effective program and also one that took into account the distress he was experiencing. In this case, it was suggested that his hands and feet be massaged regularly with medicinal cream that would ease the tingling. Mr. Kingsley was taught how to ask for this therapy whenever he felt the discomfort. He was also taught how to do this himself.

The information can lead to information about mental health risks or resilience of the individual.

It is estimated that individuals with disabilities are 2 to 4 times more likely to experience psychiatric disorders than the general population (Fletcher, Loschen, Stavrakaki, & First, 2007). Moreover, individuals with developmental disabilities are susceptible to the same range of mental health challenges as persons without disabilities. That being said, individuals with specific syndromes may be more vulnerable to particular mental health problems.

Here are a few examples:

- Persons with Down syndrome appear to have lower levels of psychopathology; however, postmenopausal females are more susceptible to depression;
- Persons with Fragile X often experience an anxiety disorder that is responsive to medications and environmental changes;
- Individuals with Prader-Willi syndrome often experience mood swings that are aided with medication;
- The behavioral characteristics of persons with Angelman syndrome (e.g., hyperactivity, frequent smiling and laughter, sleep disorders) often lead to a misdiagnosis of bipolar disorder;
- Persons with 22q11.2 deletion syndrome may be diagnosed with ADHD, impulse control disorder, obsessive compulsive disorder, social and other anxiety disorders during school age. Later, about one in four develop schizophrenia/schizoaffective disorder (Bassett et al., 2011; see more on 22q11.2 deletion syndrome in Table 10).

These potential mental health protective features and vulnerabilities or risk factors can be important to know. They can assist in appropriate diagnosis and treatment of identifiable conditions that have a known path of intervention. If there is a treatable psychiatric diagnosis, however, then generally, as for associated medical conditions, standard treatments are effective. Examples abound, for example, in 22q11.2 deletion syndrome (Bassett et al., 2011). The caveats are that the often multi-system nature of the syndrome, including the associated features and potential medication interactions, must be taken into account in the differential diagnosis and in the management of the mental health issues. An example is that of the use of clozapine for schizophrenia in 22q11.2 deletion syndrome. The efficacy of this medication is about the same as in others with other forms of schizophrenia, but the dose may be lower, and there is a need for anticonvulsant medications to prevent seizures (Butcher et al., 2015).

Table 10:
22q11.2 Deletion Syndrome

Formerly known as DiGeorge Syndrome (DGS), Velocardiofacial syndrome (VCFS)
Incidence: 1 in 2,000-4,000 live births
Etiology: Microdeletion on the long arm of one of the two chromosomes 22
How to test: Microarray (FISH test with a standard probe will detect most, but not all, 22q11.2 deletions)

Physical Characteristics (highly variable)	Behavioural/Neurologic Characteristics	Common Medical Vulnerabilities	Cognitive Implications
Long, narrow face	**Psychiatric**	Congenital heart defects	**Strengths**
Small mouth	Autism spectrum disorder	Velopharyngeal insufficiency	Rote verbal memory
Prominent nasal root	Attention deficit hyperactivity disorder (mostly inattentive type) in childhood	Hypocalcemia	Verbal IQ
Prominent nasal tip		Hypothyroidism and hyperthyroidism	Verbal recognition
Narrow eye opening	Anxiety disorders	Autoimmune conditions	Initial auditory attention and simple focused attention
Small ears with thick, overfolded helices	Schizophrenia	Recurrent respiratory and/or ear infections	Word reading and word decoding
Small hands	**Neurological**	Scoliosis	
Tapered fingers	Epilepsy, seizures	Sensory problems	**Weaknesses**
Obesity as adults	Parkinson's Disease	Anemia	Arithmetic
Dental problems	Other movement disorders	Gastroesophageal reflux disease	Non-verbal processing
			Visual-spatial skills
			Complex verbal memory
			Facial processing and recall
			Language processing
			Reading comprehension

This knowledge can also assist in appropriate differential diagnosis (i.e., identifying what is really going on and eliminating possible rival hypotheses that would lead to a misdiagnosis). The nature of the human experience is an interaction of biomedical, psychological, and social factors. An integrative biopsychosocial model is based on the premise that behavioral and emotional challenges faced by persons with developmental disabilities represent the *dynamic* influence of biomedical, including psychiatric and neuropsychiatric, psychological and social environmental factors (Griffiths et al., 1998; Griffiths & Gardner, 2002). Each factor may play not only an individual role in the expression of symptoms, but factors may interplay to influence features of the behavioral challenges.

Using the biopsychosocial model, the challenging behavior, rather than being the focus of assessment and intervention, is viewed as a symptom of other conditions. In viewing behavioral challenges as a symptom, the diagnostic and intervention attention is immediately shifted from the behavior to those conditions that produce the behavioral symptom. The behavior itself tells us nothing about the controlling conditions that influence its occurrence, severity, variability, or durability. Aggression, for example, may be influenced by medical, psychiatric, and neuropsychiatric influences, social interactions, physical and program environmental events, psychological needs or distress, or may reflect the absence of alternative ways to deal with any of the above. Thus, reduction or elimination of the behavioral challenge is not the goal of the clinical approach. Rather, identification and modification of the various conditions (causes) do represent the focus. For an example of the application of this model to a case of Fragile X, refer to Griffiths and Gardner (2002).

Behavior analysts are beginning to integrate genetic information in order to better understand specific challenging behaviors. Kennedy, Caruso, and Thompson (2001) state that "applied behavior analysis could benefit from considering a broader array of genetically regulated factors in arriving at a further understanding of the mechanisms that underlie behavioral phenomena such as food intake in Prader-Will syndrome" (p. 547). Condillac and Legree (2014) apply this approach to individuals who have Down syndrome: fatigue from sleep issues may affect the individual's ability to complete tasks at work or school. Therefore these researchers recommend encouraging the child with Down syndrome to ask for breaks from tasks and providing breaks as a reward for "asking" behaviors. They assert that because the child is fatigued, breaks will be more rewarding to the individual, and therefore be considered to be more reinforcing.

So back to Tim Kingsley: Why did we want Tim to be tested for Smith-Magenis syndrome?

Case Example 1 Revisited

> Tim Kingsley was experiencing a very restricted lifestyle because of his behavioral challenges and the fact that individuals who were supporting him did not have the understanding regarding the nature of his behavior to assist him. He was in clothing restraints (overalls zipped at the back) and was being denied time to engage in sexual satisfaction because of fear of injury. He had been on many highly intrusive behavioral programs to attempt to modify his self-injurious behavior, but without success.
>
> Moreover, he was causing considerable disruption in his home due to his sleeping problems. He was rarely taken into the community because of his behaviors and he spent much of his time in isolated activities. These restrictions were problematic for Mr. Kingsley as he very much enjoyed individual attention and demonstrated a great need to please others. He was, however, continually disappointing his family because of his perseverative behavior.

By knowing that Tim may have Smith-Magenis syndrome, several things might change:

First, the people that support him would understand that there was some internal reason that was causing his self-injury. Individuals with Smith-Magenis syndrome become more agitated if physically restrained from engaging in this behavior. Thus, instead of punishment and restraint, creative options to alter the internal sensations that were causing the self-injury would be more likely to be entertained (i.e., use of creams or massage machines to stimulate his peripheral neuropathy).

Second, research has shown that there may be some medications (e.g., melatonin) that have been shown to be effective with persons with Smith-Magenis syndrome to regulate sleep.

Third, the strengths associated with Smith-Magenis syndrome could be optimized. Although it was true that he had problems in visual short-term memory and sequential processing, Tim had an excellent long-term memory for places, people, and things. He was good at letter/word recognition and had simultaneous processing skills. He also had expressive skills that were higher than predicted by his overall cognitive functioning. His environment could be adapted to minimize reliance on areas where he had challenges and maximize his strengths. He would do best in a calm, consistent, small environment that is heavily reliant on reinforcement and attention. He needs support that is emotionally neutral toward his challenges but involves humor. Challenging behavioral responses to transitions and unexpected change need to be anticipated and planned for proactively.

Identification of a syndrome can lead to communication within clinical and medical disciplines and across disciplines to develop greater understanding and more effective treatment strategies. And it may lead to not only clinical and medical collaboration but also to research that can enhance the field and the lives of countless individuals.

Persons with developmental disabilities are a heterogeneous group. As noted in the above sections, they differ significantly as a group in terms of their socio-environmental needs, and their psychological and biomedical characteristics. Research and practice have, however, often treated this population as if they were homogeneous. Studies discuss approaches to work with persons with "developmental disabilities," "intellectual disabilities," or "mental retardation," as if the experience of all persons so labeled is the same. Similarly, classrooms and educational ventures are developed for those who have a developmental disability or an intellectual disability, without regard for individual differences. As such, there has been little discrimination made between those who will benefit from certain educational or intervention approaches because of their disability and those the system has failed to adapt to the person's individualized learning needs.

One aspect of understanding regarding the individualized needs of persons with developmental disabilities is to understand their diversity by virtue of their genetic make-up. This, however, should in no way imply that within syndromes people do not differ as well. Individuals with different syndromes are also the composite of different experiences, opportunities, and idiosyncratic features. So, syndromic identification should not replace individualized planning and support, but rather be one piece that aids in our understanding the individual better.

While still recognizing individual differences, because there are many similarities within different syndromes, opportunity is afforded to share understanding and information regarding how best to provide educational and intervention approaches that maximize skill development. Clinicians working with individuals can share strategies and as a result enhance their ability to effectively support individuals with different needs. Conferences, research, and collaborative efforts can lead to increased understanding and application to the various individuals who experience a similar syndrome. Each of the following chapters provides reference to professional resources as well as support for the various syndrome groups. The Foundation for Angelman Syndrome Therapeutics (FAST), for example, is a very active parent-professional group that raises awareness and provides funds for Angelman syndrome research.

Table 11 provides some information about common challenges associated with a particular syndrome called Angelman syndrome. Research has been able to determine the rate at which certain behaviors occur in this population (i.e., hyperactivity- 64-100%, grabbing others- 100%, frequent smiling- 96-100%, hand flapping- 84% (excited/ when walking), Inappropriate laughter- 77-91%, mouthing objects- 75-100%, Sleep disorder- 57-100%).

Table 11:
Angelman Syndrome
Formerly known as *Happy Puppet Syndrome*
Incidence: 1 in 25,000 live births
Etiology: Maternal deficiency of UBE3A gene on chromosome 15q11-q13; underlying mechanisms consist of genetic deletion, paternal uniparental disomy, mutation of UBE3A gene or imprinting centre defect
How to test: Methylation analysis followed by cytogenetic and molecular testing, if positive; mutation analysis of UBE3A

Physical Characteristics	Behavioral Characteristics	Common Medical Vulnerabilities	Cognitive and Language
Movement or balance disorder	Happy disposition Lack of speech Short attention span	Seizures- 90%	**Strengths**
Jerky, unsteady gait	Frequent laughter- unprovoked smiling and laughter (unknown if mood-based)	Seizures become less severe with age and are the only common medical problem; appear between 1 and 3 years of age	Receptive language higher than expressive language
Tremors (shakiness)			Able to use nonverbal forms of communication
Characteristic facial appearance:	Hyperactivity	Sleep disorders	Requesting skills
Long face/prominent jaw Wide mouth	Grabbing others	Scoliosis and joint contractures	Better ability for concrete tasks that require less language
Protruding tongue	Frequent smiling	Constipation	Adaptive skills for socialization
Microcephaly- small head, with flat back	Hand flapping (excited/ when walking)	**Strategies**	**Weaknesses**
Deep-set eyes	Inappropriate laughter	Keep active and mobile for as long as possible	Severe intellectual disability
	Mouthing objects	Encourage physical activity	Production of sounds and words
	Sleep disorder	Use adaptive devices to maintain mobility	Imitation of actions
	Affinity for water, shiny objects, and musical toys	Encourage fluid and fibre intake	Adaptive motor skills
		Establish good sleep routine	**Strategies**
			Provide alternative and augmentative communication strategies (i.e., picture exchange/ picture boards, speech generating devices)

Genetic information allows families to make informed decisions about reproductive choices.

This last area is one of some controversy. Society is divided on the topic of reproductive counseling, prevention of birth defects/disabilities, and therapeutic abortion. It is beyond the scope of this chapter to delve into the complexity of these ethical issues and such decisions are very personal and within the domain of individual families. Nonetheless, we outline some of the potential advantages of this advanced knowledge.

The identification of various syndromes has been scientifically and clinically possible for some time. For example, amniocentesis has allowed for routine early detection of Down syndrome during pregnancy since the 1970s. As detailed above, many advances in genetics over the past 40 years have allowed many other genetic changes to be detectable. Some professionals, advocates, family members, and individuals with developmental disabilities have expressed concerns about such advances in genetic screening and diagnosis (i.e., Chipman, 2006; Parens & Asch, 2003; Rioux, 1996; Stainton, 2003; Ticoll, 1996; Ward, 2002). Some of this concern stems from what occurred as part of the eugenics movement of the early 1900's that preceded any genetic testing capabilities.

Historically, the eugenics movement was most active in the early part of the 20th Century. It was a movement that was based on the belief that society would be improved if there could be control of genetic planning both for features that were respected (intelligence, height, beauty, health) and for features that were not valued (disability, mental illness, immorality, and criminality). This movement quickly moved to selective breeding and population control, which for hundreds of thousands of people with disabilities world-wide eventually led to sterilization and for some, especially in the Nazi regime of Germany, to genocide (Scheerenberger, 1983). As a result of such heinous actions, some advocates for persons with disabilities are cautious about the potential ramifications of modern genetics research. Some advocates have suggested that "permitting an uncontrolled barrage of prenatal genetic tests will further promote the sterotype of disabled life, and thus hinders our societal goal to recognize and promote equality and individuality" (Chipman, 2006, p. 13). However, a categorical stance on this topic fails to address that an understanding of genetic and chromosomal syndromes can greatly enhance the life of individuals with developmental disabilities. Indeed it can also be misapplied to make eugenic decisions about life itself. Thus the role of careful ethical monitoring of practice becomes paramount.

One example that may help with this discussion of the ethical issues of genetic testing is that of a mother who has PKU. As discussed above, children with PKU do not metabolize the amino acid phenylalanine. By following a specific, phenylalanine-free diet from infancy, the severe/profound developmental disabilities can be circumvented so that only subtle cognitive and attention problems exist (Channon et al., 2007). It is therefore important for mothers with PKU to control their diets before conception and through pregnancy to delivery (Waisbren et al., 2000).

The authors of this chapter see the amazing potential of genetic diagnosis and syndromic identification to aid in the quality of life of the individuals with developmental disabilities, and it is with that purpose that this chapter is dedicated.

Summary

Professionals in the field of developmental disabilities must be in a constant state of learning. In the past decade the field has been expanding exponentially regarding the knowledge of biomedical influences and genetics on behavior. It is now recognized that an individual's development is linked to the integration of a number of biomedical, psychological, and social influences (Griffiths et al., 1998), and that developmental and intellectual disabilities involve multiple genes and other factors (Gilissen et al., 2014). Knowledge gained from understanding identifiable syndromes needs to be integrated into existing knowledge about persons with developmental disabilities if clinicians are to truly employ a whole person approach to support and intervention.

Glossary of Terms

Adrenarche - *Puberty induced by hyperactivity of the adrenal cortex*

Athetosis - *Condition in which movements are involuntary, slow, squirming, and continuous. These movements occur during flexing, extending, supination (turning the palm up), and pronation (turning the palm down) of the hands and fingers. There may also be a difficulty moving the toes, feet, face, or neck*

Bruxism - *Grinding, gnashing or clenching of the teeth*

Behavioral phenotype - *a characteristic cluster of behaviors that are associated with a specific syndrome. Some of these phenotypes are unusual and unique to the syndrome.*

Cryptorchidism - *Failure of testicular descent into the scrotum*

Dyspraxia - *An impairment or immaturity of the organization of movement. Associated with this may be problems of language, perception, and thought*

Edema - *Swelling of the soft tissues caused by excess fluid*

Hyperacusis - *Impaired tolerance to normal environmental sounds. Ears lose most of their dynamic range, which is the ability of the ear to deal with quick shifts in sound loudness*

Hypercalcemia - *Excessive blood levels of calcium*

Hyperreflexia - *Reaction of the autonomic (involuntary) nervous system to over-stimula- tion, which may include high blood pressure, change in heart rate, skin color changes (pallor, redness, blue-grey coloration), and profuse sweating*

Hypertension - *Persistently high arterial blood pressure*

Hypocalcemia - *Deficient blood levels of calcium*

Hypogonadism - *Small testes*

Hypopigmentation - *Decrease in pigment production in hair and skin*

Hypospadias - *Condition where the opening of the penis is found somewhere back along the shaft, anywhere from tip to base, and it is often accompanied by other differences such as penile twisting, a "hooked" appearance because the glans bends down, and a hooded, incomplete foreskin*

Hypotonia - *Decreased muscle tone*

Kyphosis - *Curvature of the spine*

Macrocephaly - *Circumference of the head is larger than established norms for the age and gender of the infant or child*

Macroorchidism - *Enlarged testicles*

Microcephaly - *Circumference of the head is smaller than established norms for the age and gender of the infant or child*

Mitral valve prolapse - *Fairly common and often benign disorder in which a slight deformity of the mitral valve (situated in the left side of the heart) can produce a degree of leakage (mitral insufficiency). Mitral valve prolapse causes a characteristic heart sound (click) that may be heard through a stethoscope.*

Onychotillomania - *Compulsive habit of picking on the cuticles or at the nails*

Otitis media - *Inflammation of the area behind the eardrum*

Peripheral neuropathy - *Medical phrase denoting functional disturbances and/or pathological changes in the peripheral nervous system*

Pica - *Ingestion of non-food items*

Polyembolokoilamania - *Insertion of foreign objects into bodily orifices*

Postaxial polydactyly - *An extra digit is located next to the fifth digit* **Scoliosis** - *Curvature of the spine*

Sensory integration - *Disruption in the way the brain processes the intake, organization, and output of information, which can result in hypersensitivity or hyposensitivity to stimuli.*

Strabismus - *Commonly known as crossed-eyes, is a vision condition in which a person cannot align both eyes simultaneously under normal conditions. One or both of the eyes may turn in, out, up or down*

Tactile defensiveness - *Overly sensitive to touch*

Supravalvular aortic stenosis - *Localized narrowing of the aorta above the aortic sinuses*

Resources

Dykens, E.M., Hodapp, R.M., & Finucane, B.M. (2000). *Genetics and intellectual disability syndromes: A new look at behavior and interventions.* Baltimore, MD: Paul H. Brookes.

Griffiths, D., Condillac, R.A., & Legree, M. (Eds.) (2014). *Genetic syndromes and applied behaviour analysis: A handbook for practitioners.* London, UK: Jessica Kingsley Publishers.

O'Brien, G. & Yule, W. (1995). *Behavioral phenotypes.* Cambridge: Cambridge University Press.

For resources on specific syndromes, see later chapters.

References

Bassett, A. S., McDonald-McGinn, D. M., Devriendt, K., Digilio, M. C., Goldenberg, P., Habel, A. ... Vorstman, J. (2011). Practical guidelines for managing patients with 22q11.2 deletion syndrome. *Journal of Pediatrics, 159*(2), 332-339 e331.

Bassett, A. S., Scherer, S. W., & Brzustowicz, L. M. (2010). Copy number variations in schizophrenia: critical review and new perspectives on concepts of genetics and disease. *American Journal of Psychiatry, 167*(8), 899-914.

Butcher, N., Fung, W., Fitzpatrick, L., Guna, A., Andrade, D., Lang,...Bassett, A.S. (2015). Response to clozapine in a clinically identifiable subtype of schizophrenia: 22q11.2 deletions mediate side effect risk and dosage. *British Journal of Psychiatry, 206*(6) 484-491..

Channon, S., Goodman, G., Zlotowitz, S., Mockler, C., & Lee, P.J. (2007). Effects of dietary management of phenylketonuria on long-term cognitive outcome. *Archives of Disease in Childhood, 92,* 213-218.

Chipman, P. (2006). The moral implications of prenatal genetic testing. *Penn Bioethics Journal, 2*(2), 13-16.

Condillac, R.A. & Legrree, M. (2014). Understanding applied behaviour analysis. In D. Griffiths, R.A. Condillac, & M. Legree (Eds.), *Genetic syndromes and applied behaviour analysis: A handbook for ABA practitioners* (pp. 39-69). London, UK: Jessica Kingsley.

Dykens, E. M. & Hodapp, R. M. (1997). Treatment issues in genetic mental retardation syndromes. *Professional Psychology: Research and Practice, 28,* 263-270.

Dykens, E. M., Hodapp, R. M., & Finucane, B. M. (2000). *Genetics and intellectual disability syndromes: A new look at behavior and interventions.* Baltimore, MD: Paul H. Brookes.

Fletcher, R., Loschen, R., Stavrakaki, C., & First, M. (2007). Introduction. In R. Fletcher, E. Loschen, C. Stavrakaki, & M. First (Eds.), *Diagnostic manual-Intellectual disability: A textbook of diagnosis of mental disorders in persons with intellectual disability* (pp.1-10). Kingston, NY: NADD Press.

Flint, J. & Yule, W. (1994). Behavioral phenotypes. In M. Rutter, E. Taylor, & L. Hersov (Eds.), *Child and adolescent psychiatry, 3rd Edition* (pp. 666-687). Oxford: Blackwell Scientific.

Gilissen, C., Hehir-Kwa, J.Y., Thung, D.T., van de Vorst, M., van Bon, B.W., Willemsen, M.H. ... Veltman, J.A. (2014). *Genome sequencing identifies major causes of severe intellectual disability. Nature, 511*(7509), 344-347.

Griffiths, D. & Gardner, W. I. (2002). The integrated biosychosocial approach to challenging behaviors. In D. M. Griffiths, C. Stavrakaki, & J. Summers (Eds.), *Dual Diagnosis:* An *introduction to the mental health needs of persons with developmental disabilities (pp 81-114)*. Sudbury, ON: Habilitative Mental Health Resource Network.

Griffiths, D. M., Gardner, W. I., & Nugent, J. (1998). *Behavioral supports: Individual centered interventions. A multimodal functional approach.* Kingston, NY: NADD Press.

Kaufman, L., Ayub, M., & Vincent, J.B. (2010). The genetic basis on non-syndromic intellectual disability: A review. *Journal of Neurodevelopmental Disorders, 2,* 182-209.

Kennedy, C.H., Caruson, M., & Thompson, T. (2001). Experimental analysis of gene-brain-behavior relations: Some notes on their application. *Journal of Applied Behavior Analysis, 34,* 539-549.

Lowther, C., Costain, G., Stavropoulos, D. J., Melvin, R., Silversides, C. K., Andrade, D. M., ... Bassett, A.S. (2015). Delineating the 15q13.3 microdeletion phenotype: a case series and comprehensive review of the literature. *Genetics in Medicine, 17*(2),149-57.

Luria, A. R. (1966). *Human brain and psychological processes.* New York: Harper & Row.

Miller, D. T., Adam, M. P., Aradhya, S., Biesecker, L. G., Brothman, A. R., Carter, N. P.,. . . Ledbetter, D.H.,(2010). Consensus statement: chromosomal microarray is a first-tier clinical diagnostic test for individuals with developmental disabilities or congenital anomalies. *American Journal of Human Genetics, 86*(5), 749-764.

Mulle, J. G., Pulver, A. E., McGrath, J. A., Wolyniec, P. S., Dodd, A. F., Cutler, D. J.,...Warren, S.T. (2014). Reciprocal duplication of the Williams-Beuren syndrome deletion on chromosome 7q11.23 is associated with schizophrenia. *Biological Psychiatry, 75*(5), 371-377.

Nicholl, J., Waters, W., Suwalski, S., Brown, S., Hull, Y., Harbord, M.G., ... Mulley, J.C. (2014). Cognitive deficit and autism spectrum disorders: prospective diagnosis by array CGH. *Pathology, 46*(1), 41-5.

Oortveld, M.A.W., Keerthikumar, S., Oti, M., Nijhof, B., Fernandes, A.C., Kochinke, K., . . . Schenck A. (2013). Human intellectual disability genes from conserved functional modules in Drosophilia. *Public Library Of Science Genetics, 9*(10), 1-17.

Palmer, E., Speirs, H., Taylor, P.J., Mullan, G., Turner, T.,...Mowat, D. (2014). Changing interpretation of chromosomal microarray over time in a community cohort with intellectual disability. *American Journal of Medical Genetics Part A, 164A*(2), 377-385.

Parens, E. & Asch, A. (2003). Disability rights critique of prenatal genetic testing: Reflections and recommendation. *Mental Retardation and Developmental Disabilities Research Reviews, 9*, 40-47.

Rioux, M. (1996). Reproductive technology: A rights issue. *Entourage, Summer*, 5-7.

Rouch, A., Hoyer, J., Guth, S., Zweier, C., Kraus, C., Becker, C., ... Trautmann, U. (2006). Diagnostic yield of various genetic approaches in patients with unexplained developmental delay or mental retardation. *American Journal of Medical Genetics, 140A*, 2063-2074.

Sacks, O. (1995). *An anthropologist on Mars*. New York: Vintage Books.

Scheerenberger, R.C. (1983). *A history of mental retardation*. Baltimore, MD: Paul H. Brookes.

Schulze, A., Mogensen, H., Himborg-Petersen, B., Graem, N., & Brondum-Lielsen, K. (2001). Fertility in Prader-Willi syndrome: A case report with Angelman syndrome in the offspring. *Acta Paediatrica, 90*, 455–459.

Schwartz, C.E., & Neri, G. (2012). Autism and intellectual disability: Two sides of the same coin. *American Journal of Medical Genetics, 160*(2), 89-90.

Simon, E.W., Haas-Givler, B., & Finucane, B. (2014). An introduction to genetic intellectual disability syndromes: Basic concepts and applications for applied behaviour analysis professionals. In D. Griffiths, R.A. Condillac, & M. Legree (Eds.), *Genetic syndromes and applied behaviour analysis: A handbook for ABA practitioners* (pp. 17-38). London, UK: Jessica Kingsley.

Stainton, T. (2003). Identity, difference, and the ethical politics of pre-natal testing. *Journal of Intellectual Disability Research, 47*(6), 533-539.

Ticoll, M. (1996). The human genome project- A challenge for the new millenium. *Entourage, Summer*, 10-12.

Vygotsky, L. (1993). Defect and compensation. In R.W. Rieber & A.S. Croton (Eds.), *The collected works of L.S. Vygotsky: Vol. 2. The fundamentals of defectology* (pp. 52-64). New York: Plenum (original work published in 1927).

Waisbren, S.E., Hanley, W., Levy, H.L., Shifrin, H. Allred, E., Azen, C.,...Koch, R. (2000). Outcome at age 4 years in offspring of women with maternal phenylketonuria: The Maternal PKU Collaborative Study. *Journal of the American Medical Association, 283*(6), 756-762.

Ward, L.M. (2002). Whose right to choose? The "new" genetics, prenatal testing and people with learning difficulties. *Critical Public Health, 12*(2), 187-200.

Watson, S.L. (2008). "Something you have to do": Why do parents of children with developmental disabilities seek a differential diagnosis? *Developmental Disabilities Bulletin, 36,* 168-198.

Watson, S.L., Richards, D., Miodrag, N., & Fedoroff, P. (2012). Sex and genes Part 1: Sexuality and Down, Prader-Willi, and Williams syndromes. *Intellectual and Developmental Disability, 50*(2),155-168.

Demysifying Syndromes II

CHAPTER 2

Fragile X Syndrome

Marcia Braden and Brenda Finucane

Introduction

Fragile X syndrome (FXS) is a genetically complex disorder associated with a wide range of physical, cognitive, and behavioral symptoms, including attention deficits, anxiety, and autism. FXS is considered the most common inherited cause of developmental disabilities in all populations. FXS affects approximately 1 in 4,000 males and 1 in 8,000 females worldwide. Conservative estimates cite a premutation carrier rate of 1 in 813 males and 1 in 259 females (Finucane et al., 2012), and family members of people with FXS may exhibit a variety of gene-related symptoms, including infertility as well as psychiatric and neurological disorders (Hagerman & Hagerman, 2004). Given the variable features of the syndrome and the fragile X gene's multigenerational effects, providing care for individuals with FXS and their families is challenging and requires a multidisciplinary approach.

Characteristics of Fragile X Syndrome

Characteristic physical features of FXS (Figure 1) include large ears, an elongated facial appearance, and macroorchidism (enlarged testicles); the latter findings may be subtle, particularly in prepubertal boys. Ear infections (chronic otitis media) are frequent among young children with the syndrome, although overall medical health is good and lifespan is not reduced. Hand flapping, hand biting, and gaze aversion (a type of poor eye contact) are among the most commonly reported behavioral features of FXS (Hagerman, 2002). These behaviors, along with motor and language delays, are usually evident by two years of age and often raise concern about the possibility of autism spectrum disorder (ASD). FXS is strongly linked to

Demysifying Syndromes II

ASD on a behavioral and molecular level (Hagerman et al., 2009) and is among the most common known causes of ASD.

Fragile X Syndrome

Figure 1: Schematic representation of patterns of inheritance of X chromosomes with Fragile X mutation or premutation.

γ = Y chromosome, χ = X chromosome, χ_χ = X chromosome with Fragile X mutation

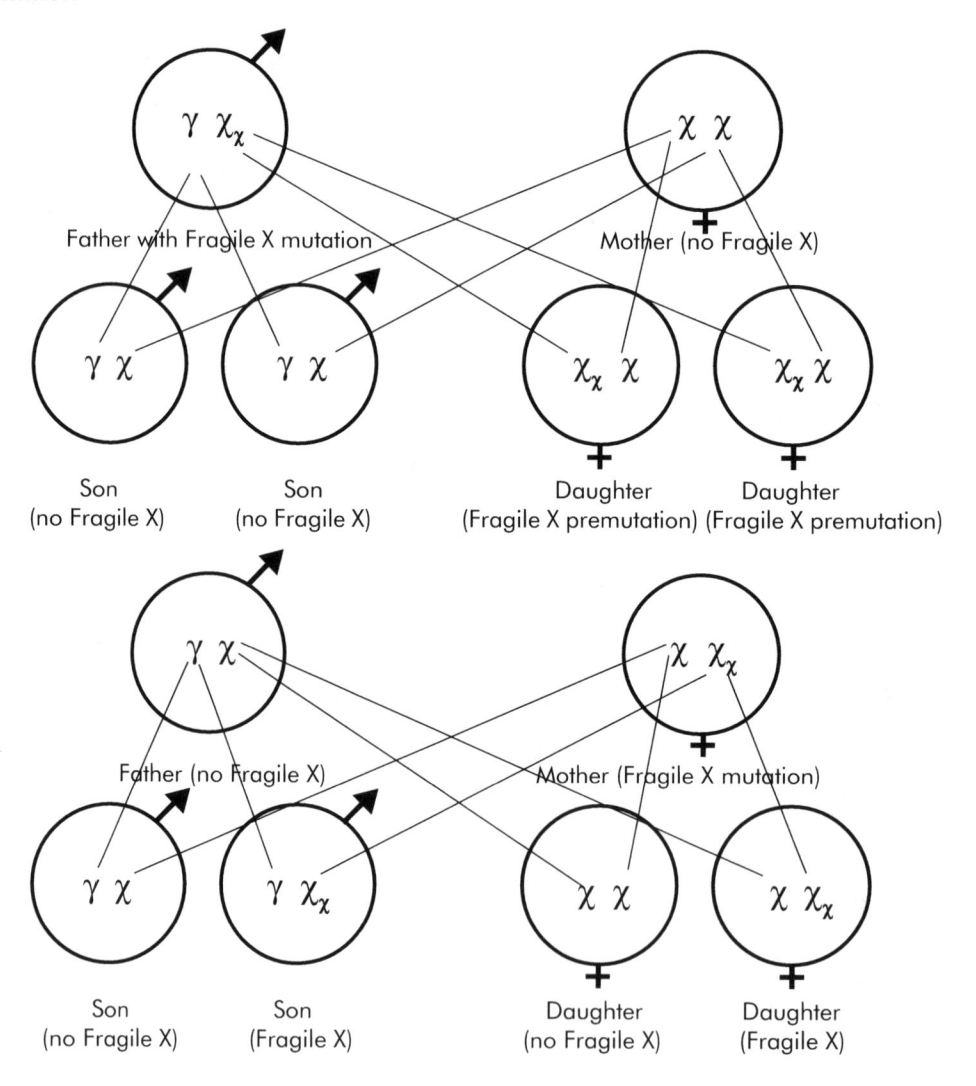

Figure 1: Facial characteristics of FXS

An association between FXS and autism has been recognized for decades (Brown, Condor, Mathrews, Wade, & Williams, 1986; Hagerman & Harris, 2008). FXS has been identified as an underlying etiology in approximately 1 in 20 children with

ASD, with a range of 2% to 8% in various studies (Brown et al., 1986; Chudley, Ciutierrez, Jocelyn, & Chodirker, 1998; Estecio, FettConte, Varella~Garcia, Fridman, & Silva, 2002; Li, Chen, Lai, Hsu, & Wang, 1993; Wassink, Piven, & Patil, 2001). Conversely, although estimates vary, up to half of male children with FXS meet criteria for ASD (Hagerman & Harris, 2008). The prevalence of ASD in girls with FXS remains unclear, as FXS occurs less commonly and with a broader range of effects in females due to its X-linked inheritance pattern.

Genetics

FXS is caused by expansion and abnormal functioning of the Fragile X Mental Retardation 1 *(FMR1)* gene on the X chromosome (Finucane et al., 2012). *FMR1* is characterized by a repetitive sequence of 3 nucleotides, known as a triplet repeat, made up of cytosine, guanine, and guanine (CGG). The usual number of *FMR1* repeats in the general population ranges from 6 to <45, with most people having ~30 CGG repeats. Slight increases in repeat number from 45 to 54 repeats are common, and these "intermediate" or "gray zone" gene sizes are most often stable and not associated with clinical symptoms or risk for significant expansion in subsequent generations of a family. CGG repeat numbers between 55 and <200 are known as fragile x premutations. Such gene expansions do not cause FXS but can result in other fragile X-related disorders, which include Fragile x Primary Ovarian Insufficiency (FXPOI) which can lead to infertility and ovarian dysfunction in females; and Fragile X-associated Tremor Ataxia Syndrome (FXTAS), a late adult onset neurodegenerative disorder in half of males and up to 20% of females with an *FMR1* premutation. These disorders do not involve cognitive impairment and are specific to fragile X premutation carriers.

FXS occurs in males and females with CGG repeat numbers over 200. Once the number of CGG repeats reaches ~200, the *FMR1* gene becomes chemically inactivated (methylated) and no longer produces Fragile X Mental Retardation Protein (FMRP). FMRP is a neuronal protein known to be involved in synaptic signaling and dendritic development (Bear, Huber, & Warren, 2004). The severity of cognitive and behavioral symptoms in FXS is not correlated with expansion size once the number of CGG repeats exceeds 200. The effect is the same whether a child has 200, 500, or 1000 repeats. Lack of FMRP causes FXS which varies widely in severity among affected males and females. The size of a full mutation does not predict the severity of fragile X symptoms. It would not be at all unusual to see a person with 850 repeats who is less affected by fragile X than one with 300 repeats.

FXS is one of several clinical disorders associated with mutations in the Fragile X Mental Retardation-1 *(FMR1)* gene, which is located on the X chromosome. Because males have only one X chromosome while females have two copies, males are more vulnerable to the effects of *FMR1* gene mutations. Fragile X DNA testing is highly accurate and widely available in North America through major commercial and academic laboratories. *FMR1* mutation analysis has long been recommended for children and adults with developmental disabilities of unknown cause (Finucane et al., 2012; Moeschler, Shevell, & American Academy of Pediatrics Committee on Genetics, 2006; Sherman, Pletcher, & Driscoll, 2005). Despite this, DNA analysis has not become routine, and most children with developmental disorders have never undergone diagnostic genetic testing. Children with undiagnosed FXS access intervention and special education services based on their presenting behavioral symptoms, including developmental delay, intellectual disability, attention deficits, and ASD.

Case Study 1

> Jim is a middle school student who is included with typical peers 40% of his school day. He was administered the Kaufman Assessment Battery for Children Second Edition (K-ABC-II) to assist with his educational planning. He demonstrated a considerable difference between his Simultaneous and Sequential processing, which is consistent with prior research using the K-ABC to assess males with FXS (Kemper, Hagerman, & Alt-Stark, 1988). The difference between his Simultaneous and Sequential scores was 17 points, which is more than 1 SD and statistically significant. His auditory sequential memory for digits, words, and motor imitation was low. Considerable strengths were in experiential problem solving, visual memory, expressive vocabulary, and gestalt processing. Jim's inability to generate a hypothesis, revise a plan, monitor it, and evaluate a strategy is far reaching and interferes with his academic progress. His inflexible cognitive set and lack of impulse control are a byproduct of his executive functioning deficits. The school staff agreed to formulate objectives to help Jim learn flexibility in his problem solving while including high interest curricular materials to hold his attention.

Early Development

Early development is delayed in children with FXS. Recent studies have tied both biological (amount of protein produced) and environmental influences together to predict outcomes of children with FXS (Dyer-Friedman et al., 2002).

Usually, infants with FXS are able to suck and access a nipple. Parents have reported that babies with FXS may not cuddle or tolerate closeness while nursing. Sometimes babies prefer a bottle propped on a pillow near them to avoid the touch of the parents while eating. Eating can be compromised if the baby has difficulty tolerating texture and taste. This can present challenges to parents when trying to introduce solid foods to better nourish the baby.

As the child moves into toddlerhood, eating issues can persist. Parents report preferences for diets high in carbohydrates such as pastas, pizza, and softer foods. The textures of most meats are difficult to tolerate and chew. If the child has difficulty swallowing solid foods it often results in gagging that can become overgeneralized to the extent that the child becomes phobic about eating solid food. When this happens, the parent is often referred to a behavioral psychologist or eating clinic. It is often necessary to provide chewable supplements to the child due to the dietary limitations.

Toileting is usually delayed (Knonk, Nolf, & Dahl, 2010). Toilet training children with FXS can be difficult and may often persist into later years. It is important to evaluate the timing of the process based on the child's readiness. Riley (2008) recommends that training can begin when the child has been dry for periods of at least two hours; there is indication that the child has a sensory awareness of having a full bladder or bowels; the child recognizes that a diaper is wet or soiled; the child has the ability to communicate about wetness or toileting need; the child has the necessary motor skills to get to the bathroom, pull pants down and sit on the toilet; the child has the ability and willingness to follow simple one-step directions; and the child has the ability to sit in one spot for several minutes at a time.

Sleep disturbances are also common. In a national survey of parents, 32 percent of children with a full mutation (1,295 children) reported sleep problems, consisting mainly of difficulty falling asleep, frequent night awakenings, and early morning waking as the most prevalent symptoms (Kronk et al., 2010). Most children (82 percent of the parents surveyed) had two or more of these sleep problems. Also reported was an association between behavior problems and sleep. Children, especially those with an already compromised nervous system, need sleep for optimal development and functioning. Ongoing support toward that end from medical providers can help play an important role in treating sleep disorders. As would be expected, individuals with lower functioning had more difficulty sleeping which translated into a higher incidence of behavioral issues during the day. (Kronk et al., 2010)

Cognitive Effects

Fragile X syndrome is the most common inherited cause of intellectual disability (Crawford, Acuna, & Sherman, 2001); thus a number of researchers have studied the cognitive characteristics in those affected by FXS. Males are usually more affected than females. Learning disabilities, particularly affecting math, are more common than intellectual disability among females.

A variety of cognitive deficits are common among males with FXS. Cognitive delays contribute to learning difficulties throughout the lifespan. Visual-motor impairments for tasks that require drawing skills are delayed (Crowe & Hay, 1990; Freund & Reiss 1991). Impairment in tasks requiring psychomotor coordination such as pegboard (Cornish, Bramble, Munir, & Pigram, 1999) has also been noted as deficient. Strengths in vocabulary (Dykens et al., 1989), long term memory for meaningful and learned information (Freund & Reiss, 1991), and face emotion perception (Turk & Cornish, 1998) have been documented.

In a hallmark study by Kemper, Hagerman, and Althshul-Stark in 1988, the cognitive phenotype for FXS emerged. They studied 20 males with FXS from the ages of 4-12 using the Kaufman Assessment Battery for Children. They compared the results from the FXS group with a control group with developmental delays. Their results indicated the following:

- FRA-X IQ < than DD controls
- FRA-X Achievement score > DD Controls
- FRA-X has more variation across subtests than DD controls
- FRA-X Simultaneous (mean 71) > Sequential (mean 62).

This study validated anecdotal observations about the learning differences between individuals with FXS and others with developmental delays. This pattern of strengths and weaknesses provided the necessary evidence to support the implementation of specific educational strategies. The fact that the IQ scores of individuals with FXS were lower than the control group was confusing considering the higher achievement score. IQ testing often predicts outcome related to learning success. This study concluded that the achievement scores were higher than those of the control group which was not expected based on the IQ scores. How could those with lower IQ's do better on the achievement testing? The answer presented a diagnostic conundrum. The best theory as to why this group performed so much better on the achievement measure is that achievement tests are based on performance of familiar tasks; those similar to those in school. IQ tests must maintain integrity by staying novel and appearing only on the standardized test. This finding provided important information about the learning style and effective intervention. When the tasks were familiar and the child had experienced repeated exposure to the task, the performance improved. When the tasks were novel the child was less able to perform; the novelty compromised performance due to increased anxiety and a reduced ability to execute the task.

The Kemper study was replicated by Dykens et al. in 1989. Other studies followed to better define the strengths and weaknesses of the males affected with FXS. Strengths in vocabulary (Dykens et al., 1989), long term memory for meaningful and learned information (Freund & Reiss, 1991) and face emotion perception (Turk & Cornish, 1998) were all documented. Weaknesses in attentional control (Munir, Cornish, & Wilding, 2000), linguistic processing (Belser & Sudhalter, 2001), and visual spatial cognition (Cornish et al., 1999) were also noted from the research.

Early studies reported a decline in IQ over time. However, a number of methodological problems were noted in the studies such as insufficient sampling and behavioral deficits (Hay, 1994). A retrospective study done by Wright-Talamante and colleagues in 1996 indicated that the decline was more likely due to a lack of cognitive development rather than any type of degeneration of the CNS.

It should be noted that it is very difficult to accurately assess the cognitive ability of those affected with FXS. It is not surprising, given the constellation of characteristics in children with FXS, that parents are frequently presented with reports and/or IEPs (Individual Education Plans) in which their child is deemed "untestable." Understanding the profile of the individual within the context of their diagnosis is clearly the first step in completing a successful assessment (Braden, 2010). What has not been explored is the integration of this information in the assessment process. Integration requires an understanding of the disorder, intentional tool selection, and appropriate administration strategies (Braden, 2010).

Language and Communication

The speech of individuals with FXS is often cluttered (fast speech with erratic rhythm) and difficult to understand. Articulation difficulties are often related to oral motor coordination problems. Patterns of language that are common in FXS include perseveration on phrases and topics, difficulty with pragmatics (use of language for communication and conversation), and poor topic maintenance (Abbeduto & Hagerman, 1997). Approximately 11% of males with FXS are non-verbal at age 5, and these individuals tend to have more severe cognitive and physical involvement (Hagerman, 1999). Most children with FXS begin speech-language intervention when they are very young (Brady, Skinner, Roberts, & Hennon, 2006). At an early age, intervention should focus on establishing prelinguistic communication skills such as the use of gestures, vocalization, and coordinated eye gaze in combination with intervention to express needs and wants. It is also important to help the child learn to signal and communicate when he or she does not understand. Lack of communication can become a behavioral issue in later years and can contribute to frustration and a sense of inadequacy. Depending on their level of development, as children grow older, delays in speech production may indicate a need for alternative and augmentative devices (Brady et al., 2006); however, because the prevalence is low, spoken communication skills is usually the focus of treatment. Intervention should emphasize the development of language and include improving the expression and comprehension of vocabulary, morphology, and syntax. For older children and adolescents with FXS, treatment goals are likely to incorporate focus on pragmatic skills, narrative language, and literacy development in meaningful contexts. Strengths in language comprehension, conversational skills, and whole word recognition should be taken into consideration when selecting intervention goals, contexts, and programs (Finestack, Richmond, & Abedutto, 2009).

Behavioral Phenotype

Individuals with FXS are often susceptible to hyperarousal or overstimulation which can be debilitating (Sudhalter, 2012). Individuals experiencing hyperarousal may become flushed, with ears, neck, and cheeks turning red. They may begin to perspire and their palms may begin to sweat. This clustering of symptoms can resemble a panic attack in which the individual also feels an increased heart rate and trouble breathing. Their behavior may become disorganized, and they may begin to engage in repetitive movements and perseverative speech. Some males become obstinate and resist the continuation of an activity or remaining in an overstimulating environment. When this happens the individual with FXS often becomes unfocused, inattentive, impulsive, aggressive, and display symptoms that mimic anxiety (Sudhalter, 2012).

We know that individuals with FXS can be provoked to states of hyperarousal when they are asked to perform novel tasks, experience sudden changes in the routine or environment, are forced to give eye contact, become the focus of attention, and/or witness a conflict or loud response pattern (Braden, 2000a). Children with FXS demonstrate irregular patterns of regulating their emotions. Providing structure in the environment is often important in the regulation process. A number of strategies have been successful in teaching self-regulation. Learning how to control impulses and expressions of emotion can reduce the tendency to escalate into a hyperaroused state.

Behavior Support

Children with FXS learn how to communicate through their behavior at an early age. Because their language development is delayed, in order to get a need met it is common to grab (to get what they want), hit (to show protest of dislike), or run away or hide (to escape a situation; Braden, 2003). Even though the behavior is aberrant, it serves an important function. In order to develop effective behavior intervention, it is necessary to understand why the behavior occurs. Given the complex neurobiological construct of those with FXS, it can be difficult to effectively change a behavioral pattern without examining the function. When the function of the behavior is acknowledged, more successful behavior intervention can ensue. The ultimate goal is to help the student with FXS become more adaptable and less disruptive by learning more adaptive ways to express his or her needs.

The idea of analyzing behavior and then applying strategies to modify behavior is not new. Applied Behavior Analysis refers to a variety of strategies to increase or decrease the frequency of certain behaviors believed to enhance or interfere with learning. Many school systems use this term when discussing the treatment of problem behavior with parents. When necessary, a behavior intervention plan (BIP) is written as part of the student's Individual Education Plan (IEP). This plan includes a variety of strategies and supports to assist the student in "modifying" his or her behavior while learning how to replace maladaptive behaviors.

Behavioral psychologists often use the ABC (Antecedent-Behavior-Consequence) model when analyzing behavior. The consequence actually becomes the intervention. Correct application of the model can make the difference between successful and unsuccessful intervention. "Antecedent" means whatever was occurring just prior to the negative behavior. When we account for the FXS behavioral phenotype in analyzing the antecedent, the intervention (consequence) will be appropriate and successful. The chart below illustrates the ABC model

Table 1:
The ABC Model without an understanding of FXS

Implementation of the A-B-C Model Without Understanding of FX Behavioral Phenotype		
Antecedent	Behavior	Consequence/Intervention
Asked to perform writing Task	Tearing paper and throwing the marker	Reinforce the student for using an alternative response set (stamp, etc.)

The following case study illustrates the difficulty of applying behavior analysis without considering the FX phenotype.

Case Study 2

John, a student with FXS is asked to write his name on his paper. When asked, he consistently threw the marker and tore up the paper. At first glance, the function of this behavior seems to be a willful attempt to escape or avoid the demands of the task. A behavior intervention plan might employ strategies to support the student to persevere through the task by offering substantial reinforcement such as a desired reward. This traditional behavior modification approach works with most children in most settings. However, this approach misses the point because John's behavior may not be willful but merely a reaction to what he experiences as overwhelming anxiety when he has to write his name. Many students with FXS have motor planning and executive functioning deficits as well as fine motor delays, making writing extremely difficult (Braden, 2006). The anxiety and discomfort created by the writing task create a fight-or-flight reaction. In this example, it is important to go beyond the typical identified function of escape or avoidance, and instead focus on determining the more relevant issue: from what is John trying to escape? When we realize what that is, we know that instead of providing motivation to have the student continue the task, it would be more effective to provide an alternative strategy to help him comply. Possible alternatives would be for him to use a stamp to write his name, or to spell his name with letter tiles. It might also be appropriate to employ backward chaining in which he can finish the last letter of his name, gradually working backward to complete the entire name. This method has proven effective because the student is able to complete the task with immediate success. This approach might eliminate his need to escape from the writing task. Ultimately, the request to write would no longer elicit such a negative behavioral response. The student would learn that the expectation was no longer insurmountable and through repeated practice and appropriate supports such as tracing, writing on a white board with a marker, completing a backward chain or using a keyboard, he would be more willing to attempt to write.

People with FXS are not generally aggressive. There are, of course, exceptions, and parents and caregivers need to plan for appropriate interventions for those instances when aggression is a problem. Aggressive behavior is usually a direct response to external factors. Clinical experience has provided clear evidence that identifying antecedents prior to aggressive behavioral episodes has significant merit in reducing aggression. In addition, there may be neurobiological factors that contribute to aggression. Therefore, it is always important to confer with a physician about medication. Aggressive incidents are described by parents, caregivers, and clinicians as a "fight-or-flight" reaction to an environmental or social condition that persists when an accommodation is not afforded. When the condition or antecedent is successfully identified and accommodations are made, the person with FXS can begin to regulate his or her reaction within a more appropriate context. If the aggression escalates and eventually becomes unmanageable, it is important to follow a crisis plan that will keep the individual with FXS and other personnel safe. Such a plan is outlined in Table 2 below.

Demysifying Syndromes II

Table 2:
Behavioral Intervention: A Three-step Approach

Step One: Responding to Common Antecedents
The first step of any behavior plan is to intervene at the antecedent level as listed below, with redirection, reduced stimulation, and introduction of a distraction or an environmental accommodation.

COMMON ANTECEDENTS
1. Environmental
   - Noisy
   - Crowded
   - Novel
   - Transition-ladened
2. Physiological
   - Red ears
   - Covering eyes
   - Sweating
   - Becoming flushed/hot
   - Pacing, excessive movement, hand-flapping
3. Social
   - Introductions
   - Answering/talking on phone
   - Receiving compliments
   - Direct questions

Step Two: Defusing Aggression
If intervening at the antecedent level is unsuccessful, it is important to institute the initial phase of a crisis management plan to defuse aggression and restore calm to the situation.

- Use fill-in strategies or side dialoguing between two staff members to set the stage. For example: "We will move the table and then turn down the lights so we can calm down."
- Remove any environmental obstructions that may become harmful to the client or others. Have other clients exit the environment.
- Reduce verbal input, remain calm, and keep voice low.

Step Three: Actively Managing Aggression
If aggression continues, discontinue all verbal input, enlist staff support, and follow the active crisis plan and procedural remedy that is sanctioned by the school district or governing agency at your facility. (Note that these procedures vary in different settings and require knowledgeable and trained staff to fully protect the well-being of the client while also shielding the facility from potential legal liability. This is one more strong argument for having well-trained staff.)

Social development has been a longtime concern for parents and caregivers of those with FXS (Braden, 2007). People with FXS want social contact, and it is best practice to advocate for inclusion with typically developing peers. While this model has served them well and offered skill development in a natural environment, once these individuals reach adolescence they face a new set of challenges in maintaining a broad array of friendships. Many of the more meaningful relationships result from therapeutic contact or friends of peers or parents.

In an attempt to provide a continuum of opportunities for those with FXS to build social relationships, a number of parents of adolescent and adult males with FXS were surveyed (Fragile X Clinical and Research Consortium, 2006). The general consensus among respondents was that these males continue to want interaction and friendships as they grow older, but they often have difficulty sustaining friendships with typically developing peers. The gap widens when those peers have gone on to explore the world of work, college, and starting their own families. The changes in age-appropriate interests as adulthood commences often bring on a different focus, diluting earlier connections. For those with FXS, it appears that the majority of friendships—those that offer opportunities to enjoy recreation, camaraderie, and true reciprocity—more often include peers who face developmental challenges of their own (Braden, 2007). This appears to be where more meaningful relationships are built and social reciprocity develops. Thus, friendships with peers who have challenges should begin before adolescence, as should involvement with common recreational opportunities. These relationships should be treated as just as valuable as those with typical peers—particularly given that they frequently outlast them. A variety of opportunities and venues were provided through the survey results. Faith-based support groups, Special Olympics, or local ARC recreational activities were listed as potentially effective in building friendships, community involvement, and recreation.

It is important to include adults in community activities so that they embed those experiences into their routines. It is far more difficult to add new activities into a life style that has become sedentary. Encouraging adults to participate in structured activities such as Special Olympics, social skills groups, and church activities provides the camaraderie that is necessary to build relationships outside their families.

Adult males with FXS can enjoy relationships with females, but the common give and take of a relationship is often difficult due to poor social reciprocity, preference to use of social media, and difficulty making phone calls (Braden, 2000b). Some males have discussed difficulty with sexual contact due to the hypersensitivity to touch. Some report that after having sexual intercourse they feel a rush of emotion that can result in being overwhelmed (Braden, 2000b).

Anxiety

Anxiety and social withdrawal are considered core features of the FXS phenotype, often noted in the literature in single case studies. Due to the presence of a second X chromosome, females can be less cognitively impaired than males but are vulnerable to behavioral and emotional problems such as anxiety (Lachiewicz 1995; Lachiewicz & Dawson 1994). Cordeiro, Ballinger, Hagerman, and Hessl (2011) documented the pervasiveness of clinical anxiety in FXS. Among those with or without ID or an ASD, male or female, anxiety is a significant and frequently untreated problem in FXS. The striking prevalence of anxiety and previous findings of physiological dysregulation in FXS necessitates clinical assessment for anxiety disorders in FXS, along with other standard neuropsychological assessments. The results uncovered debilitating anxiety symptoms, suggesting a history of diagnostic overshadowing in FXS. It is well known that anxiety can have biological roots. Fearfulness is associated with irregularities in neurotransmitters such as dopamine and serotonin. Studies in the general population show that high levels of the stress hormone cortisol release when one is anxious. Belser and Sudhalter (2001) have also researched the effect of arousal on individuals with fragile X and found similar results.

Anxiety can have far-reaching effects on the life of one with fragile X. Each experience can virtually shut down adaptive behavior. The fear can be so intense that the individual with fragile X may revert to a primal reaction of flight or fight and become unable to access an appropriate behavioral response. The best remedy to all of this is the gift of time. Building in enough preparation time to allow for a sensory diet, social story, and use of the emergency kit can slow down the process and allow a "slow motion" effect to take hold. This approach will also give the parents and caregivers sufficient time to react in a calm and supportive way, adding less stress to the interaction.

Anxiety plays an important role in negative emotions such as anger, rage and irritability. These feelings can result in behavioral episodes such as aggression and explosive outbursts. Inconsistent regulation of the arousal functions (attention, motor control, and impulses) contribute to a fear of being out of control (Belser & Sudhalter, 2001).

Case Study 3

Nathan (see Figure 2), a student with FXS, becomes anxious whenever a fellow student screams. The screaming is unpredictable and loud. Nathan reacts to the discomfort by hitting himself. The behavior is aggressive and could present a significant risk to his welfare. This self-injurious behavior is not premeditated but, rather, a reaction fueled by his anxiety. As the functional behavior analysis is completed, it becomes clear that the only time this behavior occurs is when the other student is present. The mere anticipation of that student's screaming causes Nathan to become hyper-aroused and dysregulated. Nathan needs to learn to express his discomfort in a more adaptive manner and while helping him tolerate the presence of the other student. The intervention might include graduated exposure to the other student who screams. This might be accomplished by allowing Nathan to move away from the screaming, to wear headsets to muffle the sound or to leave the classroom to complete a contrived task. Because Nathan becomes uncomfortable in the presence of the other student, it may be necessary to give Nathan the option of leaving, wearing headsets or moving into another area of the room any time the other student is present. In this case, the success of the intervention is contingent on regulating the behavior, not spending time desensitizing him to the screaming by repeated incremental exposure.

Social Anxiety

Difficulties with anxiety are most notable when the person with FXS has to engage in social expectations. When people are anxious in social settings, it is difficult to make friends. Typically, children with FXS prefer to be with adults because it is easier than age similar peers (Braden, 2000a). Adults tend to repair difficulties with social interaction and help support successful social collaboration. Many adolescents and adults with FXS dislike talking on the phone, attending social events, being with people they do not know, and taking social risks. These preferences can be debilitating because on the one hand, it is enjoyable for the person with FXS to observe social activities, but if required to participate it can result in extreme anxiety with behavioral consequences. Table 3 lists a variety of social skills that are necessary in order to build appropriate interaction. Strategies to build deficient skills accompany the targeted social competence.

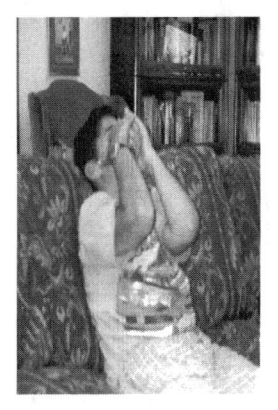

Figure 2: Nathan from Case Study

Table 3:
Strategies for Social Interaction

SOCIAL SKILL	INTERACTION STRATEGIES
Greetings: this is especially difficult when shaking hands, requiring eye contact, or tolerating any type of touch such as hugs or an arm on a shoulder.	Consistent social skill training is imperative. Use sunglasses first to help desensitize the directness of the interaction, fade the use of sunglasses to clear glass and then eventually to greeting without any visual occlusion.
Initiating and maintaining appropriate conversation.	Redirect conversation, hold up visual cue to "STOP" and return to topic of discussion. Teach rote introductory phrases that can be used to initiate conversations.
Responds appropriately to signs of emotional distress by others in the environment.	Use pictures and practice generating adaptive responses to emotional distress. Use therapeutic materials that teach emotional labeling and identification. All Feelings Are OK, Face It, Face Your Feelings (Center for Applied Psychology, 1996).
Refrains from laughing, noise making, and motor excesses during times when anxious.	Teach the individual with fragile X to replace maladaptive behaviors with self-calming strategies. Model deep breathing or blowing out a candle to initiate exhaling instead of laughing.

Refrains from aggressive or violent outbursts whenever embarrassed, complimented or criticized.	Train strategies to replace outburst when agitated. (Taking a walk, listening to music, shooting hoops or leaving the situation).
Adjusts to changes in schedule, routine, personnel, and social circumstances.	Use picture schedules, signal changes by changing pictures, introductions ahead of time, carefully planned transitions.
Practices grooming to include clean, kept hair, brushed teeth, clean mouth and nose area, use of deodorant, clean glasses lenses, and appropriate clothing. Typical peers are very cognizant of these differences and tend to discriminate against those who present as unkept or different.	Use of a pictorial chart with sequence of the grooming activity. Use a check, counter, chip or some tangible marker so that each step of the task has been accounted for and focus can be directed to the next step.

Education

Cognitive and behavioral phenotypes can compromise successful educational experiences for those affected by FXS. Matching intervention strategies with learning styles is critical to successful learning. People with FXS represent a broad spectrum of intellectual development - generalities must always give way to the specific person. Nevertheless, we know that most individuals with FXS exhibit deficits in cognitive development ranging from mild to severe. While females can demonstrate the same deficits, they tend not to be affected as widely or severely as males. Both genders tend to show weaknesses in auditory processing and what are called "executive functioning" skills. These skills include planning, attending, sustaining effort, generating problem solving strategies, using feedback, and self-monitoring. Males with FXS may exhibit strengths in verbal labeling, simultaneous learning, receptive vocabulary (which is often higher than expressive), "gestalt" learning, visual perceptive tasks, mimicry, and adaptive functioning for life skills (Braden, 2000a). Their weaknesses typically lie in higher level thinking and reasoning, complex problem solving, sequential tasks (because males with FXS tend to perceive the "whole" rather than individual parts), quantitative skills, motor planning, socialization, and communication. Part of an educational plan should include the integration of technologies including personal computers, digital devices, entertainment systems, audiovisual equipment, and games that can assist in every facet of learning. The assistive technology plan should contain software programs that can address the integration of technology and learning.

The Educational Guidelines for Fragile X Syndrome provide general applications designed to enhanced learning based on the specific cognitive and learning profile (National FX Foundation consensus paper, 2012). Modified mice/keyboards and touch screens can also be used to interface with technologies for educational purposes and to reduce motor demands, reducing limitations from motor dyspraxia and allowing responses more reflective of the ability of the individual with FXS. Games and educational apps that involve touch, as well as physical manipulation of the instrument, including a wide variety of movements (e.g., shaking, tilting), help children learn through a variety of modalities to support skill development. These technologies often allow concepts to be delivered through visual learning and visual memory strategies, an area of cognitive strength in FXS, thus enhancing learning.

Strategies for teachers that have been found to be most useful when educating children with FXS include (but are not limited to):

- To the degree possible, provide a calm, quiet classroom environment, with built-in breaks (e.g. a job in the school delivering mail to the office).
- Teach student to request a break and provide a "safe" refuge area (be cautious not to confuse this with timeout area).
- Consider distractibility and anxiety issues when arranging seating for student (e.g. avoid the middle of a group, seat the student away from doorways and a/c or heating).
- Use small-group or one-to-one instruction when teaching novel tasks.
- Explore use of calming strategies in concert with an occupational therapist trained in sensory integration. Have an occupational therapist prescribe a sensory diet to be used proactively through the day.
- Give ample time for processing and alternative methods of responding.
- Simplify visually presented materials to eliminate a cluttered or excessively stimulating format.
- Use high and low technological adaptations, such as word tiles, sticky notes and the computer, for writing assignments.
- Provide a visual schedule to prompt a transition and transitional object or task to assist in the transition.
- Use manipulatives, visual material paired with auditory input, videos, and models.
- Provide social skills lessons and social stories and have typical peers model appropriate behaviors.
- Provide completion or closure for activities and lessons.
- Capitalize on strengths in modeling, memory, and simultaneous and associative learning.
- Use indirect questioning in a triad format to include a child with FXS, a typical peer, and teacher, rather than direct questioning to the child with FXS.
- Utilize "Cloze" techniques (fill-in blanks) to help facilitate executive function skills.

- Use backward chaining—ask the student to finish the task after you begin it
- Provide visual cues—such as visual icons, color coding, numbering, and arrows—to help organize tasks.
- Use reinforcements, such as "high fives," rather than hugs or pats on the back (close physical contact tends to over-stimulate children with FXS).
- Introduce novel tasks interspersed with familiar tasks to hold attention and reduce anxiety.
- Avoid forcing eye contact or giving "look at me" prompts; reinforce eye contact by pairing yourself with positive interactions; many students with FXS increase and initiate eye contact when they are comfortable with staff.

Special Considerations in Adulthood

Even though many of the issues are the same throughout the lifespan, there are a number of considerations that must be addressed in adulthood. The issues in childhood collide with the need for independence, hormonal changes, and the move from a school environment into the community when the person with FXS becomes an adult.

Case Study 4

> David is a 27 year old with FXS. He graduated from high school, held several jobs, and was a viable member of his extended family. David has been independent in his access to the community and is able to walk to most locations to access things of interest. He is unable to drive and has recently applied to community based housing where he will share an apartment with a roommate who has developmental disabilities. During the interim he is living with his grandmother. During a recent shopping trip, David's grandmother's car would not start and she had no power to open the windows to get help from a person standing by. She asked David (because the person was on his side of the car) to get out and let the gentleman know that they did not need help. David became overwhelmed with the prospect of speaking to a stranger and refused to initiate the conversation. Instead he hid in the front seat until the man came to the other side of the car to speak with his grandmother. At that point, David fled from the car and could not be found. After his grandmother called the shopping mall security guard, David came back to the car. He had been crying and tore the shirt he was wearing and threw it away. He was completely stymied by the incident and the need to get help for his grandmother. He was simply unable to override his social anxiety in order to communicate, which in turn caused him great disappointment in himself.

As individuals with FXS progress through development, many become more able to function independently. Behavior seems to improve with age (Braden, 2000b). In some cases, older males can become more reclusive and withdrawn. In extreme circumstances, the adult can become agoraphobic and unable to leave his or her home for any reason including medical services.

Vocational Experiences

Basic guidelines to consider in determining a person's ideal work environment include his or her personal talents and preferences, learning style, and tolerance levels for various stimuli such as noise level and social interaction. Job location as it impacts transportation needs and the level of supervision required are also important. Before making phone calls to find out about potential jobs, make sure to identify the person's learning styles. For example, one of the authors found that in having conversations with one individual with FXS and his care providers, it became evident that he liked to have his job explained to him, to have it modeled for him, and then to do it side-by-side with a co-worker. Having this understanding makes the prospect of successful employment more realistic. Sometimes using a picture schedule is helpful and promotes independence from a job coach. Generally, even when the person with FXS has good communication skills, asking for help eludes him or her. This is important to keep in mind during job training.

Environment also plays an important role in successful work experiences. It is an important consideration when identifying potential jobs. Consider each of the potential jobs and evaluate them in light of the individual's skill set—including those skills that might still need to be developed. Consider the support needed—both initially and in the long term. When making the initial phone call to find out what jobs might be available, it might be important to have a trial run to see if the situation would work for both the person with FXS and the employer. Parents and caregivers often report that jobs that include movement, variety and social contacts work best. It is also important to note that standing for long periods of time may be difficult due to the low muscle tone and an underdeveloped core. Part time jobs (4-5 hours a day) may be more successful.

Figure 3: Adult in a skilled employment setting

Often individuals with fragile X syndrome enjoy cooking and working in restaurants or kitchen areas. This adult (Figure 3) has been employed in a skilled nursing center preparing and serving food and drink to the elderly.

Myths

1. FXS and ASD are unrelated conditions

It is important to understand that the diagnosis of ASD is made when the person meets certain behavioral criteria while a diagnosis of FXS is made via genetic testing. As such, ASD is a "symptom" diagnosis for which there are hundreds of different causes, FXS being one of them. People with FXS can display autistic-like behaviors that tend to have a common etiology. Eye gaze avoidance, hand flapping, as well as perseverative and repetitious verbiage often follow a highly emotionally charged experience (Braden, 2004). The avoidance of eye contact and hand stereotypies seen in FXS are thought to be associated with social anxiety and hypersensitivity to sensory input. Children and adults with FXS have been noted to exhibit a particular greeting behavior characterized by turning the head and the upper body away from a partner while shaking hands (Wolff, Gardner, Paccia, & Lappen, 1989), which may be another indication of social anxiety. The prevalence of ASD in girls with FXS remains unclear, as FXS occurs less commonly and with a broader range of effects in females due to its X-linked inheritance pattern.

2. People with FXS have no interest in sex

Adults and adolescents with FXS do demonstrate an interest in sex. Because they often imitate the actions of others, it is not uncommon for individuals to demonstrate acts associated with sexual interest such as making sexual comments they have heard, touching others or self in a sexual manner, or becoming obsessed with a person of the opposite sex (Braden, 2000b). Some may have difficulty with the tactile closeness often associated with foreplay, which has been reported by both males and females with a full mutation (Braden, 2000b). They often fall short during the courting aspect due to poor social communication and reciprocity. Many affected females marry and have children. As a legal guardian, parents may have the right to make decisions about sexuality, contraception, and reproduction for an adult son or daughter. Adult service agencies often restrict sexual activity among housemates and co-workers with FXS. People with FXS need sex education and an understanding of public and private behaviors, people and environments.

3. Males with FXS can never have children

Although FXS affects the growth of the testes, the fertility of males with FXS is generally unimpaired. Males with FXS have been known to produce offspring. However, the likelihood of becoming sexually active is decreased for severely affected males with FXS, because of their social and cognitive deficits (Hagerman, 1999). Raising and tending to a child can be very taxing especially if the children also have FXS. The ability to execute behavioral strategies and intervention can be challenging. Sensitive delivery of information regarding sexuality, including genetic implications for potential offspring, is an important part of the education process for all adolescent males with FXS. This information must be communicated in a manner that is tailored to the cognitive level of the individual.

4. Individuals who demonstrate a mosaic expression of FXS are less affected than those who do not

Some children and adults with *FMR1* mutations are said to have "mosaicism," meaning that they have more than one pattern of CGG repeats and/or methylation in their body cells. There are two different types of mosaicism in fragile X: size mosaicism and methylation mosaicism (Hagerman et al., 2002). In size mosaicism, there may be some cells with premutations and others with full mutations; or there may be a range of different premutation or full mutation sizes in the same person. Methylation mosaicism means that the *FMR1* gene may be fully methylated ("turned off") in some cells, but protein is still being produced in other cells where the gene is unmethylated. As in other genetic disorders, as a group, it appears that individuals with methylation mosaicism and those with premutation/full mutation mosaicism tend to have fewer and less severe symptoms of FXS, since some of their cells produce FMRP. *This does not mean that every child with mosaicism is mildly affected, however.* A person's blood sample may show that some cells are producing FMRP, but there's no guarantee that protein is being produced in the brain cells that determine intellectual functioning, for example. In children with mosaicism, there is a wide range of functioning, just as there is for those without mosaicism. For a child within *either* group, there is no crystal ball to exactly predict their future abilities. Each child with FXS, whether mosaic or not, will have his or her own blend of abilities and challenges.

Current Trends

Because its physiological mechanism is well elucidated and has been replicated in animal models, FXS shows particular promise for the development of targeted pharmaceuticals aimed at correcting its underlying biochemical basis (Hagerman et al., 2009). Several of these medications are currently in human clinical trials and expected to enter the drug pipeline within the next few years. The development of biochemically targeted pharmaceuticals offers hope to families affected by FXS, and they may also prove effective for the broader treatment of autism unrelated to FXS (Hagerman et al, 2009).

In the meantime, a number of interventions and strategies described in this chapter continue to be useful in providing these people and families with changes in overall functioning.

Resources

National Fragile X Foundation
www.dfraxa.org

Make-in-no-time Tasks Ltd.: Emotional Activities for Students with Autism and Other Hands-on Leaners
www.autismtasks.com

Marcia Braden, Ph.D., P.C.
www.marciabraden.com

Developmental FX: Therapy that fits
www.developmentalfx.org

New Horizons Un-Limited
www.new-horizons.org

Key developmental challenges in the range of school age individuals have been identified and, along with a detailed lesson planning guide, are available online at: www.fragilex.org/treatment-intervention/education/lesson-planning-guide/

References

Abbeduto, L., & Hagerman, R. (1997). Language and communication in fragile X Syndrome. *Mental Retardation and Developmental Disabilities Research Reviews, 3,* 313-322.

Bear, M. F., Huber, K. M., & Warren, S. T. (2004). The mGluR theory of fragile X mental retardation. *Neuroscience, 27*(7), 370–377.

Belser, R., & Sudhalter, V. (2001). Conversational characteristics of children with Fragile X Syndrome: Repetitive speech. *American Journal on Mental Retardation, 106,* 28-38.

Braden, M. (2000a). Education. In J.D. Weber (Ed.), *Children with fragile X syndrome: A parent's guide* (pp. 243-305). Woodbine House.

Braden, M. (2000b) *Fragile, handle with care. More about fragile X syndrome – Adolescents and adults.* Dillon, CO: Spectra Publishing.

Braden, M. (2003) Braden on Behavior: Communicating through behavior. *The National Fragile X Foundation Quarterly,* Summer, 9.

Braden, M. (2004) Braden on Behavior: Oppositional… or merely anxious? *The National Fragile X Foundation Quarterly,* Summer/Fall, 12-13.

Braden, M. (2006) Braden on Behavior: Reading, writing & behavior? *The National Fragile X Foundation Quarterly,* November, 8-9.

Braden, M. (2007) *Social compass: Tools for Navigating Life,* 214 E Dale #110, Colorado Springs, CO 80903.

Braden, M. (2010) Braden on Behavior: Assessment considerations. *The National Fragile X Foundation Quarterly,* March, 6-7, 24.

Brady N., Skinner, D., Roberts, J., & Hennon, E. (2006) Communication in young children with fragile X syndrome: A qualitative study of mothers' perspectives. *American Journal of Speech-Language Pathology, 15*(4), 353–364.

Brown, R., Condor, S., Mathews, A., Wade, G., & Williams, J. (1986). Explaining intergroup differentiation in an industrial organisation. *Journal of Occupational Psychology, 59,* 279-304.

Brown, W. T., Jenkins, E. C., Cohen, I. L., Fisch, G. S., Wolf-Schein, E. G., Gross, A.,- Castells, S. (1986). Fragile X and autism: A multicenter survey. *American Journal of Medical Genetics, 23*(1-2), 341-352.

Chudley, A. E., Gutierrez, E., Jocelyn, L. J., & Chodirker, B. N. (1998). Outcomes of genetic evaluation in children with pervasive developmental disorder. *Journal of Developmental and Behavioral Pediatrics, 19*(5), 321-325.

Coffee, B. Ikeda, M. Bundimirovic, D.B, Hjelm, L.N, Kaufmann, W.E, & Warren, S.T. (2008). Mosaic FMR1 deletion causes Fragile X Syndrome and can lead to molecular misdiagnosis: A case report and review of the literature. *American Journal of Medical Genetics Part A, 146A*,1358–1367

Cordeiro, L., Ballinger, E. & Hagerman, R. & Hessl, D. (2011). Clinical assessment of DSM-IV anxiety disorders in fragile X syndrome: prevalence and characterization *Journal of Neurodevelopmental Disorders, 3*, 57–67.

Cornish, K., Bramble, D., Munir, F., & Pigram, J. (1999). Cognitive functioning in children with typical cri du chat (5p−) syndrome. *Developmental Medicine & Child Neurology, 41*, 263-266.

Cornish, K., Turk, J., & Hagerman, R. (2008). The fragile X continuum: New advances and perspectives. *Journal of Intellectual Disability Research, 52*(6), 469-482.

Crawford, D., Acuna, J., & Sherman, S. (2001). FMR1 and the fragile X syndrome: Human genome epidemiology review. *Genetics in Medicine, 3*(5), 359-371.

Crowe, S. & Hay, D. (1990). Neuropsychological dimensions of the fragile X syndrome: Support for a non-dominant hemisphere dysfunction hypothesis. *Neuropsychologia, 28*(1), 9-16.

Curry, C. J., Stevenson, R. E., Aughton, D., Byrne, J., Carey, J. C., Cassidy, S., ... Opitz, J. (1997). Evaluation of mental retardation: Recommendations of a consensus conference: American College of Medical Genetics. *American Journal of Medical Genetics, 72*(4), 468-477.

Dyer-Friedman, J., Glaser, B., Hessl, D., Johnston, C., Huffman, L., Taylor, A., ... Reiss, A. (2002). Genetic and environmental influences on the cognitive outcomes of children with Fragile X Syndrome. *Journal of the American Academy of Child & Adolescent Psychiatry*, 237-244.

Dykens, E., Hodapp, R., Ort, S., Finucane, B., Shapiro, L., & Leckman, J. (1989). The trajectory of cognitive development in males with Fragile X Syndrome. *Journal of the American Academy of Child & Adolescent Psychiatry, 28*, 422-426.

Estecio, M., Fett-Conte, A., Varella-Garcia, M., Fridman, C., & Silva, A. (2002). Molecular and cytogenetic analyses on Brazilian youths with pervasive developmental disorders. *Journal of Autism and Developmental Disorders, 32*(1), 35-41.

Finestack, L.H., Richmond, E.K., & Abedutto, L. (2009). Language development in individuals with Fragile X Syndrome. *Topics in Language Disorders, 29 (2), 133-148.*

Finucane, B., Abrams, L., Cronister, A., Archibald, A.D., Bennett, R.L., & McConkie-Rosell, A. (2012). Genetic counseling and testing for FMR1 gene mutations: Practice Guidelines of the National Society of Genetic Counselors. *Journal of Genetic Counseling, 21*(6),752-760.

Fragile X Clinical and Research Consortium (2006). *The National FX Foundations Adolescent and Adult Project.* Retrieved from http://www.fragilex.org/wp-content/uploads/2012/01/adolescent_and_adult_project_01_behavior_mental_health_medications.pdf

Freund, L. & Reiss, A. (1991). Cognitive profiles associated with the Fra(X) Syndrome in males and females. *American Journal of Medical Genetics, 38*(4), 542-547.

Hagerman, R. (1996). Fragile X syndrome. Molcular and clinical insights and treatment issues. *Western Journal of Medicine, 166*(2), 129-137.

Hagerman, R. (1999). *Neurodevelopmental disorders diagnosis and treatment* (pp. 61-132). New York: Oxford University Press.

Hagerman, R. J. (2002). The physical and behavioral phenotype. In R.J. Hagerman & P. J. Hagerman (Eds.), *Fragile X syndrome, diagnosis treatment, and research* (3rd ed., pp. 3–109). Baltimore, MD : Johns Hopkins University Press.

Hagerman, P., & Hagerman, R. (2004). The fragile-X premutation: A maturing perspective. *The American Journal of Human Genetics, 74*(5), 805-816.

Hagerman, R.J., & Hagerman, P.J. (2002). *Fragile x syndrome: Diagnosis, treatment, and research* (3rd ed.). Baltimore, MD: Johns Hopkins University Press.

Hagerman, R. J. & Harris, S. W. (2008). Autism profiles of males with fragile X syndrome. *American Journal on Mental Retardation, 113*(6),427-438.

Hagerman, R., Berry-Kravis, E., Kaufmann, W., Ono, M., Tartaglia, N., Lachiewicz, A. … Tranfaglia, M. (2009). Advances in the treatment of fragile X syndrome. *Pediatrics, 123*(1), 378–390.

Hay, D. (1994). Does IQ decline with age in fragile-X? A methodological critique. *American Journal of Medical Genetics, 51*, 358-363.

Kemper, M., Hagerman, R., & Altshul-Stark, D. (1988). Cognitive profiles of boys with the fragile X syndrome. *American Journal of Medical Genetics, 30*(1), 191-200.

Kronk, R., Noll. R., & Dahl, R. (2010). Caregiver reports of sleep problems on a convenience sample of children with fragile X syndrome. *American Journal on Intellectual and Developmental Disabilities, 114*, 383-392.

Lachiewicz A. (1995). Females with fragile X syndrome: a review of the effects of an abnormal gene. *Mental Retardation and Developmental Disability Research Reviews, 1*(4), 292–297.

Lachiewicz A.M., & Dawson D.V. (1994). Behavior problems of young girls with fragile X syndrome: factor scores on the Conners' Parent's Questionnaire. *American Journal of Medical Genetics, 51*(4), 364–369.

Li, S. Y., Chen, Y. C., Lai, T. J., Hsu, C. Y., & Wang, Y. C. (1993). Molecular and cytogenetic analyses of autism in Taiwan. *Human Genetics, 92*(5), 441-445.

Moeschler, J. B., Shevell, M., & American Academy of Pediatrics Committee on Genetics. (2006). Clinical genetic evaluation of the child with mental retardation or developmental delays. *Pediatrics, 117*(6), 2304-2316.

Munir, F., Cornish, K., & Wilding, J. (2000). A neuropsychological profile of attention deficits in young males with fragile X syndrome. *Neuropsychologia, 38*, 1261-1270.

National Fragile X Foundation. (2012). Consensus of the Fragile X Clinical & Research Consortium on Clinical Practices – Educational guidelines for fragile X syndrome: Preschool through elementary students. Retrieved from https://fragilex.org/wp-content/uploads/2012/08/Educational-Guidelines-for-Fragile-X-Syndrome-Preschool-Elem2012-Oct.pdf

Riley, K. (2008). A holistic approach to toilet training. *The National Fragile X Foundation Quarterly*. San Francisco: The National Fragile X Foundation.

Shapiro, L. (1996). *All feelings are OK, it's what you do with them that counts*. King of Prussia, PA: Center for Applied Psychology.

Sherman, S., Pletcher, B. A., & Driscoll, D. A. (2005). ACMG practice guideline. FragileX syndrome: diagnostic and carrier testing. *Genetics in Medicine, 7*(9), 584–587.

Sudhalter, V. (October 2012). *Hyperarousal in fragile X syndrome*. Retrieved from http://www.fragilex.org/wp-content/uploads/2012/08/Hyperarousal-in-Fragile-X-Syndrome2012-Oct.pdf

Turk, J. & Cornish, K. (1998). Face recognition and emotion perception in boys with fragile-X syndrome. *Journal of Intellectual Disability Research, 42*(Pt 6), 490-499.

Wassink, T.H., Piven, J., & Patil, S.R. (2001). Chromosomal abnormalities in a clinic sample of individuals with autistic disorder. *Psychiatric Genetics, 11*(20), 57-63.

Wolff, R., Gardner, J., Paccia, J., & Lappen, J. (1989) The greeting behavior of fragile x males. *American Journal of Mental Retardation, 93*, 406-411.

Wright-Talamante, C., Cheema, A., Riddle, J.E., Luckey, D.W., Taylor, A.K., & Hagerman, R.J. (1996). A controlled study of longitudinal IQ changes in females and males with fragile X syndrome. *American Journal of Medical Genetics, 9*, 350-355.

Demysifying Syndromes II

CHAPTER 3

Down Syndrome

Robert J. Pary

Introduction

Clinicians have been interested in persons with Down syndrome for many years. Pueschel and Pueschel (1992) note that Esquirol described a child with what eventually would be called Down syndrome in 1838. John Langdon Down (1866) provided detail about the physical signs and later Down (1887) described behavioral characteristics such as stubbornness and self-talk. Down (1866) contrasted persons with the syndrome he called "mongolism" from those with "cretinism" (congenital hypothyroidism).

Often, it is hard for families, friends and clinicians to read about the history of this syndrome and realize that the initial descriptions referred to "mongoloids" or "mongoloid idiots." Even in the mid-20th century, Jervis (1948) wrote about "mongoloid idiocy" in a classic paper about dementia in persons with Down syndrome. Consequently, as an antidote to these pejorative terms and stereotypes, this chapter will liberally use quotes from an excellent book written by two persons with Down syndrome, Count Us In (Kingsley & Levitz, 1994).

> I'm glad to have Down syndrome. I think it's a good thing to have for all people that are born with it. I don't think it's a handicap. It's a disability for what you're learning because you're learning slowly. It's not that bad.

> There's a lot of things I did a lot of other people don't do. Like being in two different shows, going to a lot of conventions, award ceremonies like the Kennedy's, and I'm a famous actor. First of all, when I was three, that's when I started to be in the show 'This is My Son' . . . When I was three through sixteen I was filming 'Sesame Street'.

> Six years before, when I was ten, I filmed "The Fall Guy." I got to learn a sixty-four-page script. How can a Down syndrome kid memorize a sixty- four-page script? But I did it. In "The Fall Guy" I acted with Lee Majors . . . I am teaching Lee Majors how to count in three foreign languages: Spanish, French and Japanese. (Kingsley & Levitz, 1994, pp. 35-36)

Jason's quote probably is not the typical picture that most people have when they think of someone with Down syndrome. This chapter is about what people with Down syndrome can teach us as well as what is known about Down syndrome.

One of the things that people with Down syndrome can teach us is that some of their hopes and aspirations are similar to most people's dreams. The following excerpt is from an article where the lead author is a person with Down syndrome. Mike talks about his desire for a better job and what he would like about his new job.

> My name is Michael Paul Lauris. I am 35-years-old. I work at the Pittsburgh Blind Association and have worked there for eight years. I would like to move on to a better paying job, near where I live. I would like to work in a grocery store as a bagger because I would be able to meet and talk with people. I would like to help them with their groceries and ask them how they are doing. . . I have applied for a job at Foodland near where I live, and I will find out soon if I got the job. (Lauris & Pary, 1993, p. 62)

As one reads the information about biomedical features, psychological features and vulnerabilities, as well as social features and vulnerabilities, it is important not to forget these two images. One is ten-year-old Jason Kinglsey memorizing a 64-page script and teaching his cast member how to count in Japanese. The second image is that of Mike Lauris applying for a job at Foodland because it will offer better pay, be close to where he lives, and let him have more social interactions.

Biomedical Features

Cause of Down syndrome

Down syndrome is one of the most common types of genetic disorders. Approximately one child in eight hundred live births will have Down syndrome (Haydar & Reeves, 2012). The characteristics of Down syndrome result from an extra copy of chromosome 21. The extra copy occurs because of dysfunction during cell division.

There are three kinds of genetic variations leading to extra chromosome material. The most common (about 95%) chromosomal variation in Down syndrome is trisomy 21 (Zigman et al., 2008), which refers to having three copies instead of two of chromosome 21. Although the vast majority of persons with Down syndrome have three copies of chromosome 21, technically, not everyone with Down syndrome has trisomy 21. Instead of trisomy 21, some people have either translocation or mosaicism.

Translocation means that the extra chromosome 21 splits apart and attaches to another chromosome. The other chromosome may be 21, but it can also be 14 or 22. Translocation occurs in about 3-4% of Down syndrome cases (Zigman et al., 2008). The rarest chromosomal variation is mosaicism, which means that not all of the person's cells show an extra chromosome 21. Mosaicism happens in 1-2% of persons with Down syndrome (Zigman et al., 2008).

The Diagnosis of Down Syndrome

The diagnosis of Down syndrome can be made while the mother is still pregnant. The fetus' cells taken from amniotic fluid or placenta are tested. The fetus' cells will show if there is extra chromosome 21 material. Murray and Cohen (n.d.) counsel prospective parents of a newborn with Down syndrome to talk about their feelings and their fears about having a child Down syndrome. The following is an excerpt from *Count Us In* when Mitchell Levitz, who has Down syndrome, asks about his father's reaction.

> **Mitchell:** I am quite interested in knowing what your feelings are about me when I was born with Down syndrome.
>
> **Jack:** Well, the interesting thing was, that you probably don't know about, when Mommy was student-teaching during college, teaching special ed, there were a few kids in her class with Down syndrome. They had class trips and I used to go with her and we used to talk.
>
> When you're getting married, you talk about your plans, and we had said that sometimes after we had our regular family we'd like to adopt a child with Down syndrome. When you were born, the news was devastating. I thought I wouldn't have anyone to help me cut the grass or shovel the snow. And since you were my first son, I immediately thought about the Bar Mitzvah and I thought you wouldn't be able to have a Bar Mitzvah. So, even though I had once wanted to adopt a child with Down syndrome, I didn't expect you to be born with Down syndrome. So that was my reaction. (Kingsley & Levitz, 1994, p. 37)

Mitchell is puzzled; he cannot understand why his dad would want to adopt someone with Down syndrome, before his dad knew that Mitchell would come into his dad's life. This vignette captures that not only do parents have complicated feelings about their children being born with Down syndrome, but also some persons with Down syndrome wonder what his or her parents felt at the birth.

The Diagnostic Features of Down Syndrome

The most common physical features in children with Down syndrome include a) flattened face with a low nasal bridge and a small nose; b) upward slant to the eyes; c) skin folds in the inner aspects of the eyes; d) floppy muscle tone e) increased mobility of the joints; f) a small or undeveloped middle bone of the fifth finger; g) single crease across the center of the palm; h) abnormal position and/or shape of the ear; I) Brushfield spots (a ring of white spots in the iris' periphery); j) lack of a Moro reflex (when a baby is startled, the Moro reflex is for the arms to go up and away from the body).

Pueschel and Pueschel (1992) note several facial features in individuals with Down syndrome. The mouth may have one or more distinctive features such as an open mouth, protruding tongue, high-arched palate, narrow palate, and abnormal teeth. The tongue may appear to be enlarged in relationship to the small mouth. The neck can be short. The movement of the neck is supple unless there is symptomatic atlantoaxial dislocation (neck pain or evidence of spinal cord injury). In surveys of physical features of persons with Down syndrome, Pueschel and Pueschel (1992) note that congenital heart defects have been reported in between 19% to 55% of individuals diagnosed with Down syndrome. Other extremity features include short, broad hands, in-curved fifth finger, and a gap between the first and second toes. Short stature is another common feature.

Pueschel and Pueschel (1992) further discuss that the physical features of Down syndrome change over time. Epicanthal folds may become less obvious. Others, such as a fissured tongue or looking older that the chronological age, do not occur until later in life. Some features like the flattened back of the head or single palmar crease remain throughout life.

Diagnostic Test and Genetic Counseling

The genetic mystery of Down syndrome was uncovered in 1959 by Lejeune (Archaya, 2011). The diagnosis of Down syndrome can be done prenatally by sampling amniotic fluid, chorionic villus sampling or percutaneous umbilical blood sampling. Sometimes the diagnosis is not made before birth. In that case, karotyping is recommended to confirm the diagnosis of extra chromosome 21 material (Archaya, 2011). Determining the chromosomal basis for the person having Down syndrome can assist the parents in assessing the odds of having another child with Down syndrome. Although having one child with Down syndrome increases the likelihood of having other children with Down syndrome, in most situations, the risk is only 1-2% (Conn, Cozzi, Harper, Winston, & Delhanty, 1999). The exception is in the 3-4% of individuals whose Down syndrome results from translocation. When the mother is the carrier, the odds increase to 5-10%. If the translocation, however, is 21/21, then the odds are 100% (Murray & Cohen, n.d.).

The other reason to check a person's chromosomes is for persons who have been diagnosed with Down syndrome, but who do not have a typical presentation (e.g., a middle-aged adult who looks *younger* than his/her stated age). As will be discussed below, people with Down syndrome have different risks for certain illnesses (e.g., dementia or bipolar disorder) than do persons in the general population. Misdiagnosing someone with Down syndrome may make family or clinicians much more concerned about dementia than would be warranted.

Medical Risks

There is a lot of information about routine medical screening for persons with Down syndrome. Unfortunately, persons with Down syndrome are at increased risk for a number of conditions (e.g., hypothyroidism). As a guide to families and caregivers, the American Academy of Pediatrics (2001) and Cohen (1999) have published guidelines for schedule of routine supervision. Lott and McCoy (1992) advocate a screening schedule. The following has been adapted from their recommendations as well as Van Allen, Fung, and Jurenka (1999).

Down Syndrome

Table 1:
Screening Schedule Throughout the Lifespan

Neonate and Infancy
1. Check the eyes for the red reflex. This is a screen for cataracts.
2. Observe for vomiting and/or the absence of stools. Some infants with Down syndrome are born with a blockage of the gastrointestinal system.
3. Check for blue, dusky color of the skin (cyanosis). Feel the pulse and/or apical heart beat for an irregular rhythm. Listen to the heart for murmurs. Check EKG. Consider an echocardiogram. These are screens for congenital heart disease.
4. Check thyroid function tests for signs of thyroid disease.
5. Perform a hearing screen (auditory brain stem evoked response).
6. Consider referral to a parent's support group.
7. Consider referral to an early intervention program.

Pre-School (1-5 years)
1. Screen for orthopedic problems (e.g., dislocated hips).
2. Consider screen for atlanto-axial dislocation.
3. Perform dental exam.
4. Conduct ENT exam with microscopic otoscopy if ear canals do not permit routine pediatric exam.
5. Complete ophthalmologic exam.
6. Conduct annual thyroid testing.
7. Perform vaccination schedule including influenzal, pneumoccal, and hepatitis B vaccines for children at major risk.
8. Obtain speech and language assessment.
9. Consider developmental assessments (physical, occupational, and feeding/nutritional).
10. Continue early intervention programs.

Elementary and High School Years
1. Consider doing a cervical spine x-ray.
2. Conduct annual dental exam.
3. Perform annual audiogram.
4. Complete annual ophthalmological exam.
5. Check thyroid function annually.
6. Provide nutritional and dietary consultation as needed.
7. Start an individualized exercise program modified for any orthopedic or other health reasons. Provide guidance regarding participation in sports.
8. Continue speech and language programs as needed.
9. Conduct psycho-educational evaluation every three years.
10. Consider vocational training/supervised work programs.
11. Begin to develop skills for independent living and separation from family.
12. Monitor for sleep problems such as snoring or apneic spells. Consider a sleep study if obstructive sleep apnea is suspected.

Adulthood (18-50 years)
1. Consider doing a cervical spine x-ray.
2. Conduct annual dental exam.
3. Consider counseling if transition from school to workplace becomes difficult. Consider counseling to assist in separation from family and to assist in independent living if this is a reasonable goal.
4. Complete regular ophthalmological and audiological exam.
5. Check thyroid function annually.
6. Provide nutritional and dietary consultation as needed.
7. Continue an individualized exercise program modified for any orthopedic or other health reasons.
8. Consider annual complete blood count (CBC), urinalysis, renal function tests, and lipid profile.
9. Regular pelvic exam and Pap smear (frequency depends on risks of disease).
10. Chest X-ray when history and/or physical exam are suggestive of pneumonia.
11. Monitor for seizures.
12. Monitor for major depression. Observe for sleep disturbance, eating disturbance, low energy, low mood, etc.
13. Monitor for unresolved grief reactions.
14. Check for snoring and/or apneic spells. Consider referral for sleep studies.

Elderly Persons (50+ years)
1. Continue all adult screens that are appropriate (e.g., counseling for transition from school to work is not relevant).
2. Screen for osteoporosis.
3. Monitor for gait deterioration.
4. Monitor for functional decline. This includes loss of activity of daily living skills and cognitive decline. If functional decline is present, search for reversible causes (e.g., hypothyroidism). If reversible causes are not present, consider evaluation for Alzheimer disease.
5. Pay attention to development of cataracts.
6. Monitor for possibility of gastroesophageal reflux disease.
7. Check for genitourinary problems. These disorders include recurrent urinary tract infections and bladder resection.

Adherence to Health Guidelines

Despite these recommendations, it appears that many health care professionals are not familiar with the health care needs of individuals with Down syndrome. Virji-Babul, Eichmann, Kisly, Down, and Haslam (2007) surveyed 314 parents from a Canadian voluntary registry of persons with Down syndrome and over 70% responded. Generally, family practitioners and pediatricians were not familiar with the guidelines, perhaps because the guidelines did not appear in common medical textbooks. The physical examination guidelines were most followed for children five to twelve years old. Yet, less than one-third of children twelve years and younger met the guidelines for hearing tests or celiac screening. Recommendations involving discussion about behavioral health, puberty and sexual health, diet, exercise, or transition planning seldom occurred. Recommended discussions about behavioral health issues most often occurred in the 31-40 year old age group, but even then it was less than 50%.

Psychological Features

Is there a psychological and behavioral phenotype in persons with Down syndrome?

A behavioral phenotype is a pattern of particular cognitive, motor, speech, and social ways that are consistently associated with a genetic disorder. Udwin and Dennis (1995) reviewed the evidence for a psychological and behavioral phenotype in per- sons with Down syndrome. They concluded that in Down syndrome IQs center around 55 (instead of 100 in the general population). Only ten percent of persons with Down syndrome have IQs in the "normal" range. Ninety percent have IQs in the range of intellectual disability or borderline intellectual functioning. IQs tend to decline as children with Down syndrome age. Furthermore, there is a general slowing of thinking. Yet it appears that the authors of Count Us In, Jason Kingsley and Mitchell Levitz, who both have Down syndrome, stand in stark contrast to this picture of a decline of IQ. At this stage, it is not known whether the authors are very unique or whether the rich environment and high expectations they have for themselves have made the difference.

Another common trait that Udwin and Dennis (1995) mention regarding a behavioral phenotype in persons with Down syndrome is problems in speaking. Generally, people with Down syndrome understand more and have a greater desire to communicate, than they can actually enunciate because of a small jaw and prominent tongue. Jason and Mitchell discuss speaking. The stimulus is a discussion that ensues after Jason mentions that he wants to become a teacher's aide so that he can teach kids.

> **Mitchell:** From my experience, people have a hard time understanding me because of my speech.
>
> **Jason:** I have the best speech in the world ... I don't think people can't understand what I'm saying. I have a very good speech. I get speech therapy.
>
> **Mitchell:** From my point of view, the important thing is not that they don't understand you, it could help you project, help you speak better. Then, in the future more people could understand you much better if you have good fluency in order to express yourself. Like for example, if I were going to have an interview for college, I should speak more clear so they could understand the information I'd tell them so they could know ... what kind of reason I have ... (Kingsley & Levitz, 1994).

In the 1800's, John Langdon Down contributed to the quest for a behavioral phenotype when he noted that persons with the syndrome subsequently named after him were humorous, stubborn, tended to imitate, and talked to themselves.

Psychiatric or Behavioral Risks

Autism

Autism is a disorder beginning before three years of age. It consists of problems in communication, social interactions, symbolic or imaginative play and repetitive behavior (American Psychiatric Association, 2013). The lack of social imitative play may be a clue that a child with Down syndrome may also have autism. Back in the 1800's, Down noted that mimicry was a central feature of persons with Down syndrome. The association between autism and Down syndrome is unclear. Pary (1993) reviewed studies that provided percentages of autism in clinic populations. The studies were from the United States (Myers & Pueschel, 1991), England (Collacott, Cooper, & McGrother, 1992) and Sweden (Lund, 1988). The percentages of autism among persons with Down syndrome were 2/235 (0.8%), 8/371 (2.2%) and 5/44 (11%) respectively.

Major Depressive Disorder

Nearly everyone has felt sad at one time. Major depressive disorder is diagnosed only when the sadness lasts for at least two weeks and is accompanied by problems with eating, sleeping, concentrating, and feeling fatigued (American Psychiatric Association, 2013). Suicidal ideation can occur as can feelings of excessive guilt. There is the suspicion that persons with Down syndrome experience major depression more often than do others. There are numerous case reports and small studies of people with Down syndrome diagnosed with severe depression (Walker, Dosen, Buitelaar, & Janzing, 2011). Some were experiencing so much difficulty that electroconvulsive therapy was needed because medications did not work and the person was eating so little that his or her life was in danger.

In the review of psychiatric disorders in persons with Down syndrome by Pary (1993) noted above, the studies from the United States, England and Sweden revealed percentages of depression of 6%, 11%, and 0%, respectively. The 6% drops to 4% in the US study, if one includes persons with Down syndrome who were living in an institution. Pary, Strauss, and White (1996) conducted a population survey of major depression in over 11,000 persons with Down syndrome in California. Contrary to expectations, major depression was recognized and diagnosed significantly less often than in persons with other etiologies for intellectual disability.

Treatment for depression generally includes an antidepressant medication. Sometimes, treatment can include psychotherapy, with modifications to process and to accommodate for expressive language deficits. If there are psychotic symptoms, a neuroleptic may be prescribed. Rarely, electroconvulsive therapy will need to be considered when the symptoms reach a stage of life-threatening (Warren, Holroyd, & Folstein, 1989).

Walker et al. (2011) reviewed the evidence-based literature on depression treatment in persons with Down syndrome. It is sobering that there are no randomized controlled studies of antidepressants in persons with Down syndrome. Furthermore, there are no psychotherapy studies. Walker et al. (2011) found that often treatment was suboptimal when compared to known practice guidelines for the general population. Individuals with Down syndrome are often not treated to remission; significant depressive symptoms still remain. If one antidepressant fails, clinicians may not explore other alternatives.

Bipolar Disorder

Bipolar disorder is the current term for manic depression. A person experiences serious highs and lows in mood. Symptoms of mania may include demonstrating excessive energy, requiring less sleep, speaking and thinking much faster, having a greater drive for sexual activity such as compulsively masturbating, and believing that he or she possesses special powers (Pary, Friedlander, & Capone, 1999). The mood can be always joking and in excessively good spirits or there can be constant irritability. Pary et al. (1996) also looked at bipolar illness in the survey of over 11,000 persons with Down syndrome in California. They did not find any persons diagnosed with bipolar disorder.

Pary et al. (1999) reviewed clinical records and found six persons with Down syndrome and suspected bipolar disorder. Those increased the number of persons known to have bipolar disorder and Down syndrome to only 15 in publications in English. This is far, far less than would be predicted based upon the prevalence of Bipolar Disorder in the general population.

In the few cases of persons with Down syndrome and bipolar disorder, a mood stabilizer such as lithium, carbamazepine, or valproic acid would be prescribed.

Psychosis

Psychosis can be difficult to diagnose in persons with IQs under 45 (Sovner & Hurley, 1993). As with other psychiatric disorders and Down syndrome, this is another area of some controversy. Over a hundred years ago, Down noted that persons with Down syndrome tended to talk to themselves. Sovner and Hurley (1993) have cautioned that self-talk is not necessarily a sign of psychosis. Overall, it appears that schizophrenia is less common in persons with Down syndrome (Collacott et al., 1992). In clinical experience, there are some people with Down syndrome who have a major depression and also have psychotic features. In some cases, a neuroleptic medication to treat the psychotic part of the illness will also be needed.

Obsessive Compulsive Disorder

In the 1800s, John Langdon Down noted that persons with the syndrome bearing his name tended to be obstinate. Sometimes this stubbornness can reach to the degree of obsessional slowness (Pary, 1994). These are persons who take an extremely long time to do activity of daily living skills (e.g., bathing and dressing). Eating a meal can take hours. Obsessive compulsive disorder can be difficult to treat. Obsessive slowness may respond to "pacing," that is, using a clock and setting the time to complete a task. Pacing seems simple, but it can be difficult to operationalize. Pacing may well worsen symptoms initially.

Medications, such as selective serotonin reuptake inhibitors, are often tried in obsessive compulsive disorder. The results have been modest, and sometimes the medication needs to be augmented with another psychotropic medication (Charlot, Fox, & Friedlander, 2002).

Dementia

Dementia refers to memory decline associated with other cognitive features such as forgetting how to do skills previously mastered (e.g., getting appropriately dressed). The observation that persons with Down syndrome are at risk for developing dementia goes back to the 1800s, not long after the syndrome was described by John Langdon Down. In the first part of the 20th century, life expectancy for persons with Down syndrome seldom reached adulthood; therefore individuals with Down syndrome seldom lived long enough to experience dementia. However, by the mid-20th century, health care had improved and persons with Down syndrome were living longer. As they lived into their 50s and 60s, clinicians and families observed that a number of adults showed a functional decline. By 1948, Jervis concluded that persons with Down syndrome may be at increased risk for developing dementia.

Individuals with Alzheimer disease in the general population have characteristic changes in their brains. These changes include beta-amyloid plaques, neurofibrillary tangles, and neuronal loss. Similar findings can be seen in almost all postmortem brains of persons with Down syndrome who are older than 40 years old. Two genes implicated in dementia, amyloid precursor protein (APP) and dual specificity tyrosine phosphorylation kinase 1A (DYRK1A) are located on Chromosome 21. APP can be cleaved to beta-amyloid plaques. DYRK1A is involved in neruofibrillary tangles (Lott, 2012).

Nevertheless, not everyone with Down syndrome older than 40 years has dementia. Estimates of dementia in adults with Down syndrome range from 15 to 51% (Lott, 2002). The average age of developing dementia is in the early 50s.

Evenhuis (1990) described the natural history of dementia in persons with Down syndrome. Interestingly, she found that the onset of dementia did not significantly differ between persons with Down syndrome and either moderate or more severe intellectual disability. Both groups had an onset of dementia in the early 50s. Furthermore, the duration of the symptoms of dementia until death did not seem significantly different. Death occurred about five years after the onset of symptoms.

Evenhuis (1990), however, concluded that the early symptoms of dementia are different depending upon whether the person has moderate or severe intellectual disability. The hallmark of dementia is a decline in recent memory. Unfortunately, Evenhuis (1990) found, that in persons with severe intellectual disability, memory or spatial/temporal orientation could not be assessed. In persons with Down syndrome and more severe intellectual disability, the keys to the diagnosis of dementia are the early symptoms of apathy, withdrawal, and a decline in activity of daily living skills, seizures, and gait deterioration.

In distinction, Evenhuis (1990) noted that in persons with moderate intellectual disability and Down syndrome, dementia could be screened for with tests of short-term memory and orientation. Only a third of her sample (3/9) showed recent memory decline in the first year. Even fewer showed disorientation. By the third year, all nine demonstrated impairment in orientation and recent memory. The most common symptom in the early stages of both the severe and the moderate group were apathy and withdrawal. The association between dementia and depression is complex. Major depression is considered as one of the differential diagnoses to rule out when a person has a functional decline. Burt, Loveland, and Lewis (1992) catalogued the symptoms common to both Alzheimer disease and major depression in persons with Down syndrome. These symptoms include apathy, loss of self-help skills, depression, urinary incontinence, psychomotor slowing, uncooperativeness, loss of housekeeping skills, greater dependency, loss of interest in surroundings, weight loss, and sleep problems. When in doubt between major depression and dementia, some clinicians will often treat with an antidepressant because major depression is reversible with treatment and dementia cannot be cured.

The management of someone with dementia and Down syndrome includes paying attention to safety issues such as wandering, providing assistance in activities of daily living, and determining when a nursing home is needed as in persons with dementia in the general population. Drug treatment involves slowing the progression of the dementia. There is no cure for dementia and the illness probably cannot be reversed.

Strategies include memantine and anticholinesterase medications such as donepezil, galantamine, and rivastigmine. There is relatively little information about treatment. There are two studies of donepezil in persons with Down syndrome (Lott, Osann, Doran, & Nelson, 2002; Prasher, Huxley, & Haque, 2002). Prasher et al. (2002) found that 50% of the donepezil group (8 out of 16 persons) and 20% of the placebo (sugar pill) group had serious side effects, such as diarrhea, insomnia, fatigue and nausea. Furthermore, the Prasher et al. (2002) group did not find a statistically significant result, though the sample size was small. Nevertheless, they concluded that donepezil was safe and merits further study. Lott et al.'s (2002) research was a pilot study, and they found that donepezil may be helpful, also emphasizing that further study is needed.

Other Behavioral Concerns

Udwin and Dennis (1995) mention that many people think of children with Down syndrome as generally amiable. While this is often true, up to a fourth of infants can be quite difficult to engage and some could qualify for a disorder of conduct in adolescence. Challenging behaviors such as aggression have also been reported.

Although there are individuals with aggression, self-injury, and other maladaptive behaviors, the question often is whether this is a nonspecific function of having a developmental disability or are these behaviors more common in Down syndrome? Dykens and Kasari (1997) looked at the maladaptive behavior in children with Down syndrome, Prader-Willi syndrome, and nonspecific etiologies of intellectual disability. They found that children with Down syndrome had less maladaptive behaviors than persons with Prader-Willi syndrome. Interestingly, obsessions were similar to persons with nonspecific etiologies and significantly less than children with Prader-Willi syndrome. Furthermore, compulsive behavior was significantly less in those with Down syndrome compared to children with Prader-Willi syndrome. There was no behavior that separated children with Down syndrome from the other two groups. There were only a few features that were significantly different between boys and girls with Down syndrome and those with nonspecific etiologies of intellectual disability. Children with Down syndrome were significantly more likely to have speech problems and to prefer being alone. They were similar in these regards to children with Prader-Willi syndrome. Children with nonspecific etiologies of intellectual disability were significantly more likely to be hyperactive than either of the other two groups. There was no maladaptive behavior that was more common in children with Down syndrome than those with Prader-Willi syndrome.

As noted above, children with Down syndrome can often have speech difficulties, which can lead to behavioral challenges. For example, a child who wants a break from a current activity may not be able to say or sign "break." Instead, the child may throw items, tantrum, or scream. Until the teacher or caregiver can deduce that the child's behavior is actually an attempt at communicating, the child, needlessly, may be prescribed psychotropic medications. Instead the goal is to teach the child the sign, gesture, or word for "break". This is but one of the approaches that Feeley and Jones (2008) recommend to assess and address challenging behaviors in children with Down syndrome.

Social Features and Vulnerabilities

Educational Opportunities

One of the most surprising parts of *Count Us In* is in the chapter on "Our Future Plans." Jason is concerned that his friend Mitchell is rushing through his preparation for his career.

> **Jason:** ... In my opinion... I don't think he (Mitchell) should skip College. There's lots of things he might learn because a college prepares him for his future. He does not go anywhere if he skips college. He goes into an apartment with his friends to prepare him for the future. What I'm saying is that there is a big gap right before Jespy and his senior year of high school... I advise him that he should go back to college.
>
> Emily (Kingsley): Well, he did almost two years at Jespy and now he's going to move into his own place and he's starting a good job at the Peekskill/Corlandt Chamber of Commerce. He'll be working as an office assistant, answering phones, helping to give out information to walk-in customers, filing, faxing, and working on database computer projects. So he seems to be doing okay.
>
> Jason: What I'm saying is, he's getting his low-paying job at the Chamber of Commerce. To make a high-paying job is getting the skills what you need at college right before Jespy so he would have more feedback to his future. I'm really worried about Mitchell's future and his success because he doesn't go anywhere and it doesn't make sense that he skips college...
>
> Both of us want to have good high-paying jobs and a good future. (Kingsley & Levitz, 1994, p. 178)

As discussed earlier, individuals with Down syndrome often have mild to moderate intellectual disability, but with the proper supports and an understanding of their unique needs, individuals with Down syndrome can be successful in an inclusive classroom. Turner, Alborz, and Gayle (2008) found that the greatest predictors of achievement in students with Down syndrome were level of intellectual functioning and participation in inclusive settings. Kasari, Freeman, Bauminger, and Alkin (1999) found that parents of childen with Down syndrome were generally supportive of their child being in an inclusive setting and about three quarters of the sample thought that their child's needs could be met in an inclusive setting. That being said, appropriateness of the setting for their child's level of functioning and specific educational needs was a significant concern.

Teachers have also expressed concerns about their level of preparation to teach individuals with Down syndrome (Cologon, 2013), but Cologon (2013) advises building on the individual's strengths, such as linking auditory and verbal information, but also being careful not to overload auditory short-term memory. She also recommends linking learning experiences to known concepts as well as supporting learning through interests and playful engagement. Monari Martinez and Benedetti (2011) also found that secondary students with Down syndrome can be successful in solving mathematical problems and using simple algebra, although they may struggle with numeracy and require supports such as a calculator.

Sociosexual Development

Mike Lauris who has Down syndrome and was 35 years when this was written talks about his best friend.

> .... I have a roommate, who is also my best friend. His name is Ron, and I have known him for 20 years. We have been living together for about two and one half years. We share the cleaning, cooking and grocery shopping. We watch and share videos. We both like to watch football, baseball, soccer, hockey, basketball, and wrestling tapes and to listen to the oldies on the stereo. I met Ron when I was 15-years-old at the school we both went to. He was throwing a baseball and hit me in the nose. Ron and the coach came over to check my nose and it was okay. Ron and I were buddies after that.

Mike also talks about his goals in his final paragraph:

> I have accomplished a lot of things in my life and I am working very hard on losing weight. I have lost eleven pounds over the past five months. I would like to keep going the way I am with losing weight. I'm going to lose this crummy belly of mine. I feel happy; life is WOW! Exciting. The most important thing I want is to keep putting one foot ahead of the other. One last thing I want to put in this paper is I want marriage in my life. (Lauris & Pary, 1993).

Jason and Mitchell also talk about marriage. Both want to get married and have children. Mitchell talks about adopting a child, if he and his future wife could not have one by themselves. There is a need for education on sexuality. A British study found that young people with Down syndrome were inadequately prepared to consider their sexuality, including sexual relationships (Shepperdson, 1995). A recent review of medical care for adolescents with Down syndrome also emphasizes that sexuality, as well as issue of sexual abuse, pregnancy and menstrual hygiene need to be openly discussed (Rozien, 2002). Watson, Richards, Miodrag, and Fedoroff (2012) addressed the primary sexuality concerns of individuals with Down syndrome, citing both male and specific sexual issues. Males are generally sterile because of decreased gonadal functioning (Arnell, Gustaffson, Ivarsson, & Anneren, 1996) and decreased spermatogenesis (Pradham, Dalal, Khan, & Agrawal, 2006), plus many males with Down syndrome have cryptorchidism (undescended testicles). Women with Down syndrome experience low fertility rates, heavy periods, and early menopause. Watson et al. (2012) also highlight potential secondary sexual effects, such as increased sex drive due to medications the individual might be taking, such as testosterone, as well as decreased sex drive due to medications such as selective serotonin reuptake inhibitors (SSRI) for depression. Some individuals with Down syndrome may also experience precocious puberty, perhaps due to hypothyroidism (Cooley & Graham, 1991)

There is the myth that persons with Down syndrome are asexual and have little interest in sex or relationships. The above paragraph clearly disputes this myth.

Summary

This chapter has attempted to shatter some of the stereotypes about persons with Down syndrome. While there are certain medical and psychiatric concerns, the words of people with Down syndrome suggest that their dreams are not much different than the rest of us.

Resources

Canadian Down Syndrome Society

The Canadian Down Syndrome Society is a national non-profit organization providing information, advocacy and education about Down syndrome. The CDSS supports self-advocates, parents, and families through all stages of life.
New parent welcome package available online
http://www.cdss.ca
e-mail info@cdss.ca
phone: 1-800-883-5608

National Down Syndrome Society

The National Down Syndrome Society envisions a world in which all people with Down syndrome have the opportunity to enhance their quality of life, realize their life aspirations, and become valued members of welcoming communities.
www.ndss.org
800-221-4602 (Monday - Friday from 9:00 AM to 5:00 PM ET) or email info@ndss.org.

Down Syndrome Research Foundation

The mission of the Down Syndrome Research Foundation is to empower individuals with Down syndrome to reach their full potential throughout life by pioneer-

ing and providing educational programs and services, grounded in foundational research. Working with researchers, professionals and families, they are a bridge between research and practice.
http://www.dsrf.org

National Association for Down Syndrome

Founded in 1961, their mission is to ensure that all persons with Down syndrome have the opportunity to achieve their potential in all aspects of community life. They offer information, support, and advocacy.
http://www.nads.org
630-325-9112
email: info@nads.org

Educational Resources

Down Syndrome Education International

Down Syndrome Education International is a UK-based charity that transforms the lives of young people with Down syndrome by improving understanding of their particular learning needs and by helping families and professionals to provide effective support, early intervention, and education. Their goal is to improve outcomes for all children with Down syndrome, helping them to lead more independent, productive, and fulfilling lives.
http://www.dseinternational.org/en-us/

eReadingPro

eReadingPro is a reading program designed for teaching individuals with Down syndrome to read. A new app was launched on iTunes - eReadingToGo! which enables parents who already use the full program to also use this with their children to add to their vocabulary and reading skills.
http://www.ereadingtogo.com

Resources for Families

Diagnosis to Delivery: A Pregnant Mother's Guide to Down Syndrome

Nancy McCrea Iannone and Stephanie Hall Meredith

This book is specifically written for expectant mothers who are moving forward with a pregnancy after learning about a diagnosis of Down syndrome. It will answer pregnancy and birth questions, validate emotions, provide coping advice, and give hope for the future.

A revised version also includes information about prenatal screening and testing, updated resource lists and research, and new information on health insurance and social services.

An online version of this book is available for free or a text version may be purchased from the publisher, Woodbine House.
http://downsyndromepregnancy.org/book/diagnosis-to-delivery/

References

American Academy of Pediatrics. (2001). Health supervision for children with Down syndrome. *Pediatrics, 107,* 442-449.

American Psychiatric Association. (2013). *Diagnostic and statistical manual of mental disorders* (5th ed.). Washington, D.C: Author.

Archaya, K. (2011). Prenatal testing for intellectual disability: Misperceptions and reality with lessons from Down syndrome. *Developmental Disabilities Research Review,* 17(1), 27–31.

Arnell, H., Gustaffson, J., Ivarsson, S. A., & Anneren, G. (1996). Growth and pubertal development in Down syndrome. *Acta Paediatrica, 85,* 1102–1106.

Burt, D. B., Loveland, K. A., & Lewis, K. R. (1992). Depression and the onset of dementia in adults with mental retardation. *American Journal on Mental Retardation, 96,* 502-511.

Charlot, L., Fox, S., & Friedlander, R. (2002). Obsessional slowness in Down's syndrome. *Journal Intellectual Disabilities Research, 46(6), 517-24.*

Cohen, W. I. (1999, Sept.). Health care guidelines for individuals with Down syndrome. *Down Syndrome Quarterly, 4.*

Collacott, R. A., Cooper, S. A., & McGrother, C. (1992). Differential rates of psychiatric disorders in adults with Down's syndrome compared with other mentally retarded adults. *British Journal of Psychiatry, 161,* 671-674.

Cologon, K. (2013). Debunking myths: Reading development in children with Down syndrome. *Australian Journal of Teacher Education, 38*(3), 130-151.

Conn, C.M., Cozzi, J., Harper, J.C., Winston, R.M.L., & Delhanty, J.D.A. (1999). Preimplantation genetic diagnosis for couples at high risk of Down syndrome pregnancy owing to parental translocation or mosaicism. *Journal of Medical Genetics, 36,* 45-50.

Cooley, C., & Graham, J. M. (1991). Common syndromes and management issues for primary care physicians—Down syndrome: An update and review for the primary pediatrician. *Clinical Pediatrics, 30,* 233–253.

Down, J. L. (1866). Observation of an ethnic classification of idiots. *London Hospital: Clinical Lectures and Report, 3,* 259-262.

Down, J. L. (1887). *Mental affections of childhood and youth* (reprinted as *Classics in developmental medicine* (No. 5) (1990). London: MacKeith Press.

Dykens, E. M, & Kasari, C. (1997). Maladaptive behavior in children with Prader-Willi syndrome, Down syndrome, and nonspecific mental retardation. *American Journal on Mental Retardation, 102,* 228-237.

Evenhuis, H. M. (1990). The natural history of dementia in Down's syndrome. *Archives of Neurology, 47,* 263-267.

Feeley, K. & Jones, E. (2008). Strategies to address challenging behaviour in young children with Down syndrome. *Down Syndrome Research and Practice, 12*(2), 153-63.

Haydar, T. F. & Reeves, R. H. (2012). Trisomy and early brain development. *Trends Neuroscience 35(2), 81–91.*

Jervis, G. (1948). Early senile dementia in mongoloid idiocy. *American Journal of Psychiatry, 105,* 102-106.

Kasari, C., Freeman, S.F.N., Bauminger, N., & Alkin, M.C. (1999). Parental perspectives on inclusion: Effects of autism and Down syndrome. *Journal of Autism and Developmental Disorders, 29*(4), 297-305.

Kingsley, J. & Levitz, M. (1994). *Count Us In.* Orlando, FL: Harcourt.   Lauris, M. P. & Pary, R. J. (1993). Life beyond a psychiatric disorder. *Habilitative Mental Health Newsletter, 12,* 62-63.

Lott, I. T. (2002). Down syndrome and Alzheimer disease. In R. J. Pary (Ed.), *Psychiatric problems in older persons with developmental disabilities* (pp. 25-34). Kingston, NY: NADD Press

Lott, I.T. (2012). Neurological phenotypes for Down syndrome across the life span. *Progress in Brain Research, 197,* 101-121.

Lott, I. T., & McCoy, E. (1992). *Down syndrome advances in medical care.* New York: Wiley-Liss.

Lott, I. T., Osann, K., Doran, E., & Nelson, L. (2002). Down syndrome and Alzheimer disease: Response to donepezil. *Archives of Neurology, 59,* 1133-1136.

Lund, J. (1988). Psychiatric aspects of Down's syndrome. *Acta psychiatrica Scandinavica, 178,* 369-374.

Monari Martinez, E. & Benedetti, N. (2011). Learning mathematics in mainstream secondary schools: Experiences of students with Down's syndrome. *European Journal of Special Needs Education, 26*(4), 531-540.

Murray, N., & Cohen, W. (n.d.). *When your baby has Down syndrome.* Pittsburgh, PA: The Down Syndrome Center, Children's Hospital of Pittsburgh.

Myers, B. A., & Pueschel, S. M. (1991). Psychiatric disorders in persons with Down syndrome. *Journal of Nervous and Mental Disease, 179,* 609-613.

Pary, R. J. (1993). Psychiatric disorders in adults with Down syndrome. *Habilitative Mental Health Newsletter, 12,* 26-27.

Pary, R. J. (1994). Obsessional slowness. *Habilitative Mental Health Newsletter, 13,* 49-50.

Pary, R.J., Friedlander, R., & Capone, G. T. (1999). Bipolar disorder and Down syndrome: Six cases. *Mental Health Aspects of Developmental Disabilities, 2,* 59- 63.

Pary, R. J., Strauss, D. J., & White, J. F. (1996). A population survey of bipolar disorder in persons with and without Down syndrome. *Down Syndrome Quarterly, 1(3),* 1-4.

Pradham, M., Dalal, A., Khan, F., & Agrawal, S. (2006). Fertility in men with Down syndrome: A case report. *Fertility and Sterility, 86,* 1765e1–1765e3.

Prasher, V. P., Huxley, A., & Haque, M. S. (2002). A 24-week, double-blind, placebo-controlled trial of donepezil in patients with Down syndrome and Alzheimer's disease: Pilot study. *International Journal of Geriatric Psychiatry, 17,* 270-278.

Pueschel, S. & Pueschel, J. (1992). *Biomedical concerns in persons with Down Syndrome.* Baltimore, MD: Paul H. Brookes Publishing Co.

Rozien, N. J. (2002). Medical care and monitoring for the adolescent with Down syndrome. *Adolescent Medicine, 13,* 345-358.

Shepperdson, B. (1995). The control of sexuality in young people with Down's syndrome. *Child Care Health Development, 21,* 333-349.

Sovner, R. & Hurley, A. D. (1993). "Psychotoform" psychopathology. *Habilitative Mental Health Newsletter, 12,* 112-113.

Turner, S., Alborz, A., & Gayle, V. (2008). Predictors of academic attainments of young people with Down's syndrome. *Journal of Intellectual Disability Research, 52(5),* 380-392.

Udwin, O. & Dennis, J. (1995). Down syndrome. In G. O'Brien & W. Yule (Eds.), *Behavioural Phenotypes* (pp. 105-109). Cambridge, England: MacKeith Press.

Van Allen, J. I., Fung, J., & Jurenka, S. B. (1999). Health care concerns and guidelines for adults with Down syndrome. *American Journal of Medical Genetics, 89,* 100-110.

Virji-Badul, N., Eichmann, A., Kisly, D., Down, J., & Haslam, R.H.A. (2007). Use of health care guidelines in patients with Down syndrome by family physicians across Canada. *Paediatric Child Health. 12(3), 179–183.*

Walker, J.C., Dosen, A., Buitelaar, J.K., & Janzing, J.G. (2011). Depression in Down syndrome: A review of the literature. *Research in Developmental Disabilities. 32(5),* 1432-40

Warren, A. C., Holroyd, S., & Folstein, M. F. (1989). Major depression in Down's syndrome. *British Journal of Psychiatry, 155,* 202-205.

Watson, S.L., Richards, D., Miodrag, N., & Fedoroff, P. (2012). Sex and genes Part 1: Sexuality and Down, Prader-Willi, and Williams syndromes. *Intellectual and Developmental Disability, 50(2),*155-168.

Zigman, W. B., Devenny, D. A., Krinsky-McHale, S. J., Jenkins, E. C., Urv, T. K., Wegiel, J., Schupf, N., & Silverman W. (2008). Alzheimer's disease in adults with Down syndrome. *International Review Research Mental Retardation, 36, 103–145.*

CHAPTER 4

Williams Syndrome

Brenda Finucane

Introduction

Williams syndrome (WS) has fascinated geneticists and behaviorists for decades, and it is among the most well-researched of the genetic intellectual disability (ID) syndromes (Pober, 2010). The condition is associated with an unusual combination of cognitive strengths and weaknesses, as well as a distinctive behavioral phenotype. Co-morbid psychiatric symptoms, particularly attentional disorders, anxiety, and phobias, are common among children and adults with the syndrome. The discovery of a specific genetic abnormality linked to WS (Ewart et al., 1993) has led to more accurate diagnosis and an increase in research on molecular correlations with the clinical phenotype.

WS is estimated to occur in 1 in 20,000 births, although a Norwegian survey suggests a much higher prevalence in Scandinavia (Stromme, Bjornstad, & Ramstad, 2002). Most individuals with the disorder fall within the 1% of the population having ID, and its incidence among children and adults with developmental disabilities is approximately 1 in 200. WS is thought to account for 6% of those with diagnosed genetic ID syndromes. Professionals working with special needs populations, including those with dual diagnosis, are therefore likely to encounter at least a few people with WS over the course of their careers.

Interest in WS in the popular press and on television has proven to be a double-edged sword. On the positive side, increased public awareness of WS has resulted in the diagnosis of many more children and adults with the condition. This awareness not only benefits families, but as the number of those diagnosed grows, researchers gain a clearer understanding of the condition across the full range of age and severity Unfortunately, some of the unique characteristics of WS have been exaggerated in the media, and a stereotypical perception has emerged implying that all people with WS show extraordinary musical and linguistic talents. While these appear to be areas of relative strength for some people with WS, affected individuals show a wide range of abilities, and most do not exhibit unusual linguistic and/or musical talents when compared to typically developing individuals. Moreover, despite decades of research interest in WS, a critical review of published data revealed that because of significant limitations in research methodology, accurate characterization of the neurobehavioral phenotype in WS has been hampered (Martens, Wilson, & Reutens, 2008).

Clinical and Laboratory Diagnosis

WS was first described as a clinical entity in 1961 by Charles Williams, a physician in New Zealand (Williams, Barrett-Boyes, & Lowe, 1961). The condition is sometimes referred to as Williams-Beuren syndrome because it was almost simultaneously described in the medical literature by a German team (Beuren, Apitz, & Harmjanz, 1962). These initial reports focused on the cute and attractive facial appearance (Figure 1) seen in affected children, and for several years, the disorder was referred to as the "pixie" or "elfin facies" syndrome, until it was more appropriately renamed WS in the 1980's. In Europe, WS has also been called infantile hypercalcemia syndrome because of its association with elevated calcium in the blood of some affected infants.

The clinical characteristics of WS, particularly the hallmark cardiovascular and facial features, are well-described. Until 1993, when the underlying genetic basis for WS was discovered (Ewart et al., 1993), the diagnosis was reliably made by geneticists based on known clinical criteria (Preus, 1984). Laboratory testing now allows objective confirmation of the WS diagnosis. The vast majority of people with WS have a microdeletion (submicroscopic missing segment) of the chromosomal locus 7q11.23 (Bayes, Magano, Rivera, Flores, & Perez Jurado, 2003). The deleted region contains a few dozen genes, including the gene for elastin (ELN) which is thought to be directly responsible for many of the syndrome's characteristic physical findings (Lowery et al., 1995). The 7q11.23 microdeletion can be detected using a molecular FISH probe when the diagnosis is clinically suspected. Laboratory confirmation is recommended for all children and adults meeting clinical criteria for WS, particularly those with characteristic cardiovascular findings (Committee on Genetics, 2001). Over the past decade, the increasingly routine use of chromosomal microarray analysis for infants and children with developmental delay has allowed more complete ascertainment of WS in this population. Since the majority of cases occur sporadically with no known familial or environmental risk factors, the diagnosis of WS is rarely intentionally checked for before birth. Babies with WS are almost always born to unaffected parents whose chance of having a second child with the disorder is not increased over that of couples in the general population. Individuals with WS have a 50% chance of passing the condition to their offspring. In the past, few adults with WS had children, but as opportunities for socialization and independence for people with developmental disabilities increase, familial cases of WS (Morris, Thomas, & Greenberg, 1993) are likely to become more common. Prenatal testing for WS is available, either through targeted FISH testing or chromosomal microarray. Detection through maternal blood sampling, a technique known as non-invasive prenatal testing or NIPT, is currently being offered for several chromosomal disorders and will likely include WS in the near future (Lau et al., 2014).

The deleted chromosomal region in people with WS contains more than two dozen genes, only a handful of which have been clearly linked to the clinical phenotype. ELN, which codes for the protein elastin, plays a role in connective tissue elasticity. Some of the syndrome's major findings, including cardiovascular anomalies, joint laxity, and abnormalities of the walls of the bladder and bowel, can potentially be explained by deletion of ELN on one of the two number 7 chromosomes in people with WS (Lowery et al., 1995). Several other genes in the 7q11.23 region, specifically *CYLN2, GTF2IRD1, GTF2I,* and *LIMK1,* are known to be expressed in brain tissue and have specifically been linked to the WS neurocognitive profile in animal studies and case reports (Antonell et al., 2010; Frangiskakis et al., 1996; van Hagen et al., 2007). Ongoing research efforts are aimed at characterizing genes within the deleted 17q11.23 chromosomal region and identifying molecular correlations with the clinical phenotype, particularly the cognitive and behavioral manifestations of WS.

Physical Findings and Medical Issues

The facial characteristics of people with WS are distinctive and easily recognized in most cases by clinicians familiar with the disorder (fig 1). The facial appearance in young children and infants is characterized by full lips, puffy cheeks, a relatively long philtrum, and a small jaw. In adolescents and adults, the loss of subcutaneous fat gives the face a more elongated appearance. The eyes often show a starburst (stellate) pattern in the iris, which is particularly noticeable in blue or light-colored eyes. Many individuals with WS have a characteristic raspy, hoarse voice. Short stature is typical, and both children and adults may exhibit joint contractures, sloping shoulders, spinal curvature, and/or a slumped posture.

Sensory impairments are common among children and adults with WS. Almost two thirds of those affected develop esotropia (inward deviation of the eye) (Kapp, von Noorden, & Jenkins, 1995), sometimes requiring surgery. Hyperopia (far-sightedness), possibly related to ocular elastin abnormalities, is common and may severely affect vision. Chronic ear infections compound language delays in many

Figure 1
photo courtesy of the Williams Syndrome Association

young children with WS, although these tend to occur less frequently with age (Klein, Armstrong, Greer, & Brown, 1990). Hyperacusis, or increased sensitivity to sound, is an unusual feature of WS found in over 90% of those affected (Klein et al., 1990). Children and adults with WS exhibit abnormal responses to sounds that do not usually cause fear or discomfort to people in the general population. People with WS may react to distressing sounds by crying, screaming, and/or covering their ears. Extreme fear responses to benign sounds, such as vacuum cleaners, motorcycles, and lawn mowers, can result in anticipatory anxiety (e.g., a child who refuses to attend school fearing a fire drill), which disrupts daily activities. In addition, hyperacusis may be an underlying factor in the attentional deficits seen in many people with this syndrome. With age, some adults with WS seem to become partially desensitized to distressing sounds and may be better able to tolerate noisy environments (Dykens, Hodapp, & Finucane, 2000).

WS is associated with several known medical complications and anomalies, which can affect health throughout the lifespan, as shown in Table I. Congenital cardiovascular anomalies are found in approximately 80% of people with WS. Most often, these involve stenosis (narrowing) of blood vessels of the heart, but can include arteries going to the kidneys and other body organs (Pober, 2010). The most common cardiovascular abnormality is supravalvular aortic stenosis (SVAS) in which narrowing of the aorta disrupts blood flow. The condition often becomes more severe with age and requires careful monitoring by a cardiologist. Peripheral pulmonary artery stenosis is also common in infancy but usually improves over time. (Morris et al., 1988).

Table 1.
Medical / Developmental Characteristics of Williams Syndrome*

INCIDENCE	FINDING	AGE SEEN		
		INFANT	CHILD	ADULT
FREQUENT: > 75%	CHARACTERISTIC FACIAL APPEARANCE	X	X	X
	DEVELOPMENTAL DELAY	X	X	
	INTELLECTUAL DISABILITY (usually mild)		X	X
	CARDIOVASCULAR DISEASE (mostly supravalvular aortic stenosis)	X	X	X
	CHARACTERISTIC COGNITIVE PROFILE		X	X
	HYPOTONIA (central)	X	X	
	LOOSE JOINTEDNESS	X	X	
	HYPERACTIVE DEEP TENDON REFLEXES		X	X
	HYPERACUSIS	X	X	X
	DENTAL ABNORMALITIES		X	X
	SOFT, STRETCHY SKIN	X	X	X
	PREMATURELY GRAY HAIR			X
	GENERALIZED ANXIETY DISORDER		X	X

COMMON: 50 TO <75%	FEEDING DIFFICULTIES	X	X	
	CHRONIC OTITIS MEDIA	X	X	
	ATTENTION DEFICIT HYPERACTIVITY DISORDER		X	
	EARLY PUBERTY		X	
	HYPEROPIA		X	X
	STRABISMUS	X		
	ENURESIS		X	
	UMBILICAL HERNIA	X		
	JOINT CONTRACTURES	X	X	X
	AWKWARD GAIT		X	X
	HYPERTONIA (peripheral)		X	X
LESS COMMON: 25 TO < 50	HYPERCALCIURIA	X	X	X
	CHRONIC URINARY TRACT INFECTIONS			X
	CONSTIPATION	X	X	X
	COLON DIVERTICULAE		X	X
	INGUINAL HERNIA	X		
	RENAL ARTERY STENOSIS	X	X	X
	LORDOSIS		X	X
OCCASIONAL < 25%	IDIOPATHIC HYPERCALCEMIA	X		X
	STRUCTURAL URINARY TRACT ABNORMALITIES	X	X	X
	NEPHROCALCINOSIS	X	X	X
	RECTAL PROLAPSE	X	X	
	KYPHOSIS			X
	HYPOTHYROIDISM	X	X	X
	DIABETES MELLITUS			X
	ARNOLD-CHIARI MALFORMATION	X	X	X
	BORDERLINE TO AVERAGE INTELLIGENCE		X	X

* adapted from Committee on Genetics, 2001.

Approximately 15% of infants with WS have documented hypercalcemia (abnormally elevated levels of calcium in the blood). Hypercalcemia is most often transient and disappears by the fourth year of life. However, a minority of older children and adults with WS experience persistent hypercalcemia that requires monitoring because of the potential for secondary health problems, such as calcium accumulation in the kidneys (nephrocalcinosis), related to abnormal calcium metabolism (Pober, Lacro, Rice, Mandell, & Teele, 1993).

Hypertension (high blood pressure) is present in almost half of children and adults with WS, even in the absence of cardiovascular or renal disease (Broder et al., 1999). The etiology of hypertension in this population is unknown, and it does not appear to be related to the generalized anxiety seen in most people with the condition. Hypertension in WS is significantly correlated with infantile hypercalcemia, potentially implicating subtle abnormalities in calcium metabolism. Abnormalities of the blood vessels due to the underlying elastin microdeletion could also theoretically contribute to hypertension in this disorder (Broder et al., 1999).

Chronic constipation is common among people with WS and may account for stomach pain and feeding problems in infants and children. Stool softeners are often needed to maintain regularity and to avoid secondary gastrointestinal complications, such as rectal prolapse. Many older children and adults with WS experience incontinence and urinary tract infections, sometimes related to structural bladder changes such as diverticula ("pockets" in the bladder wall) (Morris, Leonard, Dilts, & Demsey, 1990). Renal abnormalities, ranging from mild to severe, are found in approximately 18% of those affected (Pober et al., 1993). Although most of the associated medical issues in WS can be successfully managed, early identification, and monitoring are key for ensuring optimum health. Health care directives for people with WS have been published and are helpful for guiding medical management of children and adults with this disorder (Committee on Genetics, 2001).

Natural History

Infants with WS often come to medical attention because of cardiovascular abnormalities in the first year of life. Many cardiologists are familiar with the association between SVAS and WS, and babies born with SVAS are likely to be referred for genetic testing. Individuals with other more common types of heart defects, as well as those who are free of cardiac anomalies, are less likely to receive an early diagnosis (Huang, Sadler, O'Riordan, & Robin, 2002). Newborns with WS tend to be relatively small in weight as compared to other babies in the family. Growth remains slow, and many infants experience failure to thrive during the first year of life. Typically, they are cranky, fussy babies in the first year, possibly related to infantile hypercalcemia and/or gastrointestinal problems.

Both motor and language development are delayed in children with WS. Hypotonia (low muscle tone) and joint laxity are likely contributors to motor delays in young children. Older children and adults often show increased tone and stiffness. Many individuals develop contractures of both large and small joints, resulting in a crouched, awkward gait and impairments in fine motor function (Kaplan, Kirschner, Watters, & Costa, 1989). Spinal curvatures, particularly kyphosis and lordosis, are relatively common among older children and adults with WS. Adult height is usually less than expected for the family background.

Language acquisition is delayed, and young children with WS benefit from early intervention services, including speech therapy. As they age, however, language becomes an area of relative strength for most people with WS. Relatively sophisticated language abilities may mask cognitive deficits in other areas, particularly visuospatial tasks. The majority of school-aged children with WS require special education, particularly for Math and Reading. Most test within the mild range of ID, with some individuals having average intelligence and others more severe degrees of intellectual impairment (Dykens et al., 2000). Some adults with WS are employed in the community, most often with the support of a job coach and/or supervision from a sponsoring agency. Many find work in traditional sheltered workshop settings. Although they may seem capable of more challenging work, a significant number of adults with WS have difficulty maintaining competitive employment due to visuospatial deficits, distractibility, and psychiatric issues, particularly anxiety (Davies, Howlin, & Udwin, 1997; Morris, Demsey, Leonard, Dilts, & Blackburn, 1988). As with most other genetic syndromes, little is known about long-term functioning into later adulthood and old age in people with WS. Based on the limited number of cases reported, there is no evidence for an increased incidence of Alzheimer disease, as in Down syndrome, or other neurodegenerative conditions.

Cognitive Strengths and Weaknesses

Individuals with WS show a wide range of cognitive abilities. The average IQ among those affected is between 50 and 60, with most functioning in the mild to moderate range of ID (Bellugi, Mills, Jernigan, Hickok, & Galaburda, 1999). A small percentage of those with the syndrome test within the average range of intellectual functioning, while some fall within the severe range of ID. There is significant scatter in the cognitive profile of people with WS, which cannot be fully appreciated by simply considering an overall IQ score. Relative strengths include language abilities, facial recognition, and short term auditory memory. By contrast, the syndrome is associated in most people with significant deficits in visuospatial construction, perceptual planning, and fine motor control (Farran & Jarrold, 2005).

In practical terms, educational and vocational interventions for individuals with WS are often complicated by their uneven abilities and associated impairments, such as hyperacusis and attentional disorders (Mervis & John, 2010). Relatively advanced language abilities may mask cognitive impairments and give the impression of higher overall functioning. Visuospatial deficits coupled with fine motor difficulties may make it impossible for a person to WS to perform a work task, which he or she can otherwise describe in exacting detail. Research is currently focused on identifying and describing specific aspects of the WS cognitive profile. Such efforts will ideally lead to the development of appropriate strategies and interventions to address their educational needs in the future.

Language

WS has been a source of great interest to researchers studying the connection between intelligence and language. Some studies of WS show preserved language abilities in the context of significantly impaired cognition, calling into question the interdependency of the two (Bellugi, Wang, & Jernigan, 1994). Vocabulary, for example, appears to be a relative strength for individuals with WS, although discrepancies between verbal and nonverbal abilities may not become apparent until later childhood or adolescence (Jarrold, Baddeley, & Hewes, 1998). In most people with WS, however, vocabulary still falls below that of CA-(chronological age) matched controls without ID. Some studies have shown grammar (the ordering of words in a sentence) and other aspects of syntax to be areas of relative strength for people with WS (Bellugi, et al., 1994; Losh, Bellugi, & Reilly, 2000), while other researchers have confirmed significant impairments in syntax as compared with CA-matched, and in some cases, MA (mental age)-matched controls (Karmiloff-Smith et al., 1997; Volterra, Capirci, Pezzini, Sabbadini & Vicari, 1996).

Studies have also shown conflicting results with regard to semantics, that is, the meaning and organization of words. Anecdotally, people with WS prefer the use of unusual words and phrases in conversation. Unusual word choices were confirmed by Bellugi et al. (1994), who found that adolescents and adults with WS produced more low-frequency words than MA-matched controls on word fluency tests. When asked to name as many animals as possible in a 60 second period, for example, children with WS included uncommon animals such as ibex, condor, and saber-toothed tiger among their choices. Subsequent studies by other research groups (Scott et al., 1995; Volterra et al., 1996) found no differences between children with WS and MA-matched controls on word fluency tasks, suggesting that semantic abilities in people with this disorder are commensurate with cognitive functioning. More recent studies (Stojanovik, Perkins, & Howard, 2004; Vicari et al., 2004) have identified significant atypicalities in grammatical skills and language use in individuals with WS, calling into question the concept of language as a relative strength in this population.

The debate over language in WS continues and may be resolved by further research. Most researchers agree that while linguistic abilities may not be completely spared, certain aspects of language represent areas of relative strength for people with WS, at least as compared to those with similar levels of cognitive impairment. In addition, exaggerated linguistic affect may give a false impression of highly developed language abilities in people with WS. Their use of exclamations, dramatic inflection, and other storytelling devices creates interest and adds to their positive interactive style (Losh et al., 2000).

Musical Ability

Only a handful of studies have formally examined the musical abilities of individuals with WS. As compared to individuals with autism and Down syndrome, people with WS showed greater emotional responses to music, manifested interest in music at younger ages, and spent more time listening to music (Levitin et al., 2004). Dykens, Rosner, Ly, and Sagun (2005) surveyed parents and found that children with WS were significantly more likely to take music lessons and play a musical instrument. Rhythmic abilities among some children with WS were found to be equal to those of typically developing controls (Levitin & Bellugi, 1998), with the Williams group showing an impressive ability to improvise. Musical abilities among people with this syndrome may in part be related to hypertimbria, an enhanced ability to distinguish the subjective quality of a sound (e.g., different musical instruments playing the same note). Anecdotally, parents report that their children with WS have an uncanny ability to identify the exact origin of sounds in their environment (e.g., distinguishing different types of aircraft based on their engine sounds). This capability may be a variant of perfect pitch, the ability to precisely recognize musical notes, which in turn could be related to the known association between WS and hyperacusis. Although these preliminary studies and observations are intriguing, further research is needed to determine the extent to which musical abilities are part of the WS phenotype.

Visuospatial Perception

Visuospatial perception refers to the ability to process and interpret visual information related to the location of objects in space. Deficits in this cognitive function have a practical impact on a wide range of daily activities, from drawing and writing to tying shoelaces. People with WS tend to perform very poorly on visuospatial tasks as compared to both typically developing children and those with other types of developmental disabilities, such as Down syndrome (Mervis, Morris, Bertrand, & Robinson, 1999). Impairments in motor planning, spatial orientation, and eye-hand coordination may explain their difficulty with relatively simple tasks, such as orienting blocks to match a model (Dykens et al., 2000). Several studies have shown that children with WS have severe perceptual-motor deficits on tests which require figure copying and drawing. In 1994, Bellugi, Wang, and Jernigan asked children with WS to both describe and draw specific objects and animals. Their verbal descriptions were richly detailed and accurate, but their drawings were disorganized and unrecognizable. Debate continues as to whether this represents an age-related delay in drawing development or a syndrome-specific area of abnormal cognitive functioning.

Recent studies have suggested that visuospatial deficits in WS may be localized to the parieto-occipital region of the brain, which is believed to process visual information related to space and motion. By contrast, preliminary research suggests that people with WS are adequately able to process visual information about the form and color of objects, a skill believed to be mediated by the temporal region of the brain. For example, Nakamura, Kaneoke, Watanabe, and Kakigi (2001) found that performance on line copying tasks improved in a small cohort of children with WS when colored dots were used as guides. Such research suggests that efforts to better understand the underlying pathophysiology of cognitive deficits in WS may eventually lead to practical interventions.

Behavior and Personality

People with WS have long been noted to be friendly and outgoing. These positive personality attributes are mentioned in even the earliest reports of the syndrome and have become a hallmark of the behavioral phenotype. Some researchers have speculated that the friendly demeanor in WS can be partly explained by its characteristic facial appearance, which includes a wide mouth, upturned nose, and a stellate iris pattern resulting in "sparkly", animated eyes (Pober, 2010). People with WS tend to have an unusual interest in faces from an early age, and research has confirmed a relative strength in their ability to recognize and remember faces (Bellugi et al., 1994). This interest, combined with their heightened linguistic affect, gives the impression of an attentive, charming, and enthusiastic listener (Levine & Wharton, 2001). Families report that their children with WS are often the "greeters" at social functions, initiating conversation, and asking social questions to newcomers ("What's your name? Where are you from?"). Their attractive, happy appearance may also engender positive, friendly reactions from those who interact with them, reinforcing outgoing, gregarious behavior from an early age. WS is, therefore, an excellent model for how inherent physical and personality characteristics can become reinforced and even exaggerated through the environmental responses they generate.

Individuals with WS come across as unusually empathic and emotionally sensitive. Researchers have speculated that they may have an intact "theory of mind", the ability to take on the perspective and infer the mental state of another person. This ability is known to be impaired in people with autism and other types of developmental disabilities. People with WS have been found to perform better than MA-matched controls, and in some cases as well as typical peers, on various tasks designed to assess theory of mind (Karmiloff-Smith, Klima, Bellugi, Grant & Baron-Cohen, 1995; Tager-Flusberg, Boshart, & Baron-Cohen, 1998). These findings support the anecdotal impression of a sensitive, caring personality phenotype in WS.

Despite charming and friendly personalities, many people with WS have difficulty with social interaction. They are sometimes overly friendly, even with strangers, to the point that their social style becomes intrusive. They may be socially uninhibited, leading to indiscriminate and inappropriate interactions with others. They frequently have difficulty sustaining friendships, in part because they "come on too strong" and tend to become infatuated with friends. They can also be emotionally labile and physically over-demonstrative, putting them at risk for sexual exploitation. Children and adults with WS can benefit from social skills training (e.g., role playing, structured interactions) to help them understand social boundaries (Davies, Udwin, & Howlin, 1988).

Associated Psychopathology

Over the course of their lifetimes, most individuals with WS meet the criteria for both ID and at least one psychiatric disorder (Levitas, Finucane, Dykens, & Kates, 2007). Some of the associated psychopathology seems to be age-related. Young children with WS are often diagnosed with Attention Deficit Hyperactivity Disorder, while motor hyperactivity rarely persists into adulthood. Adults continue to have short attention spans and distractibility, however, even in the absence of hyperactivity.

Anxiety disorders are common among both children and adults with WS. Over half of those studied using standard psychiatric interviews were considered chronic "worriers", while almost all had some persistent anxiety-producing fears (Dykens, 2003). Specific phobias are often related to noise (e.g., thunder, motorcycles), natural disasters, illness, and fears about the future. The high incidence of phobias in WS contrasts strongly with the relatively low prevalence (<5%) of these conditions in people with nonspecific ID (Dykens et al., 2000). By contrast, autistic symptoms are only rarely seen in association with WS. Many of the characteristic behavioral features of autism and WS are mutually exclusive (e.g., poor versus intact theory of mind, facial emotion recognition, language). Some autism researchers have a keen interest in studying WS because its many contrasting characteristics could potentially provide insights into the underlying neurological basis for autism.

As with most other genetic syndromes, there have been virtually no controlled trials to study the effectiveness of specific medications on psychiatric symptoms in WS. Pharmacological treatment is symptomatic and may include stimulant drugs for attentional disorders as well as anti-anxiety medications. Non-pharmacological strategies include reassurance, counseling, and cognitive-behavioral approaches which capitalize on the linguistic and musical strengths of people with the syndrome (Dykens et al., 2000). Because of the complexity of their medical, sensory, behavioral, and intellectual needs, children and adults with WS usually require a long-term coordinated network of multidisciplinary supports. Fortunately, the many positive aspects of the behavioral phenotype foster a high degree of dedication and interest among caregivers who often consider it a privilege to work with these unique and fascinating individuals.

Resources

Williams Syndrome Association (WSA)
www.williams-syndrome.org
The WSA is the most comprehensive resource for people and families living with Williams syndrome as well as for doctors, researchers, and educators. The WSA website has a wealth of practical resources for families and professionals.

The Martens, Wilson and Reutens (2008) reference cited below provides an exhaustive review of the neurocognitive profile and research findings in WS. It is an indispensable resource for professionals interested in behavioral and cognitive aspects of WS.

Williams Syndrome Changing Lives Foundation
www.wschanginglives.org
The Foundation was formed to enhance the lives of children and adults with Williams syndrome by providing needed financial assistance with medical, educational, developmental, therapeutic and recreational resources.

References

Antonell, A., Del Campo, M., Magano, L.F., Kaufmann, L., de la Iglesia, J.M., Gallastegui, F.,…. Pérez-Jurado, L.A. (2010). Partial 7q11.23 deletions further implicate GTF2I and GTF2IRD1 as the main genes responsible for the Williams-Beuren syndrome neurocognitive profile. *Journal of Medical Genetics, 47*(5), 312-320.

Bayes, M., Magano, L.F., Rivera, N., Flores, R., & Perez Jurado, L.A. (2003). Mutational mechanisms of Williams-Beuren syndrome deletions. *American Journal of Human Genetics, 73*, 131–51.

Bellugi, U., Mills, D., Jernigan, T.L., Hickok, G., & Galaburda, A. (1999). Linking cognition, brain structure, and brain function in Williams syndrome. In H. Tager-Flusberg (Ed.), *Neurodevelopmental disorders* (pp. 111–136). Cambridge: MIT Press.

Bellugi, U., Wang, P., & Jernigan, T.L. (1994). Williams syndrome: An unusual neuropsychological profile. In S.H. Browman & J. Grafram (Eds.), *Atypical cognitive deficits in developmental disorders* (pp. 23-56). Mahwah, NJ: Lawrence Erlbaum Associates.

Beuren, A.J., Apitz, J., & Harmjanz, D. (1962). Supravalvular aortic stenosis in association with mental retardation and a certain facial appearance. *Circulation, 26*, 1235-1240.

Broder, K., Reinhardt, E., Ahern, J., Lifton, R., Tamborlane, W., & Pober, B. (1999). Elevated ambulatory blood pressure in 20 subjects with Williams syndrome. *American Journal of Medical Genetics, 83*, 356-360.

Committee on Genetics, American Academy of Pediatrics (2001). Health care supervision for children with Williams syndrome. *Pediatrics, 107,*1192-1204.

Davies M., Howlin, P., & Udwin, O. (1997). Independence and adaptive behavior in adults with Williams syndrome. *American Journal of Medical Genetics, 70*, 188-195.

Davies, M., Udwin,O., & Howlin, P. (1998). Adults with Williams syndrome. *British Journal of Psychiatry, 172*, 273-276.

Dykens, E.M. (2003). Anxiety, fears, and phobias in Williams syndrome. *Developmental Neuropsychology, 23*(1-2), 291-316.

Dykens, E.M., Hodapp, R.M., & Finucane, B.M. (2000). *Genetics and mental retardation syndromes: A new look at behavior and interventions.* Baltimore, MD: Paul H. Brookes Publishing Company

Dykens, E.M., Rosner, B.A., Ly, T., & Sagun, J. (2005). Music and anxiety in Williams syndrome: A harmonious or discordant relationship? *American Journal on Mental Retardation, 110*, 346-358.

Ewart, A.K., Morris, C.A., Atkinson, D., Jin, W., Sternes, K., Spallone, P.,…Keating, M.T. (1993). Hemizygosity at the elastin locus in a developmental disorder, Williams syndrome. *Nature Genetics, 5*, 11-16.

Farran, E.K., & Jarrold, C. (2005). Evidence for unusual spatial location coding in Williams syndrome: An explanation for the local bias in visuo-construction tasks? *Brain and Cognition, 59*, 159–172.

Frangiskakis, J.M., Ewart, A.K., Morris, C.A., Mervis, C.B., Bertrand, J., Robinson, B.F.,…Keating, M.T. (1996). LIM-kinase1 hemizygosity implicated in impaired visuospatial constructive cognition. *Cell, 86*, 59-69.

Huang, L., Sadler, L., O'Riordan, M.A., & Robin, N.H. (2002). Delay in diagnosis of Williams syndrome. *Clinical Pediatrics, 41,* 257261.

Jarrold, C., Baddeley, A.D., & Hewes, A.K. (1998). Verbal and nonverbal abilities in the Williams syndrome phenotype: Evidence for diverging developmental trajectories. *Journal of Child Psychology and Psychiatry and Allied Disciplines, 39,* 511-523.

Kaplan, P., Kirschner, M., Watters, G., & Costa, M.T. (1989). Contractures in patients with Williams syndrome. *Pediatrics, 84,* 895-899.

Kapp, M.E., von Noorden, G.K., & Jenkins, R. (1995). Strabismus in Williams syndrome. *American Journal of Ophthalmology,119,* 355-360.

Karmiloff-Smith, A., Grant, J., Berthoud, I., Davies, M., Howlin, P., & Udwin, O. (1997). Language and Williams syndrome: How intact is "intact"? *Child Development, 68,* 246-262.

Karmiloff-Smith, A., Klima, E., Bellugi, U., Grant, J., & Baron-Cohen, S. (1995). Is there a social processing module? Language, face processing, and theory of mind in individuals with Williams syndrome. *Journal of Cognitive Neuroscience, 7,* 196-208.

Klein, A.J., Armstrong, B.L., Greer, M.K.,& Brown, F.R.[3rd] (1990). Hyperacusis and otitis media in individuals with Williams syndrome. *Journal of Speech and Hearing Disorders, 55,* 339-344.

Lau, T.K., Cheung, S.W., Lo, P.S., Pursley, A.N., Chan, M.K., Jiang, F., Zhang, H.... Choy, K.W. (2014). Non-invasive prenatal testing for fetal chromosomal abnormalities by low-coverage whole-genome sequencing of maternal plasma DNA: review of 1982 consecutive cases in a single center. *Ultrasound in Obstetrics and Gynecology, 43*(3), 254-64.

Levine, K. & Wharton, R. (2001). Williams syndrome and happiness. *American Journal on Mental Retardation, 105,* 363-371.

Levitas, A., Dykens, E., Finucane, B., & Kates, W.R. (2007). Behavioral phenotypes of genetic disorders. In R. Fletcher, E. Loschen, C. Stavrakaki, & M. First (Eds.) *Diagnostic manual – Intellectual disability: A textbook of diagnosis of mental disorders in persons with intellectual disability* (pp.33-62). Kingston, NY: NADD Press, 2007.

Levitin, D.J. & Bellugi, U. (1998). Musical abilities in individuals with Williams syndrome. *Music Perception, 15,* 357-398.

Levitin, D.J., Cole,K., Chiles,M., Lai, Z., Lincoln,A., & Bellugi, U. (2004). Characterizing the musical phenotype in individuals with Williams Syndrome. *Child Neuropsychology, 10*(4), 223-47.

Losh, M., Bellugi, U., & Reilly, J (2000). Narrative as a social engagement tool: The excessive use of evaluation in narratives from children with Williams syndrome. *Narrative Inquiry, 10*(2),265–290.

Lowery, M.C., Morris, C.A., Ewart, A., Brothman, L.J., Zhu, X.L., Leonard, C.O., Carey, J.C., Keating, M., & Brothman, A.R. (1995). Strong correlation of elastin deletions, detected by FISH, with Williams syndrome: evaluation of 235 patients. *American Journal of Human Genetics, 57*(1), 49-53.

Martens, M.A., Wilson, S.J., & Reutens, D.C. (2008). Research review: Williams syndrome: A critical review of the cognitive, behavioral, and neuroanatomical phenotype. *Journal of Child Psychology and Psychiatry, 49*(6), 576-608.

Mervis, C.B. & John, A.E. (2010). Cognitive and behavioral characteristics of children with Williams syndrome: Implications for intervention approaches. *American Journal of Medical Genetics C, Seminar in Medical Genetics,* 154(2), 229-248.

Mervis, C.B., Morris, C.A., Bertrand, J., & Robinson, B.F. (1999). Williams syndrome: findings from an integrated program of research. In: H. Tager-Flusberg (Ed.), *Neurodevelopmental disorders: Contributions to a framework from the cognitive sciences* (pp. 65-110). Cambridge: MIT Press.

Morris, C.A., Demsey, S.A., Leonard, C.O., Dilts, C., & Blackburn, B.L. (1988). Natural history of Williams syndrome: Physical characteristics. *Journal of Pediatrics, 113,* 318-326.

Morris, C.A., Leonard, C.O., Dilts, C., & Demsey, S.A. (1990). Adults with Williams syndrome. *American Journal of Medical Genetics Supplement, 6,*102-107.

Morris, C.A., Thomas, I.T., & Greenberg, F. (1993). Williams syndrome: Autosomal dominant inheritance. *American Journal of Medical Genetics, 47,* 478-481.

Nakamura, M., Kaneoke, Y., Watanabe, K., & Kakigi, R. (2002). Visual information process in Williams syndrome: Intact motion detection accompanied by typical visuospatial dysfunctions. *European Journal of Neuroscience, 16,* 1810-1818.

Pober, B.R. (2010). Williams-Beuren syndrome. *New England Journal of Medicine, 362,* 239–52.

Pober, B.R., Lacro, R.V., Rice, C., Mandell, V., & Teele, R.L. (1993). Renal findings in 40 individuals with Williams syndrome. *American Journal of Medical Genetics, 46,* 271-274.

Preus, M. (1984). The Williams syndrome: Objective definition and diagnosis. *Clinical Genetics, 25,* 422-428.

Scott, P., Mervis, C.B., Bertrand, J., Klein, B.P., Armstrong, S.C., & Ford, A.J. (1995). Semantic organization and word fluency in 9- and 10-year-old children with Williams syndrome. *Genetic Counseling, 6,* 172-173.

Stojanovik, V., Perkins, M., & Howard, S. (2004). Williams syndrome and specific language impairment do not support claims for developmental double dissociations and innate modularity. *Journal of Neurolinguistics, 17,* 403–424.

Stromme, P., Bjornstad, P.G., & Ramstad, K. (2002). Prevalence estimation of Williams syndrome. *Journal of Child Neurology, 17,* 269-271.

Tager-Flusberg, H., Boshart, J., & Baron-Cohen, S. (1998). Reading the windows to the soul: Evidence of domain-specific sparing in Williams syndrome. *Journal of Cognitive Neuroscience, 10,* 631-639.

van Hagen, J.M., van der Geest, J.N., van der Giessen, R.S., Lagers-van Haselen, G.C., Eussen, H.J., Gille, J.J., ... Zeeuw, C.I. (2007). Contribution of CYLN2 and GTF2IRD1 to neurological and cognitive symptoms in Williams syndrome. *Neurobiology Disease, 1,*112-24.

Vicari, S., Bates, E., Caselli, M.C., Pasqualetti, P., Gagliardi, C., Tonucci, F., & Volterra, V. (2004). Neuropsychological profile of Italians with Williams syndrome: An example of a dissociation between language and cognition? *Journal of the International Neuropsychological Society, 10,* 862–876.

Volterra, V., Capirci, O., Pezzini, G., Sabbadini, L., & Vicari, S. (1996). Linguistic abilities in Italian children with Williams syndrome. *Cortex, 32,* 663-677.

Williams, J.C., Barrett-Boyes, B.G., & Lowe, J.B. (1961). Supravalvular aortic stenosis. *Circulation, 24,* 1311-1318.

CHAPTER 5

Smith-Magenis Syndrome

Elliott W. Simon, Barbara Haas-Givler, & Marcy Schuster

Introduction

The behavioral phenotype of Smith-Magenis syndrome (SMS, Smith et al., 1986) results from a complex interplay among biomedical, psychological, and psychosocial factors. Our understanding of these factors and their interrelationship can inform supports for SMS and other genetically based developmental disorders (Simon & Finucane, 1998). The SMS phenotype includes sensory deficits, neurological findings, a sleep disorder, and a characteristic pattern of facial features. Intellectual impairment is present, and resulting deficits in adaptive behavior during the developmental period lead to a diagnosis of intellectual disability. Deficits in intellectual and adaptive behavior are usually mild or moderate but associated behavioral and psychiatric disorders can be quite severe and often include self-injury. SMS is likely underdiagnosed. Parents and Researchers interested in Smith-Magenis Syndrome (PRISMS has recently published a comprehensive SMS guidebook for schools (Haas-Givler & Finucane, 2014) that is available from that organization. SMS is a model for the way in which biomedical factors can impact psychological, cognitive, behavioral, and psychosocial functioning.

Etiology/Incidence

The majority of individuals with SMS have chromosomal deletions in the area of 17p11.2 that includes the RAI1 gene (Greenberg et al., 1991), which means that a portion of one of the two number 17 chromosomes is missing or deleted. Approximately 10% of individuals with SMS do not have a chromosomal deletion but instead have a heterozygous point mutation (Slager, Newton, Vlangos, Finucane,

& Elsea, 2003) in the retinoic acid induced 1 gene (RAI1). Individuals with SMS, therefore, have one normal and one affected chromosome 17 in each of their cells. SMS is also termed a continuous gene syndrome in that the missing genetic material is continuous on the chromosome, and, in the case of SMS, varying numbers of genes in this region may be missing. Although the missing genes in SMS are positioned close to each other, they may have very different functions. This variation results in the complex SMS physical and behavioral phenotype. Differences in phenotype are beginning to be identified between individuals with the deletion and individuals with the RAI1 mutation (Edelman et al., 2007). Based on small sample size investigations, people with the RAI1 mutation have obesity, are taller, and do not share the same systemic problems as people with the deletion (Girirajan, Elsas, Devriendt & Elsea, 2005; Slager et al., 2003).

The missing genes in SMS in this region are only detectable by high resolution chromosome analysis. Therefore karyotype analyses, which confirm gross genetic findings such as the extra chromosome 21 in Down syndrome, will not reveal the SMS deletion. If no deletions can be detected, the RAI1 gene should be sequenced to identify mutations (Elsea & Girirajan, 2008). Almost all cases of SMS are the result of deletions that are not inherited and the chance of a parent having a second child with SMS is usually no greater than for an individual who has not had a child with SMS. There have been a few cases of asymptomatic individuals who are mosaic for the deletion (the deletion is not present in all cells) bearing children with the full SMS deletion (Zori et al., 1993).

The general incidence statistic for SMS may be as high as 1/15000 live births (Elsea & Girirajan 2008). SMS is, however, under-diagnosed (Lockwood et al., 1988) and the incidence of SMS may be very common in individuals with intellectual disability. During a five year period in a population of approximately 1,000 individuals with intellectual disability, 23 people were diagnosed with SMS (Finucane & Simon, 1999).

Features Associated with SMS
Physical and Medical Findings
A pattern of physical and cognitive characteristics as well as associated medical implications are present in SMS. These characteristics include facial and body features as well as specific medical findings, some of which are related to the SMS behavioral profile.

Infants with SMS have significant low muscle tone and are characterized as floppy babies; however hypotonia does not emerge as a significant symptom in individuals who have an RAI1 mutation (Finucane & Haas-Givler, 2009). Poor eating during infancy may result in some babies with SMS being diagnosed with failure to thrive. Other feeding difficulties include impairment in oral motor functioning and the sucking reflex (Elsea & Girirajan, 2008). Some cranio-facial findings include under-developed cheekbones, a low nasal bridge, unusually formed ears, abnormalities of the palate (at times cleft), a prominent jaw in older children and adults, a down turned mouth, and a protruding upper lip (Lockwood et al., 1988; Smith et al., 1986). Skeletal characteristics include short fingers and toes, broad hands, webbing of the toes (particularly toes 2 and 3), fingertip pads, abnormal palmar creases, scoliosis, and a small stature. Facial characteristics become more pronounced with age but are subtle in children with SMS. See Figure 1.

Figure 1

Neurologically, abnormal EEG patterns and seizures have been reported but are not considered a hallmark of SMS (Goldman et al., 2006). Brain malformations can be present in individuals with SMS though none have been reported with any significant frequency. A partial absence of vermis and dystrophic calcifications of the frontal lobe were found in 52% of individuals with SMS (Greenberg et al., 1996). An important neurological finding with behavioral implications for the self-injury present in SMS is a decreased sensitivity to pain and reduced deep tendon reflexes with peripheral neuropathy (Greenberg et al., 1991; Greenberg et al., 1996; Zori et al., 1993). Peripheral neuropathies are characterized by reduced and abnormal sensations in the extremities.

Visual system findings include strabismus and nearsightedness (Chen, Lupski, Greenberg, & Lewis, 1996; Finucane, Jaeger, Kurtz, Weinstein, & Scott 1993). Finucane et al. (1993) also reported 10 individuals with retinal detachment. Individuals with SMS should be considered at risk for retinal detachment especially as they enter adolescence. Hearing deficits and recurrent otitis media are also common if not almost universal in SMS (Greenberg et al., 1996). The facial and palate structure of individuals with SMS result in a reduction in sinus cavity capacity, which increases the susceptibility to otitis media that may contribute to the genesis of self injurious head banging.

Cardiac and renal findings are also prevalent in SMS. Greenberg et al. (1996) found kidney abnormalities (including ectopic kidneys and renal agenesis) in 35% of people studied and cardiac malformations (including mitral regurgitation septal defects and aortic stenosis) in 37%. If a diagnosis of SMS is not made, these medical conditions may go undiagnosed with resulting permanent damage. This danger is especially true for the renal findings.

As more individuals with SMS are identified, greater variability in the physical and medical phenotype is being reported. Potocki, Shaw, Stankiewicz, and Lupski (2003) examined 58 people with SMS and found that the only commonality among all individuals was a sleep disturbance and decreased intellectual and adaptive functioning. A majority of people did, however, have scoliosis, were shorter in height than average, and had ophthalmological, otolaryngological, and audiological problems. Slightly less than half of the individuals had cardiac issues and less than 20% had problems with renal function.

Based upon these physical and medical findings, an accepted medical protocol has been developed for the initial and annual physical examination of individuals with SMS (GeneClinics, 2012) See Table 1.

Table 1.
Recommended physical exam for SMS (GeneClinics, 2012)

Newly Diagnosed	Annual Evaluations
• Physical and neurological exam	• Routine physical
• Renal ultrasound	• Thyroid function
• Audiological evaluation	• Fasting lipid profile
• Spinal radiographs	• Urinalysis
• Ophthalmological evaluation	• Scoliosis
• Otolaryngological evaluation	• Ophthalmology
• Echocardiogram	• Audiological
• Assessment for velopharyngeal incompetence	• Monitoring for elevated levels in cholesterol
• Routine blood chemistries	
• Quantitative Immunoglobulins	
• Fasting lipid profile	
• Thyroid functioning	

Behavioral and Psychological Phenotype

The cognitive and behavioral aspects of SMS have been identified as the most salient characteristics of the syndrome (Smith, Dykens, & Greenberg, 1998a). These features include a specific pattern of self-injury, stereotypies, and developmental delays. A severe sleep disorder is also present in many individuals with SMS and complicates behavioral and psychiatric presentations. These patterns of behavior can cause a large amount of stress on the family and the person's support system. Maladaptive behaviors are the result of a complex combination of intrinsic and environmental factors. Self-injury and aggression are often triggered by low levels of attention from adults and are subsequently positively reinforced once attention is provided (Finucane & Haas-Givler, 2009; Wilde, Silva & Oliver, 2013). In the first study to critically examine attention seeking behavior in individuals with SMS, Wilde et al. (2013) compared the behavior of children with SMS to children with Down syndrome. Children with SMS focused their attention on adults and looked towards them more than they looked towards their peers. An interdisciplinary treatment approach that includes good communication and understanding of SMS in the context of the special education or intellectual disability service system is indicated for long term support to be most effective. The family, medical, and behavioral professionals and school or work setting will in most instances need education and direction concerning the behavioral and psychological aspects of SMS.

Self-Injury. A wide array of specific self-injurious behaviors has been reported in individuals with SMS (Arron, Oliver, Moss, Berg, & Burbidge, 2011; Finucane, Dirrigl, & Simon, 2001; Sloneem, Oliver, Udwin, & Woodcock, 2011). Self-injury may be complicated by a decreased sensitivity to pain (Elsea & Girirajan, 2008). Commonly reported self-injury topographies include head banging and face slapping (Finucane et al., 2001; Finucane & Haas-Givler, 2009). Head banging, skin picking, and wrist biting can be observed as early as 15-18 months (Elsea & Girirajan, 2008). Picking at fingernails and toenails until they bleed (onychotillomania) and inserting objects in body orifices (polyembolokoilomania) are seen more frequently in individuals with SMS than other genetic syndromes and can become quite severe. In some cases, toenails and fingernails have been removed completely and object insertion has necessitated surgery. The presence of these two types of self injury in individuals with intellectual disability is indication to screen for SMS (Finucane & Haas-Givler, 2009).

Dykens and Smith (1998) found the prevalence of self-injury in SMS to be over 90%, with hand and wrist biting most common. Onychotillomania and polyembolokoilomania have been reported in one third to one half of individuals. The developmental course of self-injury in SMS has also been described. Parents reported that about 25% of children with SMS under the age of 12 engaged in onychotillomania while 85% of the parents of older children reported this behavior. Age-related increases in slapping self and skin picking were also noted by parents (Finucane et al., 2001).

Stereotypies. Dykens, Finucane, and Gayley (1997) utilized the *Reiss Screen of Maladaptive Behavior* (Reiss, 1988) and determined that 7 of the 10 individuals with SMS in their sample engaged in unusual motor movements. Most common were the "self-hug" and "lick and flip." The self-hug was first described by Finucane, Konar, Haas-Givler, and Kurtz (1994) and was usually exhibited when an individual with SMS was happy or excited. The behavior has been observed more frequently in children than adults and is described as a midline tic-like movement. Some individuals wrap their arms around their chests as if hugging themselves and then tense their bodies in quick tic-like movements. Other individuals clasp their hands together in front of their bodies in a twisting motion quickly pressing both clasped hands against their chest tensing their body while grimacing facially.

The movements appear involuntary and often occur in quick spasmodic like flurries. Although this behavior does not interfere with purposeful hand use it is an important diagnostic marker and should prompt an evaluation for SMS.

Dykens et al. (1997) also reported an unusual repetitive behavior they termed the "lick and flip." Nine of ten individuals engaged in a repetitive sequence of page turning when testing materials were placed in front of them. This sequence involved an exaggerated wetting of the fingers by placing four fingers of one hand in their mouth and then using the wetted hand to turn pages in succession. Other reported stereotypical behaviors include teeth grinding, placing hands in the mouth, body spinning, and twisting objects (Elsea & Girirajan, 2008).

Adaptive Behavior. Individuals with SMS engage in many behaviors that interfere with their adaptive functioning aside from the characteristic self-injury profile. Hyperactivity, tantrums, attention seeking, and aggressive and destructive behaviors have been reported as present in as high as 80% of individuals with SMS (Dykens et al., 1997; Greenberg et al., 1996, Smith et al., 1986). Martin, Wolters and Smith (2006) found that children with SMS had specific deficits in communication, daily living skills, and socialization. However, socialization was higher than expected based on assessed intellectual ability. Madduri, Peters, Voigt, Llorente, and Potocki (2006) similarly found a relative strength in socialization and a weakness in daily living skills for 58 individuals with SMS. The extent of deficits in adaptive behavior did not correlate with the size of the 17p11.2 deletion. There was a diverse range of adaptive behavior with some individuals not meeting the criteria for a diagnosis of intellectual disability.

Sleep Disturbance. Another hallmark of SMS is an almost universal severe sleep disturbance (Smith et al., 1998a) that has been described in 75-100% of individuals with SMS. Sleep disorders can be an early clue to the diagnosis (Elsea & Girirajan, 2008) and can dramatically affect those around the individual with SMS (Foster, Kozachek, Stern & Elsea, 2010). The sleep disturbance will exacerbate the maladaptive behavioral profile. Therefore control, though very difficult, aids in supporting individuals with SMS and positively impacts their quality of life. It is pervasive, expressed in several sleep domains, and varies depending on age. Hypersomnolence typically occurs during infancy, while difficulty falling asleep, shortened REM sleep, and significant daytime drowsiness is observed in older children (Elsea & Girirjan, 2008).

Dykens and Smith (1998) determined that the presence of a sleep disorder was the strongest predictor of problem behaviors. Most individuals with SMS take frequent naps during the day, have difficulty falling asleep, are easily awakened, and once awake find it difficult to fall back asleep. The sleep disorder appears to be maintained by a disruption in melatonin. Melatonin is a hormone that is involved in the regulation of an individual's circadian rhythm. Hagerman (1999a) suggests that people with SMS evidencing a sleep disturbance should receive a melatonin trial of 3 mg at bedtime, and, if ineffective, a trial of clonidine or trazodone at bedtime should be considered.

Alternatively, it has been suggested that as the light sensitive pineal gland is involved in melatonin regulation, light therapy would be of benefit. Smith, Dykens, and Greenberg (1998b) report on one such successful treatment in a 6 year old who responded to 20 minutes of light therapy administered each morning at 6 a.m. beginning in January. Dramatic improvement was noted in behavioral and sleep problems. In May of the same year, the light therapy was decreased to 10 minutes per day with an increase in behavioral problems. When light therapy was increased to 15 minutes per day behavior improved within 48 hours.

De Leersnyder and Munnich (1999) studied 20 children with SMS between the ages of 4 and 17. They found that all of the children were asleep by 9 p.m., had frequent awakenings, and were awake before dawn. Children had frequent daytime naps and all were very tired by dinnertime. Twenty-four hour melatonin levels were monitored in 8 of the children. In the normal course of melatonin, levels of the hormone rise from 9 p.m., peak at midnight, and taper off until dawn. The 8 children with SMS evidenced a reverse pattern; melatonin levels rose during the morning hours and peaked at noon. De Leersnyder and Munnich (1999) believe that the hyperactivity with which some individuals with SMS present is due to fighting against sleep. Further research from this group (De Leersnyder, 2006; De Leersnyder et al., 2003) has effectively trialed the beta blocker, acebutolol, with melatonin. A regimen of morning administration of acebutolol and evening administration of melatonin was found to be most effective. Improved sleep, decreased aggression, and increased concentration were reported.

Cognition. Cognitive delay in individuals with SMS is evident very early in life with most individuals assessed to function within the mild and moderate levels of intellectual disability. There is, however, large variability in both IQ and adaptive levels of functioning with specific deficits in short term memory and sequential processing (Elsea & Girirajan, 2008).

In one of the few examinations of the SMS cognitive profile, Dykens et al. (1997) administered a series of cognitive and intellectual measures to 10 individuals with SMS. All 10 individuals evidenced a weakness in sequential processing skills. Sequential processing involves the ability to place items in an order and to remember lists of auditory and visual stimuli. Deficits in these abilities may be related to underlying processing problems or to hyperactivity and inattention. Simultaneous processing skills involve the ability to perceive a whole from its parts, such as naming a partially completed drawing, and were a relative strength. Strengths were also found in long-term memory for places, people and things and letter/word recognition. Expressive language development was higher than would be predicted based on overall level of cognitive functioning. Despite the cognitive limitations that individuals with SMS experience, Finucane and Haas-Givler (2009) report relative cognitive strengths, which include reading and long-term memory.

Sensory Processing. Recently, the sensory processing abilities of individuals with SMS have been assessed (Hildebrand & Smith, 2012). Based on parent reports for a cohort of 34 children aged 3 to 14 years of age, initial findings revealed significant deficits in sensory processing abilities when compared to a national norm group of children with and without disabilities. Visual (e.g., ability to put puzzles together) and oral (e.g., responses to touch and taste in the mouth) processing were relative strengths. A majority of the children were reported to need more protection from life and as being overly affectionate when compared to other children. Age was found to interact with gender in the ability to modulate sensory input that affects emotional responses. Younger females (aged 3-5 years) were more similar to typically developing children than were older females. The "seeking" pattern of sensory processing, that reflects a high sensory threshold and active self-regulation, was found to decrease with age in a small subset of individuals followed longitudinally.

Speech. Speech in individuals with SMS is delayed and is often impacted by oral-motor impairments and hearing loss (Finucane & Haas-Givler, 2009). Most individuals with SMS develop expressive language, but they may struggle with articulation. Speech difficulties can negatively impact behavior and increase the level of frustration for individuals with SMS due to communication difficulties (Elsea & Girirajan, 2008).

Social. Social skills as measured by standardized assessments are delayed, with researchers (Dykens et al., 1997; Greenberg et al., 1996) finding an average socialization age of approximately 5 years. People with SMS are very demanding attention seekers and have difficulty in sustaining attention. This aspect of their behavior impinges negatively on their social interactions. In addition, children with SMS generally seek adult as opposed to peer attention and are very sensitive to the emotional state of others. It is not uncommon for these individuals to compete with their peers and siblings for attention. It is important to note that the social behavioral phenotype of SMS is based largely on anecdotal reports from teachers, direct support workers, and parents.

Haas-Givler and her colleagues (1994; 1996; 2014) have reported observations of the social behavior of children with SMS from the perspective of a classroom special education teacher and behavior analyst. The child with SMS is characterized as an insatiable attention seeker who is adult oriented, extremely affectionate, and who is very sensitive to the emotions of others. This affection is sometimes inappropriately overly demonstrative, with indiscriminate hugging of strangers and known adults in a rib crushing hug. This need for attention is often times at the root of behavioral disturbances in the classroom due to diminishing attention, which will result in self-injury or tantrums escalating to aggression. Other characteristics observed in the classroom include responsiveness to routine and structure, an eagerness to please, communication through sign, pictures, or speech, and a developed sense of humor. Children are easily motivated by food, sticker rewards, attention, and access to preferred items or activities.

Psychiatric Disorders. Given the behavioral presentation of individuals with SMS, it is no surprise that many meet the criteria for and are diagnosed with psychiatric disorders. Dykens et al. (1997) found 6 of 10 individuals with SMS with clinically significant psychopathology scores on the Reiss Screen (Reiss, 1988). Difficulties with attention and hyperactivity result in many children with SMS being diagnosed with attention deficit disorder and or hyperactivity disorder (Finucane & Simon, 1999). The high prevalence of self-injury and stereotypies coupled with a failure to develop peer relationships appropriate to their developmental level, language delay, and overall general developmental delay has previously resulted in many children meeting the criteria for Pervasive Developmental Disorder Not Otherwise Specified (PDD-NOS). The sociability and attention that individuals with SMS crave has in the past obviated a diagnosis of classic autistic disorder, although Vostanis, Harrington, Prendergast and Farndon (1994) did report on a 14 year old boy with SMS who met the DSM-III-R (American Psychiatric Association, 1987) criteria for autistic disorder.

Changes in the diagnostic criteria for the neurodevelopmental disorders in the DSM-5 (American Psychiatric Association, 2013) and the removal of the PDD-NOS category may result in increasing numbers of people with SMS being diagnosed with Autistic Spectrum Disorder (ASD). *The Social Responsiveness Scale* (SRS, Constantino & Bruber, 2005) and the *Social Communication Questionnaire* (SCQ, Rutter, Bailey, & Lord, 2003) are widely used measures of ASD. These tools were utilized by Laje, Morse, et al. (2010) to assess ASD symptomatology in a cohort of 20 children with SMS aged 4.2 to 49.9 years. Using these instruments, it was determined that 18/20 children scored within the ASD range.

When diagnosing ASD according to DSM-5 in a person with SMS, the diagnosis should read ASD associated with SMS. In addition, a diagnosis of ASD necessitates further specification with regard to verbal and cognitive abilities and the severity of ASD symptoms. This diagnosis differs for the person with SMS but without ASD who receives a diagnosis of intellectual disability (intellectual developmental disorder), the DSM-5 term for intellectual disability (formerly mental retardation). In that case, the person would not have their diagnosis of SMS associated with their diagnosis of intellectual disability (intellectual developmental disorder); in this instance, the SMS diagnosis as an etiological factor should be listed separately with other medical diagnoses.

Dykens and Smith (1998) found that individuals with SMS are particularly emotionally labile when compared to individuals with intellectual disability of mixed etiology and to individuals with Prader-Willi syndrome. Anecdotal reports of quickly changing affect with tantrum and aggression followed by over-apologetic behavior coupled with the high prevalence of sleep disturbance has also resulted in diagnoses of cyclical mood disorders.

Treatment for Smith-Magenis Syndrome
Psychopharmacological Approaches
There is currently no medication approved for use that specifically treats SMS, and no individual with SMS should be prescribed a psychotropic medication simply because he or she has SMS. However, as the behavioral profiles of individuals with SMS can include attentional problems, hyperactivity, self-injury, aggression, sleep disorder, and mood lability, psychotropic medications are often in use and

polypharmacy is not uncommon. If an individual with SMS has a known psychiatric disorder, then medication appropriate for that disorder should be considered. As previously stated, many individuals with SMS meet the criteria for attention deficit disorder with or without hyperactivity. Hagerman (1999a; 1999b) reports that there is anecdotal evidence that the stimulants methylphenidate, adderall, and dextroamphetamine can positively affect these symptoms (Allen, cited in Hagerman, 1999a).

Given the mood swings and sleep disorder that are present, individuals with SMS also can meet the criteria for bipolar disorder. The SSRI medications have been suggested as effectively treating these mood swings (Smith & Gropman, 2010). Greenberg et al. (1996) recommend that the anticonvulsant mood stabilizers carbamazepine or valproic acid be tried in these instances. Hagerman (1999a) also suggests that risperidone has been used with some success.

There have been no controlled drug trials of psychotropic medication in people with SMS and the syndrome itself does not appear to predict medication class efficacy. Laje, Bernert, Morse, Pao, and Smith (2010) evaluated psychotropic efficacy in 62 people with SMS across 7 medication categories. Support providers were asked to rate the efficacy of specific medications drawn from the following classes: stimulants, antidepressants, antipsychotics, sleep aides, mood stabilizers, alpha 2 agonists and benzodiazepines. A 5 point Likert scale that ranged from "symptoms much worse" to "symptoms much better" with a "no change" center score was utilized. Six of the 7 medication categories showed no positive or negative effect in the aggregate while benzodiazepines were rated as making symptoms slightly worse. In addition to biomedical approaches, a variety of educational, behavioral, and family support approaches have been shown to be helpful.

Support Approaches

There are no substitutes for a well-informed interdisciplinary team approach when supporting individuals with SMS. Knowing that an individual has SMS makes support easier, and there is a rich literature for the team to draw on in developing a system of supports. Early and appropriate assessment regarding cognitive, developmental, and behavioral strengths and needs is very important when supporting individuals with SMS.

In addition to the team members that are indicated by the behavioral, cognitive, educational, vocational, and physical needs of the individual, it is most helpful to include as a team consultant a genetic counselor. The inclusion of this professional serves to educate members of the individual's habilitative team who may not be familiar with SMS, discuss the known features with the individual, their family and other interested parties, as well as promote a linkage with the national support group PRISMS. As the habilitation team becomes familiar with SMS and is guided to utilize the available knowledge base and ongoing support provided by the SMS community, it becomes focused in its approach and the difficult treatment planning process of developing a unified integrated interdisciplinary biopsychosocial approach. Often times in support planning for individuals with developmental delay and behavioral/psychiatric disorders, families, psychiatrists, primary physicians, behavior analysts, social workers, educators, and vocational counselors work in isolation and even opposition. Refocusing the team approach in support of an individual with SMS allows access to a knowledge base and approach that is more specific than the more generic approaches used to support individuals with intellectual disability, autism, and psychiatric disorders.

Much progress has been made in detailing the phenotype of SMS. However, little research has been completed that investigates specific interventions targeted for the SMS behavioral phenotype. Much of the specific SMS intervention knowledge is still anecdotal. It is crucial that the efficacy of specific behavioral, psychopharmacological, and educational interventions be assessed for individuals with SMS. Such research would enable the development of specific interventions and intervention hierarchies targeted for the SMS behavioral phenotype. Although we still may be a long way from specific SMS clinical pathways, there are certain intervention approaches that logically follow from a thorough knowledge of the syndrome.

Educational. Interventions in early childhood should include a focus on speech and communication development as well as addressing any feeding issues that may be present (Elsea & Girirajan, 2008). Incorporating sign language strategies to support speech therapy can assist in speech development and reduce an individual's frustration related to deficits in expressive language (Elsea & Girirajan, 2008).

Educational and teaching strategies should build on the strengths and meet the needs of an individual. As Dykens et al. (1997) have shown a specific SMS cognitive processing style, it is important to know the extent to which a given individual fits the syndromic profile of strength in long term memory and weakness in sequential processing abilities. Once a comprehensive educational assessment is completed, it should form the basis for an Individualized Education Plan (IEP).

Based on the observations of Haas-Givler and Finucane (1996) and Finucane and Haas-Givler (2009), several strategies can be used to promote an IEP that best utilizes the syndromic strengths of SMS. Table 2 presents the basics of this approach. As children with SMS are very sensitive to the emotional state of others, exaggerated emotional expressions by the teacher can serve to trigger a behavioral outburst or distract the attention of the child with SMS from the lesson. Exaggerated positive or negative teacher emotions can be problematic. The teacher who constantly praises even a minor accomplishment in an effervescent way can serve to over excite the child with SMS. Likewise, exaggerated negative emotional expression can serve to trigger tantrum or self-injury. Instructions are best given in a neutral tone without over-exaggeration. Children with SMS should certainly be praised for accomplishments, but it should be done in a way that does not result in over-stimulation. A neutral tone, calling attention to the accomplishment and task at hand, is best. Likewise, when correction is being used, minimal attention to the error and emphasis on the correct answer is preferred. The attention seeking behavior of children with SMS is best controlled in classes with a close staff-to-student ratio, as classmates are viewed as competitors for the teacher's attention.

Table 2.
Recommended classroom strategies for children with SMS (Haas-Givler & Finucane, 2014).

- Staff training to ensure consistency of intervention approaches
- Systematic data collection and analysis
- Focus on positive behavior support, with consistent and frequent reinforcement of appropriate behavior
- Individual and class behavior support plans, including protocols for crisis intervention
- Emphasis on prevention of behavioral outbursts rather than consequence based intervention
- Opportunities for academic, social and life skills development, as well as community based instruction

The sequential processing deficit common in SMS results in difficulty with following multi-step instructions and weaknesses in mathematical abilities. Multi-step verbal task instructions or directions are difficult for children with SMS to process and execute. A series of instructions such as "pick up the paper, throw it in the trash and return to your seat" can be impossible for a child with SMS to completely process. Instructions are best given in simple single step phrases. The use of pictures and visual aids to represent the steps of a task can greatly aid instruction. Picture schedules for activities are also useful, as a child finishes one aspect of a task, the next aspect can be pointed to on the task schedule. This approach also allows the teacher to better control the child's needs for attention and assure that each task of a sequence is completed correctly. The use of computers and educational software should be considered. Special adaptations and simplifications of the keyboard and assuring that the monitor is of a high enough quality and large enough size to accommodate any visual problems must be taken into consideration.

Children with SMS will inevitably need a formalized classroom behavioral support plan to address problem behaviors. Attention, as one would expect, is highly valued by individuals with SMS and can be implicated in some way in many behavioral outbursts. Judicious use of one-on one attention is an important classroom management technique for children with SMS. The teacher must be aware that paying "one-to-one attention" to another classmate without the child who has SMS having a preferable activity to do may result in problem behavior. Children with SMS are at their best, behaviorally, when involved in a preferable one-to-one activity with an adult. Teachers must also be aware that when the one-to-one activity ends, the probability of a behavioral outburst is high, especially if the withdrawal of attention is sudden. Slow withdrawal of the one-to-one attention and substitution of the attention with a preferred solo activity is a strategy to avoid the attention withdrawal motivated tantrum. Antecedent strategies to decrease the occurrence of problem behaviors are recommended as this will provide more opportunities to practice desirable behaviors and interactions in the classroom.

For learning motivation and reinforcement, visual rewards and attention are preferred and brightly colored stickers and trinkets can be highly motivating. The sequential processing problems also argue for more holistic teaching strategies than reinforcing steps in a sequential task analysis. One would expect that children who have SMS would benefit more from approaches based on modeling and participation with a visual presentation than from highly-verbal based sequential instruction.

Behavioral Support. Virtually all people with SMS will need behavioral support beginning in childhood and continuing throughout adulthood. A functional behavioral analysis from a behavioral analyst familiar with the SMS phenotype is crucial in developing behavioral supports that are appropriate. Given the sometimes florid behavioral presentation of self-injury, it is noteworthy that there have been no controlled behavioral studies that have examined the treatment of self-injury in SMS. There are, however, many features of the SMS phenotype that can be used to develop functional behavioral hypotheses and assist in determining the triggers for many of the challenging behaviors that require support.

The sleep disorder must be viewed as a contributing factor in the behavioral problems experienced by people with SMS. A sleep chart should always be kept and in many cases a sleep study at a sleep clinic should be considered. If the sleep disturbance can be controlled in the ways previously mentioned, behavioral interventions should have a higher probability of success. The visual and auditory deficits associated with SMS must also be viewed as contributory factors. Uncorrected vision or hearing should be investigated. The high incidence of otitis media should also be examined as a factor in self injurious behavior. Finger-/toenail picking and yanking should first be viewed in the context of peripheral neuropathy. Clinically, lotion to hydrate cuticles and skin and keeping nails clipped short have been used successfully to minimize this behavior. What may start in the context of peripheral neuropathy may acquire operant characteristics given the reinforcement history.

Sequential processing attention deficits and other processing issues should be examined as contributing to observed problem behavior. Again, the use of visuals, favored activities interspersed with less favored, with clear simple instructions is the best way to structure the time of an individual with SMS. For individuals with expressive language problems, a communication system based on visuals is a must. Picture schedules and picture exchange systems can be of enormous help in aiding an individual to communicate with others and avoiding behavioral incidents that result from an inability to communicate wants and needs. Behavioral interventions should include these components.

For individuals with SMS in living, educational, or vocational settings the extent that competition for caregiver attention contributes to the problem behavior should be assessed. In settings where there are other people receiving supports, the fewer people with support needs present, the less likely it is that a problem behavior will develop, due to less competition for attention from peers.

The best way to support an individual with SMS is to make use of syndromic strengths and weaknesses as an aid to developing a behavioral support plan that minimizes contributory factors and maximizes strengths. Even in a SMS "friendly" environment that takes into account biological and behavioral profiles, there are apt to be some instances of self injurious behavior and tantrums. In these instances it is important to intervene as early as possible. It is often easy to tell that a person with SMS is escalating his or her behavior to the "point of no return" and that a tantrum will occur. If the behavioral course can be addressed before the tantrum escalates, there is often a good chance that the full-blown tantrum can be avoided by distracting and then engaging the person in an appropriate activity.

Haas-Givler and Finucane (2014) have proposed that positive reinforcement based behavioral interventions are less effective in addressing problem behaviors for people with SMS than for other individuals with special needs. They point out that while the use of positive contingencies for people with SMS can be highly motivating, they are typically not enough to prevent a target behavior from occurring. Manipulating antecedents to target behaviors is viewed as a much more powerful and appropriate intervention than manipulating consequences. They recommend that behavioral support be "front loaded" with antecedent-based interventions to set a stage for success. Three instructions for success in behaviorally supporting individuals with SMS were proposed:

Choose your battles. Implementing a training program to teach a fine motor skill that is very difficult due to peripheral neuropathy has a high probability of resulting in a major behavioral outburst. Look for alternative ways to accomplish the same goal and if, a fine motor skill must be taught, do so in small sessions with frequent breaks.

Consider the big picture. Develop individual training and support plans based on the functional needs of the individual and complete a risk benefit analysis. Self-care and activities of daily living should be given more weight than difficult academic or fine motor skills.

Life is not always fair. People with SMS, due to their significant behavioral support needs, will almost always need more attention and support than a person without SMS of the same cognitive ability.

There will of course be times where a major tantrum cannot be avoided. In these instances it is best to withdraw attention and let the person know that you will be there for them when they are ready to interact with you. Because the tantrum may stem from a situation where others are competing for attention, removing the individual from the environment where the tantrum has begun, if possible, can sometimes aid the dissolution of the behavior. If the function was for attention, then removal of the individual from the situation may resolve the immediate challenge. However, long term resolution lies in the teaching strategies addressed earlier in this section.

Family Support. Families with a member who has SMS clearly have increased stressors. Although supporting any individual with a developmental disability is stressful for the family, the severe behavioral presentation of SMS can be particularly stressful. Parents of children with SMS report sleeping in shifts to ensure their child's safety. Hodapp, Fidler, and Smith (1998) and Foster et al. (2010) have examined the stress and coping in 41 families of children with SMS using standardized assessments of stress and behavior. High levels of both stress and family support were found, with the size of the family support system the best overall predictor of family stress: the more family friends and the larger number of individuals in the family support circle, the lower the stress. Families made use of professional support to a great degree, with 76% reporting a professional in their family support circle. Given these results, the use of outside family support services such as friends and professionals is very important for the overall welfare of the family (See resources below).

Summary and Conclusions

SMS is a clearly defined genetic syndrome with characteristic behavioral, psychological, medical, and physical features. These features affect the way individuals process information, react to the environment, and are perceived by those around them. It is becoming apparent that there are specific developmental pathways to these features. Specific recommendations for the support of individuals with SMS with regard to physical health, classroom structuring, behavioral support, and teaching strategies already exist. PRISMS, an active support group for parents, researchers and individuals with SMS, continues to be the primary resource for developing supports for people with the syndrome.

Resources

Families should be made aware of the following organizations:

Parents and Researchers Interested in Smith-Magenis Syndrome, PRISMS, can be contacted at PRISMS, Inc., 21800 Town Center Plaza, Suite #266A-633, Sterling, VA 20164 Tel: 972-231-0035 Fax: 972-499-1832 Email: info@prisms.org There is also a national conference sponsored by PRISMS. Information on the national conference and the many other services available through this organization is available on their Internet Web site: http://www.prisms.org. PRISMS also has a Facebook page that can be accessed at https://www.facebook.com/prisms.smithmagenis.

The Smith-Magenis Research Foundation can be contacted at The SMS Research Foundation, 18620 SW 39th St. Miramar, FL 33029. Tel: (203) 450-9022: Email: info@smsresearchfoundation.org The SMS Foundation's mission is "to support research to improve the knowledge and understanding of SMS so that viable therapeutic options can be developed in order to improve the quality of life of those with SMS." The SMS Foundation has a webpage that details it s research efforts and advocacy work that can be accessed here: http://www.smsresearchfoundation.org/ Their Facebook page can be accessed at https://www.facebook.com/Smith-MagenisResearchFoundation.

At **Geisinger's Autism & Developmental Medicine Institute** (ADMI) in Lewisburg, PA, families can access a variety of medical, behavioral, genetic counseling, and assessment services. In addition, ADMI's team of specialists is available to provide local and long distance consultations to help schools, agencies, and families address the complex needs of children and adults with SMS. Learn more about their full range of services for people affected by SMS at www.geisingeradmi.org/patients-caregivers/specialty-clinics/smith-magenis-clinic/ or call 570.522.6287.

References

American Psychiatric Association. (1987). *Diagnostic and statistical manual of mental disorders* (3rd ed., revised). Washington, DC: Author.

American Psychiatric Association. (2013). *Diagnostic and statistical manual of mental disorders (5th ed.).* Washington, DC: Author.

Arron, K., Oliver, C., Moss, J, Berg, K., & Burbidge, C. (2011). The prevalence and phenomenology of self-injurious and aggressive behaviour in genetic syndromes. *Journal of Intellectual Disability Research, 55,* 109–20.

Chen, K. S., Lupski, J. R., Greenberg, F., & Lewis, R. A. (1996). Ophthalmic manifestations of Smith–Magenis syndrome. *Ophthalmology, 103,* 1084-1091.

Constantino J. N., Bruber, C. P. (2005). *Social Responsiveness Scale (SRS) Manual.* Los Angeles, CA: Western Psychological Services.

De Leersnyder, H. (2006). Inverted rhythm of melatonin secretion in Smith-Magenis syndrome: From symptoms to treatment. *Trends in Endocrinology and Metabolism, 17,* 291-298.

DeLeersnyder, H. & Munnich, A. (1999). Abnormal sleep patterns and behavioral difficulties in patients with Smith-Magenis Syndrome are due to an inversion in the circadian rhythm of melatonin. Paper presented at the 49th Annual Meeting of the American Society of Human Genetics, San Francisco, CA, October 1999.

De Leersnyder, H., Bresson, J. L., De Blois, M. C., Souberbielle, J. C., Mogenet, A., Del-hotal-landes, B… Munnich, A. (2003). Beta 1-adrenergic antagonists and melatonin reset the clock and restore sleep in a circadian disorder, Smith-Magenis syndrome. *Journal of Medical Genetics, 40,* 74-8.

Dykens, E. M., Finucane, B. M., & Gayley, C. (1997). Brief report: Cognitive and behavioral profiles in persons with Smith-Magenis Syndrome. *Journal of Autism and Developmental Disorders, 27,* 203-211.

Dykens, E. & Smith, A. C. (1998). Distinctiveness and correlates of maladaptive behavior in children and adults with Smith-Magenis syndrome. *Journal of Intellectual Disability Research, 42,* 481-489.

Edelman, E. A., Girirajan S., Finucane B., Patel P. I., Lupski J. R., Smith A. C., & Elsea S. H. (2007). Gender, genotype, and phenotype differences in Smith-Magenis syndrome: A meta-analysis of 105 cases. *Clinical Genetics, 70,* 1540–50.

Elsea, S. H., & Girirjan, S. (2008). Smith-Magenis syndrome. *European Journal of Human Genetics, 16,* 412-421.

Finucane, B., Dirrigl, K. H., & Simon, E. W. (2001). Characterization of self-injurious behaviors in children and adults with Smith-Magenis syndrome. *American Journal of Mental Retardation, 106,* 52-58.

Finucane, B. & Haas-Givler, B. (2009). Smith-Magenis syndrome: Genetic basis and clinical implications. *Journal of Mental Health Research in Intellectual Disabilities, 2,* 134-148.

Finucane, B. M., Jaeger E. R., Kurtz, M. B., Weinstein, M., & Scott C. I. (1993). Eye abnormalities in the Smith-Magenis contiguous gene deletion syndrome. *American Journal of Medical Genetics, 45,* 443-446.

Finucane, B. M., Konar, D., Haas-Givler, B., & Kurtz, M. B. (1994). The spasmodic upper body squeeze: a characteristic behavior in Smith-Magenis syndrome. *Developmental Medicine and Child Neurology, 36,* 78-83.

Finucane, B., & Simon, E. W. (1999). Genetics and dual diagnosis: Smith-Magenis Syndrome. *The NADD Bulletin, 2,* 8-10.

Foster, R. H., Kozachek, S., Stern, M. & Elsea, S. H. (2010). Caring for the caregivers: an investigation of factors related to well-being among parents caring for a child with Smith-Magenis syndrome. *Journal of Genetic Counseling, 19,* 187–98.

GeneClinics (2012). *Smith-Magenis syndrome [del(17)(p11.2)].* Retrieved on (April 10,2015) from http://www.ncbi.nlm.nih.gov/books/NBK1310/

Girirajan, S., Elsas L., Devriendt K., & Elsea, S. H. (2005). RAI1 variations in Smith-Magenis syndrome patients without 17p11.2 deletions. *Journal of Medical Genetics, 42,* 820-8.

Goldman, A.M., Potocki, L., Walz, K., Lynch, J.K., Glaze, D.G., Lupski, J.R., & Noebels, J.L. (2006). Epilepsy and chromosomal rearrangements in Smith-Magenis Syndrome [del(17)(p11.2p11.2)]. *Journal of Child Neurology, 21*(2),93-98.

Greenberg F., Guzzetta V, De Oca-Luna R. M., Magenis R. E., Smith A. C. M., Richter S. F.,… Lupski, J. (1991). Molecular analysis of the Smith-Magenis syndrome: A possible contiguous-gene syndrome associated with del(17)(p11.2). *American Journal of Human Genetics, 49,* 1207-1218.

Greenberg, F., Lewis, R. A., Potocki, L., Glaze, D., Parke, J., Killian, J., … Lupski, J. R. (1996). Multi-disciplinary clinical study of Smith-Magenis syndrome (deletion 17p11.2). *American Journal of Medical Genetics, 62,* 247-254.

Haas-Givler, B. (1994). Educational implications and behavioral concerns of SMS: From the teacher's perspective. *Spectrum, 1,* 36-38.

Haas-Givler, B. (1996). Observations on the behavioral and personality characteris- tics of children with Smith-Magenis syndrome. *Genetwork, 2,* 4-5.

Haas-Givler, B., & Finucane, B. (1996). What's a teacher to do? Classroom strategies that enhance learning for children with SMS. *Genetwork, 2,* 6-10.

Haas-Givler, B. & Finucane, B. (2014). On the road to success with SMS: A Smith-Magenis guidebook for schools. Sterling, VA: PRISMS.

Hagerman, R.J. (1999a). Psychopharmacological interventions in fragile X syndrome, fetal alcohol syndrome, Prader-Willi syndrome, Angelman syndrome, Smith-Magenis syndrome, and velocardiofacial syndrome. *Mental Retardation and Developmental Disabilities Research Reviews, 5,* 305-313.

Hagerman, R. J. (1999b). Smith Magenis Syndrome. In R.J. Hagerman (Ed.), *Neurodevelopmental disorders: Diagnosis and treatment* (pp. 341-364). New York: Oxford University Press.

Hildebrand, H. L. & Smith, A. C. M. (2012). Analysis of the Sensory Profile in Children with Smith–Magenis Syndrome. *Physical & Occupational Therapy in Pediatrics, 32*, 48-65.

Hodapp, R. M., Fidler, D. J. & Smith, A. C. M. (1998). Stress and coping in families of children with Smith-Magenis syndrome. *Journal of Intellectual Disability Research, 42*, 331-340.

Laje G., Bernert R, Morse R, Pao, M., & Smith, A. C. (2010). Pharmacological treatment of disruptive behavior in Smith-Magenis syndrome. *American Journal of Medical Genetics C: Seminars in Medical Genetics, 154*, 463–8.

Laje, G., Morse, R., Richter, W., Ball, J., Pao, M., & Smith, A. C. (2010). Autism spectrum features in Smith-Magenis syndrome. *American Journal of Medical Genetics C: Seminars in Medical Genetics, 154*, 456–62

Lockwood, D., Hecht, F., Dowman, C., Hecht, B. K., Rizkallah, T. H., Goodwin, T.M. & Allanson, J. (1988). Chromosome subband 17p11.2 deletion: A minute deletion syndrome. *Journal of Medical Genetics, 25*, 732-737.

Maddurri, N., Peters, S. U., Voigt, R. G., Llorente, A. M. & Potocki, L. (2006). Cognitive and adaptive behavior profiles in Smith-Magenis syndrome. *Journal of Developmental and Behavioral Pediatrics, 27*, 188-92.

Martin, S. C., Wolters, P. L., & Smith, A. C. (2006). Adaptive and maladaptive behavior in children with Smith-Magenis Syndrome. *Journal of Autism and Developmental Disorders, 36*, 541-52.

Potocki, L., Shaw, C.J., Stankiewicz, P., & Lupski, J.R. (2003). Variability in clinical phenotype despite common chromosomal deletion in Smith-Magenis syndrome [del(17)(p11.2p11.2)].*Genetic Medicine, 5(6)*, 430.

Reiss, S. (1988). *Reiss Screen for Maladaptive Behavior*. Chicago, IL: International Diagnostic Systems Inc.

Rutter, M. Bailey, A. & Lord C. (2003). *The Social Communication Questionnaire (SCQ) Manual*. Los Angeles, CA: Western Psychological Services.

Simon, E. W., & Finucane, B. (1998). Etiology and dual diagnosis: Notes on a biologically based syndromic approach. *The NADD Bulletin, 1*, 63-65.

Slager, R. E., Newton, T. L., Vlangos, C. N., Finucane, B., & Elsea, S. H. (2003). Mutations in RAI1 associated with Smith-Magenis syndrome. *Nature Genetics, 33*, 466-8.

Sloneem, J., Oliver, C., Udwin, O., & Woodcock, K. A. (2011). Prevalence, phenomenology, aetiology and predictors of challenging behaviour in Smith-Magenis syndrome. *Journal of Intellectual Disability Research, 55*, 138–51.

Smith, A. C., Dykens, E., & Greenberg, F. (1998a). Behavioral phenotype of Smith-Magenis syndrome (del 17p11.2). *American Journal of Medical Genetics (Neuropsychiatric Genetics), 81,* 179-185.

Smith, A. C., Dykens, E., & Greenberg, F. (1998b). Sleep disturbance in Smith-Magenis syndrome. *American Journal of Medical Genetics, 81,* 186-191.

Smith, A. C. & Gropman, A.L. (2010). Smith-Magenis Syndrome. In S. Cassidy, & J. Allanson (Eds.), *Management of genetic syndromes, 3rd ed.* (pp. 739-767). New York: Wiley-Blackwell.

Smith, A. C. M., McGavran, L., Robinson, J., Waldstein, G., Macfarlane, J., Zonona, J., & Reynolds, J.F. (1986). Interstitial deletion of (17) (p.11.2) in nine patients. *American Journal of Medical Genetics, 24,* 421-432.

Vostanis, P., Harrington, R., Prendergast, M., & Farndon, P. (1994). Case reports of autism with interstitial deletion of chromosome 17 (p11.2 p11.2) and monosomy of chromosome 5 (5pter->5p15.3). *Psychiatric Genetics, 4,* 109-111.

Wilde, L., Silva, D., & Oliver, C. (2013). The nature of social preference and interactions in Smith-Magenis syndrome. *Research in Developmental Disabilities, 34,* 4355–4365.

Zori, R. T., Lupski, J. R., Heju, Z., Greenberg, F., Killian, J. M., Gray, B. A. … Zackowski J. L. (1993). Clinical, cytogenetic, and molecular evidence for an infant with Smith- Magenis syndrome born from a mother having a mosaic 17p11.2p12 deletion. *American Journal of Medical Genetics, 47,* 504-11.

Demysifying Syndromes II

CHAPTER 6

Autism Spectrum Disorder

Sandra Fisman

Introduction

Patrick is 4 years old. He has been referred to an inter-professional children's treatment center because of his unusual language and his lack of social development. His mother sensed that "something was not right with Patrick" since his early infancy. He was content to be left alone in his crib, arching his back when lifted out of his crib to be held. He did not smile responsively and seemed to stare into space. He showed no stranger anxiety and failed to stretch out his arms to be picked up. As a toddler, he failed to point and showed no other interest in other children. Rather than engaging in imaginative play, he had shown a preference for carpet tassels, ignoring his toys as a toddler except to line them up in rows and spin the wheels on his toy trunk. Both parents questioned Patrick's hearing abilities at this time as he appeared to ignore them and did not respond to his name. However, other sounds such as the vacuum cleaner or lawn mower seemed very upsetting to him and he would cup his hands over his ears screaming at high pitch. Between age 2 and the present, Patrick increasingly became fascinated by letters and numbers. Patrick's motor milestones were all achieved on time. His language development (both expressive and receptive) had been quite delayed and his present language is largely composed of repetitive chunks and echoes, and he largely held monologues with himself. Patrick was proving very difficult to toilet train and insistent on having his bowel movements with a diaper on. Patrick has a diagnosis of Autistic Spectrum Disorder (ASD)—previously Autism or Autistic Disorder. Patrick has a socially awkward 12 year old paternal first cousin, James, who had recently received a diagnosis of Asperger's Disorder after struggling for several years with social, learning and behavioral difficulties, in spite of being tested to have overall above average cogenitive ability. He had a fascination with the design of buildings and had eloped on numerous occasions from home and school to pursue his interest, unaware of the lack of safety of many of his ventures. He was mercilessly teased by his same age peers (other than another 12 year old boy who shared his passion for Minecraft). He was frequently disciplined by teachers who thought him "sassy."

It was Leo Kanner in 1943 and Hans Asperger in 1944 who provided the descriptions of autism that became the basis for the classification system in the *Diagnostic and Statistical Manual* (4th Edition) of the American Psychiatric Association (DSM-IV) (1994) and more recently the DSM-5 (2013). However, descriptions of individuals akin to Kanner's autism date back to the late eighteenth century. Amongst these descriptions are feral children who were abandoned to the wild and recaptured into society. Itard, the savior of Victor the wild boy of Aveyron in France, provides us with a comprehensive case history that is strongly suggestive of ASD. Itard's struggles to educate and socialize Victor, his frustrations and his joy with small accomplishments resonate for those who care for, teach, and train this hard to serve population. It is with these caretakers and professionals in mind that this chapter has been written.

Autism spectrum disorders (ASD) are a group of childhood neurodevelopmental disorders with difficulties in social interaction, communication, and repetitive behaviors. The prevalence of ASD is estimated to be 1 in 68 (0.6%; Centers for Disease Control and Prevention,2014) with a male to female ratio of 4:1 (Fombonne, 2005). Much earlier epidemiological prevalence estimates were significantly lower (4.6 per 10,000; Lotter, 1996) This increase in prevalence likely relates to a combination of a true increase in incidence coupled with broader diagnostic criteria. This chapter will trace the evolution of diagnostic practices over several decades and the increasing understanding of the biology of these disorders derived from genetic, neuroimaging and neuropathological studies. Increasingly these studies are suggesting there are alterations in neuronal organization, cortical connectivity, neurotransmitter pathways and brain growth (Grafodatskaya, Chung, Szatmari, & Weksberg, 2010).

Diagnostic Features

Diagnostic Conceptions and Misconceptions

Prior to 1980 when the Pervasive Developmental Disorders (PDDs) were first included as a separate category in the third edition of the American Psychiatric Association Diagnostic and Statistical Manual, autism was conceptualized as a form of childhood psychosis (Creak, 1963), which led to the lumping together of a heterogeneous group of children with impaired relating, abnormal perceptual sensitivities, poorly modulated anxiety, disordered language, and a lack of sense of self.

Kanner's description of 11 children in his 1943 paper titled "Autistic Disturbances of Affective Contact" in the journal *Nervous Child* provided a durable account of classic autism. The triad of deficits in social relatedness, insistence on sameness, and language abnormalities continue to guide our diagnostic systems. However, Kanner (1943) provided some false research leads that delayed progress in this field. His use of the term "autism," borrowed from Bleuler's use of the term in adult psychiatry to refer to lack of affective contact in individuals with schizophrenia, suggested that these children were part of an inclusive view of schizophrenia. This issue was only resolved in 1971 when the differentiation of these children from individuals with schizophrenia was clearly established through emphasis on age of onset, clinical course, and family history (Kolvin, 1971).

A second false lead was in the area of cognition. Kanner believed that the "islets of ability" that he observed in these children, including phenomenal rote memory for names and rhymes and the recollection of complex patterns, sequences, and earlier events, bespoke above average intelligence. It took several decades to dispel this idea. With the notion of an autism spectrum, it became evident that some children have preserved intellectual skills while other children with autism scored in the "mentally retarded" range on psychometric evaluation. Intelligence, together with functional language, both serve as prognostic factors.

The third and final false lead has probably been the greatest source of heartbreak for the parents of these children. The idea that the cause of autism originated in problematic parent-child interactions where parents were thought to be high achieving professional individuals, was congruent with the psychoanalytic ethos of the nineteen fifties and nineteen sixties. The term "refrigerator mother" encapsulates the essence of this idea. As controlled studies were conducted in the 1970s, clear evidence emerged that parents of children with autism were neither deficient in their caregiving (Cantwell, Rutter, & Baker, 1978), nor as a group did they present with higher levels of occupational and educational achievement.

Evolution of Diagnostic Concepts

It was not until 1980 that the PDDs were recognized as a distinct group of disorders separate from schizophrenia. In the DSM-III, autism was included under the umbrella of the PDDs. Criteria for the diagnosis of childhood schizophrenia were subsumed with the adult disorder (DSM-III; American Psychiatric Association, 1980). In the DSM-III, age of onset prior to or after 30 months of age (i.e., infantile autism versus childhood onset PDD) and the absence of delusions and hallucinations were recognized as important defining characteristics of this group of disorders.

The concept of an autistic spectrum, rather than age of onset, influenced the diagnostic criteria for PDD in the third, revised edition of the DSM-DSM-III-R (American Psychiatric Association, 1987). This concept evolved from an epidemiological survey of children with intellectual and physical disabilities conducted in Camberwell, a borough of inner London (Wing & Gould, 1979). In the Camberwell study, social impairment was defined as an inability to engage in two-way social interaction. The quality of this impairment was captured in three distinct descriptors: aloof, passive, and active but odd. Accompanying the impaired two-way social interaction were abnormalities in verbal and non-verbal communication and restricted interests carried out in a repetitive fashion. The three clusters of difficulty were referred to as the "autistic triad." It was acknowledged that children could have varying degrees of difficulties in these three areas. Those who showed abnormalities in all aspects of the triad were considered part of the autistic spectrum disorders (Wing, 1981; 1986). It was suggested that Asperger's Disorder was at one end of the continuum and low functioning autism at the other. However, the DSM-III-R provided only two diagnostic options: autistic disorder representing classic Kanner's autism and the much broader category of Pervasive Developmental Disorder Not Otherwise Specified (PDD-NOS), which resulted in a classification system that was highly sensitive but low in specificity. (Volkmar, Cicchett, Bregman, & Cohen, 1992).

Perhaps in an effort to create more diagnostic specificity, a categorical approach to the diagnosis of the PDDs was subsequently reflected first in the 10th edition of the ICD Classification of Diseases (1990) and repeated in the DSM-IV (American Psychiatric Association, 1994). Other categories grouped with autistic disorder in the PDD class included Asperger's Disorder, Rett's Disorder, Childhood Disintegrative Disorder, and Pervasive Developmental Disorder Not Otherwise Specified (PDD-NOS) (including Atypical Autism). The PDD-NOS category was used when criteria for one of the specific pervasive developmental disorders were not met but there was a severe and pervasive impairment of two way social interaction or of verbal and non-verbal communication, or the presence of stereotyped behavior, interests and activities. Thus the concept of the "autistic triad" of symptoms was maintained in the DSM-IV.

Current Diagnostic Concepts

In 2013 the DSM-5 (American Psychiatric Association) was published. This most recent classification returns us to a spectrum with three different levels of severity and places autism spectrum disorder (ASD) in the section of Neurodevelopmental Disorders. We still recognize the original "autistic triad" in the autism spectrum disorder umbrella in which impaired social interaction and communication alongside stereotyped behaviors and interests, become evident from early childhood (Morrison, 2014). DSM-5 has chosen to lump together communication and socialization under Criterion A. Stereotyped interests and activities fall under Criterion B.

Specifically **Criterion A** describes persistent deficits in social communication and social interaction across multiple contexts, as manifested by the following, currently or by history with illustrative examples:

1. Deficits in social-emotional reciprocity, ranging, from abnormal social approach and failure of normal back-and-forth conversation; to reduced sharing of interests, emotions, or affect; to failure to initiate or respond to social interactions.

2. Deficits in nonverbal communicative behaviors used for social interaction, ranging, from poorly integrated verbal and nonverbal communication; to abnormalities in eye contact and body language or deficits in understanding and use of gestures; to a total lack of facial expressions and non-verbal communication.

3. Deficits in developing, maintaining, and understanding relationships, ranging, from difficulties adjusting behavior to suit various social contexts; to diffi-

culties in sharing imaginative play or in making friends; to absence of interest in peers.

Specifically **Criterion B** describes restricted, repetitive patterns of behavior, interests, or activities, as manifested by at least two of the following, currently or by history with illustrative examples:

1. Stereotyped or repetitive motor movements, use of objects, or speech (e.g. simple motor stereotypes, lining up toys or flipping objects, echolalia, idiosyncratic phrases).

2. Insistence on sameness, inflexible adherence to routines, or ritualized patterns of verbal or nonverbal behavior (e.g., extreme distress at small changes, difficulties with transitions, rigid thinking patterns, greeting rituals, need to take same route or eat same food every day).

3. Highly restricted, fixated interests that are abnormal in intensity or focus (e.g., strong attachment to or preoccupation with unusual objects, excessively circumscribed or perseverative interests).

4. Hyper- or hypo- reactivity to sensory input or unusual interest in sensory aspects of the environment (e.g., apparent indifference to pain/temperature, adverse response to specific sounds or textures, excessive smelling or touching of objects, visual fascination with lights or movement).

In addition, DSM-5 requires that:

Symptoms must be present in the early developmental period (but may not become fully manifest until social demands exceed limited capacities, or may be masked by learned strategies in later life).

They must cause clinically significant impairment in social, occupational, or other important areas of current functioning.

These disturbances are not better explained by intellectual disability (intellectual developmental disorder) or global developmental delay. Intellectual disability and autism spectrum disorder frequently co-occur; to make comorbid diagnoses of autism spectrum disorder and intellectual disability, social communication should be below that expected for general developmental level.

Individuals with a well-established DSM-IV diagnosis of autistic disorder, Asperger's disorder, or pervasive developmental disorder not otherwise specified should be given the diagnosis of autism spectrum disorder. Individuals who have marked deficits in social communication, but whose symptoms do not otherwise meet criteria for autism spectrum disorder, should be evaluated for social (pragmatic) communication disorder.

ASD Levels of Severity

DSM-5 specifies the level of severity (1 through 3) for Criterion A and B. Levels of severity provide a guide to the individual intensity of support and intervention required. (See severity levels for autism spectrum disorder-DSM-5, American Psychiatric Association, 2013). Level 1 requires support, Level 2 substantial support and Level 3 requires very substantial support.

ASD Associated Disorders

Key to understanding the spectrum concept is that ASD comprises a variety of neurodevelopmental disorders with varied manifestations that have genetic and biological causes. DSM-5 requires that these be specified, (See Comorbid Neurodevelopmental Specifiers-DSM-5 American Psychiatric Association, 2013). Included in this list of specifiers are other associated neurodevelopmental, mental, or behavioral disorders. These include anxiety disorders (especially common) and depression, obsessive compulsive disorder (also common) and attention deficit hyperactivity disorder (most common). Intellectual disability affects about 50% of individuals with ASD and 25-50% have seizures. Physical disorders may include phenylketonuria, fragile X syndrome, tuberous sclerosis, and a history of perinatal distress. Sleep difficulties (both initial insomnia and reduced need for sleep) are very common and add to levels of stress in the home.

The Associated Disorders for Autism Spectrum Disorder are further specified in DSM 5 coding as:

With or without accompanying intellectual impairment

With or without accompanying language impairment

Associated with a known medical or genetic condition or environmental factor

Associated with another neurodevelopmental, mental, or behavioral disorder

With catatonia

Patrick and James

> Returning to 4 year old Patrick, his mother noticed his lack of social responsiveness from very early infancy. Parents often become concerned in the second 6 months when their infant lacks social responsiveness. Lack of eye contact, absence of reciprocal smiling, and discomfort with cuddling, all cued Patrick's mother to something not being right. From early development, contact with others is affected by deficits in social relatedness and language, which are reciprocally linked with one another. Each of these vary in parallel from mild to almost complete lack of interaction. Patrick's first cousin, James, had relatively much milder symptoms. His preoccupations and stereotypical interests, while intense and preoccupying much of his waking time, were more esoteric. However, he was still significantly socially and behaviorally impaired, although not to the extent that Patrick was.
>
> Patrick's early pattern of development and his continued trajectory are typical of the more severe levels of Criteria A and B, in keeping with Level 3 impairments in social interaction and communication, as well as stereotyped interests and activities, while James's difficulties in each of these areas were more in keeping with Level 1 impairments.

ASD and Social (Pragmatic) Communication Disorder: Diagnostic Dilemmas

DSM-5, in its shift from Developmental Language Disorders to a broad category of Communication Disorders, has incorporated children that were labeled by speech and language pathologists as "semantic pragmatic disorder" (Bishop, 1989, p. 107). As a group these children were said to "shade into autism at one extreme and normality at the other" (Brook & Bowler, 1992, p. 62). Specifically, Social (Pragmatic) Communication Disorder (SCD) describes individuals who despite adequate vocabulary and syntax (ability to form sentences) have difficulty with the practical use of language (semantics and pragmatics).

Difficulties are usually identified in a social context by age 4 or 5 and concerns may be raised about ASD, intellectual disability or ADHD. Later concerns may be raised about social anxiety disorder. SCD can occur on its own or with other communication disorders, specific learning disorders, or intellectual disability.

Both children and adults with SCD have difficulty understanding and using the pragmatic aspects of social communication to the point where their conversations can be socially inappropriate, but they do not have the restricted interests and repetitive behaviors that would qualify them for a diagnosis of ASD (Morrison, 2014). Table 1 outlines the main diagnostic features of SCD.

Table 1:
Characteristic Pragmatic Difficulties in Social Communication Disorder

a) Task oriented language
- Greeting
- Maintaining a conversation
- Requesting

b) Adapting language
- Changing language in different circumstances

c) Following the rules of conversation
- Turn taking
- Staying on topic
- Use of nonverbal and verbal signals
- Respecting personal space

d) Understanding implied conversation
- Metaphors
- Idioms
- Innuendoes
- Humour

Demysifying Syndromes II

The Neurobiology of the Autism Spectrum Disorders

It is not surprising, given the heterogeneous clinical presentation ASD to discover that diverse mechanisms of central nervous system dysfunction have been implicated in the etiology of these disorders. Ideally this diversity should reflect the spectrum of clinical presentation. While our current state of knowledge reflects descriptive phenomenology of these disorders rather than a precise understanding of their pathogenesis, DSM-5 may help to overcome this problem by grouping individuals affected by autism into a single category of ASD, with mild, moderate, or severe specifiers, as well as identification of associated disorders (some with known etiology; Butler, Youngs, Roberts, & Hellings, 2012).

Although the specific abnormalities of brain function in ASD remain elusive, there have been considerable advances in the genetic and neuropsychological studies of these disorders. While gene discovery has led to only modest understanding of biological pathways in ASD, several lines of study may unite findings across different disciplines (e.g., genetics, neuropathology, and neuroimaging). These findings are beginning to converge and point to a final common etiological pathway for ASD: specifically defective synaptic functioning, excitation-inhibition imbalance and brain connectivity (Ecker, Spooren & Murphy, 2013). Adding to our understanding of these disorders and possibly identifying biomarkers for specific ASD subcategories, these findings are providing some rationale for biological treatments, particularly pharmacotherapy and other therapies that may herald a better quality of life.

Genetic Considerations

Autism and its related disorders have among the highest heritability rates for neuropsychiatric disorders with concordance rates of 90% reported for identical twins in some studies (Ritvo et al., 1989; Smalley, Asarnow, & Spense, 1988). The current focus is not on autism as a genetic disorder but rather which specific genes and genetic mechanisms might be involved. The earlier evidence for a strong genetic basis for these disorders came from twin and sibling studies particularly those studies of multiplex families where more than one child is affected or has a variant. There have been four general-population based twin studies of autism: two British studies (Bailey et al., 1995; Folstein & Rutter, 1977), a Norwegian study (Steffenburg et al., 1989) and a U.S. study in Utah (Ritvo et al., 1985). The concordance rate for monozygotic twins ranged from 64 to 98% and 0 to 38% for the dizygotic twin pairs.

Smalley, Asarnow, and Spence (1988) summarized six studies of sibling risk for autism and estimated the risk to be 2.7%. In a population study of autism in Utah, however, Ritvo et al. (1989) reported a sibling risk of 4.5% and a recurrence risk of 8.5% in a family. This higher risk for siblings in the Utah study may be explained by the presence of a large Mormon population in Utah who are not deterred from having further children after the birth of a child with a developmental disability. In most societies, there is a tendency for parents with children who have early onset burdensome conditions to not have any further children.

This stoppage effect, evidenced by the tendency for children with autism to be born late in their sibships or to be only children, may explain the above discrepant sibling risk figures. Even if the true risk for siblings was only 1%, this would still increase their risk, compared to the general population by as much as 25 times (Jones & Szatmari, 1988).

Using DSM-IV criteria, the overall risk for PDDs to the siblings of PDD probands was 5-6% (Szatmari et al., 1993) while the risk for the lesser variant PDD (equating to Level 1 ASD or not meeting the criteria for full syndrome) was much higher. Bolton et al. (1994) found that 20% of siblings of autistic probands had social or communication impairments or a restricted pattern of interests compared to 3% of Down syndrome (DS) control siblings. Piven et al. (1994) reported that parents of autistic children were often rated as more aloof, tactless, and unresponsive on a standardized personality interview than parents of DS controls. The lesser variant PDD/ASD has also been found in second and third degree relatives of PDD probands, suggesting that biological rather than environmental factors were operative in the family patterns of PDD transmission (Pickles et al., 1995).

Advances in Genetic Research

With the sequencing of the human genome and the advances in genomic technologies, significant insights have been made into the cellular and molecular mechanisms underlying ASD (Gupta & State, 2007). Search for candidate genes has been only modestly helpful. It has been more recent work with de novo mutations, which are submicroscopic variations in chromosomal structure (especially significant increases in copy number variations or CNVs), that is moving the genetic field forward in ASD. This is particularly the case in simplex families (i.e. with only one individual affected with ASD) as compared with multiplex families (where there is a positive family history). In one study (Sebat et al., 2007), 10% of individuals with autism from simplex families had CNVs compared with only 3% of individuals with autism in multiplex families. Only 1% of the individuals were seen in typically developing children who were controls. The majority of the CNVs were deletions (as opposed to duplications).

Evidence suggests that environment also plays an important role in interaction with genetic risk. Neurodevelopmental disorders, including the expression of different phenotypes from identical gene factors (pleiotropy), different genes causing the same phenotype (genetic heterogeneity), and between gene (epistasis) and gene-environment interactions, are generated by a complex interplay between gene and environment. Research that disentangles the effect of environment in creating different phenotypes requires methodologies that incorporate both genetic and environmental factors and take into account the developmental timing of exposure (Kim & Leventhal, 2015). Epigenetic modifications that alter gene expression without changing primary DNA sequence may play a role in the etiology of ASD. Epigenetics may play a role in integrating genetic and environmental influences to dysregulate neurodevelopmental processes (Grafodatskaya et al., 2010).

There is good evidence for both genetic and etiological heterogeneity in these disorders. As an example, autism can be associated with several known genetic disorders (e.g., fragile X syndrome, tuberous sclerosis, neurofibromatosis, and phenylketonuria). It can also be associated with congenital syndromes caused by rubella and cytomegalovirus. Several other genetic syndromes associated with ASD including Rett's, Prader-Willi and CHARGE Syndrome demonstrate epigenetic mechanisms. Abnormal epigenetic dysregulation is associated with syndromic (15q 11-13) maternal duplication and also with non-syndromic forms of ASD. Overall, with advances in genetic testing and syndromic recognition of individuals with ASD, an underlying cause can now be identified in about 50% of cases (Schaefer, & Mendelsohn, 2008; Schaefer et al., 2010).

Mitochondrial Dysfunction in ASD

Over the past decade evidence has accumulated that some individuals with ASD have an underlying mitochondrial dysfunction (MD) (Rossignol & Frye, 2012). The mitochondria are distinct cellular organelles that serve to provide the cell's energy demands. They are the only organelle in mammalian cells that have their own genome. The number of mitochondria in each cell depends on the cellular energy demands. Low energy cells (such as skin cells) have fewer mitochondria, while cells with high energy demands (such as brain, liver, muscle, GI cells) have many mitochondria. Nerve synapses are areas of high energy consumption and especially dependent on mitochondrial function. Mitochondria are very vulnerable to oxidative stress and damage. The brain contains non-replicating cells that may be permanently dysfunctional or die (by apoptosis) if damaged. In the brain, neurons that have the highest firing rate such as GABAminergic interneurons may be the most vulnerable. Biochemical markers for MD that signal metabolic breakdown are many but include lactate, pyruvate, carnitine, and creatinine kinase among others.

For ASD the prevalence of MD has been found to be 5% as compared with 0.01% in the general population. In the Rossignol and Frye (2012) study, some biomarkers correlated with ASD severity. The prevalence of developmental regression, seizures, motor delay, gastrointestinal abnormalities, gender, and elevated lactate were high and mostly not associated with genetic abnormalities. ASD/MD may represent a particular ASD subgroup with possible treatment implications (Rossignol & Frye, 2011).

Neuroimaging in ASD

Early neuroimaging studies demonstrated changes in brain structure and metabolism with the tools available at that time (see Table 2). Neuroanatomical changes that were described in autism and Asperger's disorder were primarily described in overall brain volume. One of the most consistent neuroanatomical findings in individuals with autism has been an increase in brain volume (Piven et al., 1995). This brain volume had been described in an autopsy study that demonstrated a 100 to 200 gram increase in brain weight in individuals with autism (Bailey et al., 1995).

In a single-photon emission computed tomography (SPECT) study, Zilbovicius et al. (1995) found lower frontal regional cerebral blood flow at age 3 years in participants with autism as compared to controls. This blood flow normalized at age 6 years, which may indicate delayed frontal maturation in autism consistent with the frontal lobe cognitive findings that have been described.

The thalamus is a subcortical brain center that acts as a sensory or attentional filter to higher cortical centres including the prefrontal cortex. It is possible that abnormal frontal cortical development in PDD may be the result of an early thalamic lesion. Szelazek et al. (2000) found decreased prefrontal activity and increased thalamic activity using functional MRI in participants with Asperger disorder compared with their control siblings. Early thalamic-cortical dysfunction may also explain abnormalities in brain hemispheric lateralization that have been described in autism (Cantor, Thatcher, Hrybyk, & Kaye, 1986) and Asperger's disorder (Semrud-Clikeman & Hynd, 1990).

The temporal lobe of the brain is involved in the control of language and memory. It has important connections with the limbic system, which is involved in emotion and motivation and has connections with the frontal lobe. Using SPECT, Gillberg, Bjure, Uvebrant, and Vestergren (1993) found decreased blood flow in the temporal lobes of individuals with high functioning autism.

Changes have been found in the cerebellum in imaging and post mortem studies. The cerebellum is associated with functions such as the conscious control of fine motor movement, speech, and calculations. Piven, Saliba, Bailey, and Arndt (1997) have suggested that any increase in volume of the cerebellum is similar to the increased volume of the temporal, occipital, and parietal lobe.

Study results have been inconsistent, findings varied widely, and they were found in only a minority of cases due to different methods of imaging and small numbers of heterogeneous subjects. Future research is therefore required to clarify the role that these brain structures play in ASD.

Table 2:
Earlier Brain Imaging Techniques

Imaging Modality	Imaging Technique	Imaging Interpretation
Structural	Computer-axial tomography (CAT)	Computer construction of x-ray image
Functional	Computer analysis of electroencephalogram (EEG)	Brain mapping by computer analysis of EEG
	Position emission topography (PET)	Images generated by intravenously injected radioactively labeled substances in the brain; measures regional brain blood flow, glucose metabolism and neurochemical activity

	Single photon emission computed tomography (SPECT)	Images generated by intravenously or inhaled radioactively labeled substances in the brain; measures regional brain blood flow
Structural and Functional	Magnetic Resonance Imaging (MRI)	Non-invasively images molecular changes in brain cells exposed to a strong magnetic field

Recent Advances in Neuroimaging

Over the past decade, newer imaging and statistical techniques have told us more about the structure and function of the brain in ASD (see Table 3). These sophisticated techniques, particularly functional MRI and magnetic resonance spectroscopy, have begun to shed light on both the structure and neurochemistry of the brain in these disorders (Horder & Murphy, 2012). Multivariate statistical analysis shows promise in picking up both structural and functional differences within the autism spectrum and assists in more accurate categorization of different subgroups. In the near future, the combination of imaging modalities made possible by advances in computer hardware and software will allow both structural and functional/neurochemical studies to be done in the same imaging session (Chugani, 2012).

While early changes in over proportional white matter (WM) and grey matter (GM) with increased overall brain volume and amygdala overgrowth continue to be described, there is a subsequent WM and GM volume reduction in older children, adolescents and adults with ASD compared with healthy controls (Ben Bashat et al., 2007). Given that core clinical symptoms often appear as early as the second year of life and are evident by the age of 4 years, developmentally informed neuroimaging studies of ASD can potentially inform our knowledge about etiology and early intervention (Wolff & Piven, 2013).

Table 3:
Advanced Brain Imaging Techniques

Imaging Modality	Imaging Technique	Imaging Interpretation
Structural	Longitudinal structural morphology	Developmental changes in brain structure and volume of cerebral cortex
Functional	Functional MRI	Disease specific alterations in brain function
	Functional connectivity MRI (fc MRI)	Resting state spontaneous neuronal activity
	Diffusion tensor imaging (DTI) and voxel-based morphometry (VBM)	Provides neurobiologic correlates for brain architecture and function; may be evaluative tools for therapeutic approaches and potential early markers

| Structural and Functional | Multivariate pattern classification | Detects relationship between structure and function of different brain regions |
| Neurochemical | Proton MR specificity ([1H] MRS) | Detection of mitochondrial defects |

Do We Understand the Neurocognitive Deficits in ASD?

The accumulating evidence using multiple neuroimaging techniques across a variety of presentations and ages has in common impaired structural and functional connectivity between brain regions (Travers et al., 2012). This discovery is congruent with earlier findings that individuals with autism may have weak central coherence, which means that they tend to process information in individual parts rather than in a context (Bailey, Phillips, & Rutter, 1996), and there is deficient integration and synchronization of brain regions (Just, Cherkassky, Keller, & Minshew, 2004).

Recent studies have focused on altered connectivity in ASD using functional and structural imaging techniques (Vissers, Cohen, & Geurts, 2012). While an in depth review of this research is beyond the scope of this chapter, suffice it to say that considerable work is still required, both cross-sectional and longitudinal, and across low and high functioning phenotypes to more fully understand the complexities of neuroimaging findings across these disorders. Both long range under connectivity (between regions across different lobes of the brain or more than one cubic centimetre within a region) and local over connectivity (within a brain region of less than one cubic centimetre) are described. These studies have mainly implicated the frontal regions using a variety of fMRI paradigms including executive functioning, working memory for faces, and facial affective expression processing (Ecker et al., 2013). The most consistent finding in neuropsychological studies of people with high functioning ASD is an abnormality of executive function, which leads to problems with planning, sequencing, impulse control, and attention. The prefrontal cortex of the brain plays an important role in these functions. This region of the brain is also involved in novel goal directed behavior and speech. Ozonoff and McEvoy (1994) suggest that tests of executive function such as the Wisconsin Card Sort test and The Tower of Hanoi demonstrate perseveration, difficulty shifting cognitive set, poor planning, and deficits in working memory in individuals with autism.

Other neurocognitive theories have involved deficits in theory of mind. Theory of mind is described as the capacity to attribute thoughts, feelings and desires to oneself and other people (Baron-Cohen, 1989). This theory distinguishes between first order thinking ("he thinks that…") and second order thinking ("he thinks that she thinks that …"). Developmentally typical children master first order tasks by age seven. It is hypothesized that the lack of social reciprocity and communication failure in autism arises in the context of an inability to understand intentions and beliefs of others. Deficits compatible with theory of mind deficits have been found in 80% of verbal children with autism.

How About Neurochemical Changes?

Neurotransmitters in autism have been studied for over 50 years. Neurotransmitters are best described as specialized chemical messengers that are synthesized and secreted by neurons to communicate with other neurons. Among the numerous excitatory and inhibitory neurotransmitters in the nervous system, serotonin, dopamine, gamma-aminobutyric acid (GABA) and more recently N-acetylaspartate (NAA), glutamate, and glutamine have been implicated in autism.

Measurement of neurotransmitters in autism has ranged from initial studies of serum, urine, and cerebrospinal fluid to more recently molecular imaging, genetic measurement of genes involved in neurotransmitter synthesis, transporters, receptors and signaling pathways. The primary neuroimaging technologies that have been used for in vivo investigation have been position emission tomography (PET), single-photon emission computed tomography (SPECT), and magnetic resonance spectroscopy (MRS) (Chugani, 2012). Unlike PET and SPECT, MRS does not require the administration of radio labeled tracers, but rather uses the magnetic properties of stable atomic nuclei within the brain tissue itself such as hydrogen, phosphorus, and carbon. As the technology advances, the development of the combined capacity to assess neurochemistry in vivo with neuroimaging will enable the identification of new biomarkers that will guide new pharmacology interventions for ASD.

In the search for biomarkers, the most consistent findings have been in the serotonin system, with elevated whole blood serotonin being the most consistent biological marker described to date (Martineau, Barthelemy, Jouve, Muh, & Lelord, 1992). Hyperserotonemia segregates in families; the presence of a hyperserotonemic autistic child has been related to a 2.5 fold increase in the likelihood of a hyperserotonemic relative (Leventhal, Cook, Morford, Ravitz, & Freedman, 1990). This relationship is of interest given the broader phenotype of autism in families.

Two fundamentally different types of serotonergic abnormality have been found in children with autism, using a tryptophan-derived tracer with PET measuring whole brain serotonin synthesis. These abnormalities include global as well as focally abnormal asymmetric development in the serotonin system, which may relate to handedness, language, and hemispheric asymmetry, all described in autism (Chandana et al., 2005).

Using a SPECT tracer reduced serotonin transporter binding has been found in both adults and children with autism. Reduction in binding in the anterior and posterior cingulate cortex has been correlated with impairment in social cognition, while the reduction in serotonin transporter binding in the thalamus has been correlated with repetitive or obsessive behaviour (Nakamura et al., 2010).

Medications affecting the serotonin system that have been used include serotonin agonists, most commonly citalopram, as well as serotonin antagonists (risperidone, olanzapine, quetiapine, and more recently aripiprazole). Only citalopram, risperidone, and aripiprazole have been tested in Randomized Control Trials (RCTs) in children and adolescents. Citalopram has not shown benefit for repetitive behaviors and only slight benefit for irritability/agitation. A high proportion of children become activated with SSRIs (in keeping with the elevated levels of serotonin in ASD), which compounds pre-existing difficulties with irritability/aggression. Other activation symptoms include decreased need for sleep, impulsivity and increased energy, and mood lability.

Risperidone and aripiprazole, on the other hand, significantly reduce irritability/ aggression, in keeping with serotonin, as well as dopamine, antagonism. They may also target hyperactivity and stereotyped behaviors. Risperidone is significantly more robust in its effectiveness compared with placebo, while aripiprazole trials show benefit with aripiprazole, but also more placebo response. These benefits are offset by the side effects of weight gain particularly with risperidone, sedation, and extra pyramidal effects, as well as occurrence of agitation with aripiprazole.

In adults and particularly with Asperger's Disorder, fluoxetine and fluvoxamine have demonstrated effectiveness targeting obsessive compulsive symptoms (Lounds et al., 2012).

Altered dopaminergic function has been found in the frontal cortical regions (but not the striatum) in autistic children and adults with autism. An increase in the dopamine metabolite homovanillic acid (HVA) was found in children with autism when compared with controls (Barthelemy, Bruneau, & Conet-Eymard, 1988; Gillberg & Svennerholm, 1987). Increased HVA levels seemed to correlate with neurological impairment rather than a diagnosis of autism (Hameury et al., 1995). Using PET with a radioactive dopamine precursor (FDOPA) taken up, metabolized, and stored by dopaminergic neurones, Ernst, Zamatkin, Matochik, Pascualvaca, and Cohen (1997) found a 39% reduction by the anterior medial prefrontal cortex compared with the parietal cortex in children with autism compared with controls. This reduction also correlated with cognitive impairment. Subsequently, whole brain increase in dopamine transporter binding was found using SPECT in an age matched study of boys with autism aged 3-10 years (Xiao-Mian, Jing, Chhongxuna, Min, & Hui-Xing, 2005). This finding was confirmed in young adults with autism (Nakamura et al., 2010).

Controlled studies of medications that antagonize dopamine have been found to improve some of the behavioral symptoms of ASD including hyperactivity, aggression, temper tantrums, stereotypies, and lack of social relatedness. Dopamine antagonists include haloperidol, pimozide, risperidone, olanzapine, clozapine, and, more recently, aripiprazole. As indicated, risperidone and aripiprazole have the highest level of evidence.

Drugs that are dopamine agonists such as stimulants may worsen pre-existing symptoms in children with autism. In RCTs, methylphenidate had less benefit and more side effects in ASD with ADHD than ADHD alone (McPheeters et al., 2011). Atomoxetine has much less evidence for robust effectiveness in ASD with ADHD (Harfterkamp et al., 2012).

Significant abnormalities in norepinephrine and epinephrine levels and their metabolites have not been found in these disorders, but some medications that decrease activity of the sympathetic nervous system may have a role in the treatment of ASD. These medications include Beta-adrenergic blockers, propranolol and nadolol (which target anxiety and aggression), and Alpha-adrenergic blockers, clonidinee and guanfacine, which target hyperactivity and impulsivity.

Excessive brain opioid activity resulting in increased endorphins could account for some of the symptoms seen in autistic disorder, including social deficits and decreased pain sensitivity (Panksepp & Sahley, 1987). However, studies of endorphin levels have been very variable and the response of individuals with autism to naltrexone, an opioid antagonist, has been equally variable.

Finally, with the use of MRS and cytogenetic studies, findings are emerging pointing to decreased NAA levels in children and adults with autism in several brain areas (Chugani, 2012). Although the function of NAA in the brain is still unclear, decrease in NAA in brain regions with decreases in serotonin synthesis and fMRI activation may point to dysfunction of the corticothalamocortical system. Studies of glutamate and glutamine as well as GABA are still in their very early stages. Decreased GABA receptor binding has been demonstrated in all of the genetic disorders in which autistic behavior is present.

The Diagnostic and Assessment Process in ASD

The interdisciplinary assessment of cognitive, social, communication, and adaptive behavior skills are essential for planning intervention. A comprehensive initial assessment (see Table 4) will provide a profile of the child's strengths and weaknesses. Intervention using a goal-focused approach that facilitates adaptation and minimizes interfering behaviors will then flow from the assessment process.

Important Issues to Consider in the Assessment Process

There are five key issues to consider when assessing a child for ASD.

- **A developmental perspective** is essential in the assessment in order to interpret cognitive and adaptive functioning in relation to normative expectations for the age of the child. The tests that are chosen should be developmentally appropriate and be able to maximize the sampling of a wide-range of the child's skills. For example, using a cognitive test that is heavily dependent on language will skew the assessment results in a non-verbal child with non-verbal intellectual ability. A measure of non-verbal intellectual ability such as the Leiter International Performance Scale (Leiter, 1948) will provide a more valid measure of the child's developmental profile and will better guide intervention strategies.
- **Understanding delays and deviance** in the child's developmental profile will provide a more accurate profile from which to plan interventions. **Delays** will be identified using standardized instruments of intellectual

functioning combined with measures of adaptive behavior. Information regarding deviant behaviors may be obtained from diagnostic instruments such as the Autism Diagnostic Interview- Revised (ADI-R) (Lord, Rutter, & Le Couteur, 1994) or the use of the Autism Diagnostic Observation Schedule (ADOS) (Lord et al., 1989). These instruments are administered in a semi-structured fashion. The ADI-R focuses on parents' descriptions of their child's behavior in multiple areas. It assists the diagnostic process and provides relevant information about the child's developmental and behavioral history, current difficulties in social, communicative, and behavioral areas and the parents' perceptions of the child's behavior and difficulties. The ADI-R has excellent validity and reliability and is a useful clinical as well as a research tool. As the name implies, the ADOS is used to observe the child's communicative and social behaviors. The ADOS was developed for children who had a mental age of at least 3 years. A prelinguistic form of the instrument, PL-ADOS, has been developed.

- **Establishing the variability of the child's skills profile** provides a better assessment of the child's capacity for learning and adaptation than simply focusing on the numerical results of standardized assessment. There are two antithetical issues to consider: first of all, it is important to delineate the child's strengths and deficits in the context of very variable test scores. Secondly, there should not be an expectation of generalization of ability from one exceptional splinter skill. For example, the precocious ability to recognize letters and words may not correlate with the ability to combine these letters into words and sentences, with reading comprehension or with the use of these words for the purpose of communication. Similarly, an unusual ability with number computation may not transfer to the understanding of basic money concepts such as making change. On the other hand the child's assets and strengths can be used to maximize his/her learning potential and optimize the learning environment.

- **Developing an inventory of functional skills** will provide an understanding of the child's everyday adaptation and response to real life demands. Use of a structured interview such as the Vineland Adaptive Behavior Scales (Sparrow, Balla, & Cicchetti, 1984) with the child's caregivers will provide standard scores, percentiles and age equivalents for adaptive behavior, communication, socialization, daily living, and motor skills. The assessment information can then be used to inform program planning.

- **IQ and Adaptive Behavior** are not well correlated; tested IQ in a high functioning individual is generally one or two levels beyond the level of adaptive skills especially in the social realm.

Demysifying Syndromes II

Table 4:
Overview of the Initial Assessment
- History of presenting difficulties
- Communication/imagination/play
- Social reciprocity
- Behaviour
- Developmental history
- Pregnancy/delivery/neonatal period
- Social emotional development
    - Infant temperament/early attachment
    - Eye contact
    - Social smiling/anticipatory gestures
    - Stranger/separation anxiety
    - Development of relationships
- Language development
    - Pre-language skills
    - Intent to communicate
    - Expressive/receptive language milestones
    - Deviant language (e.g., echolalia, pronoun reversal)
- Motor development
- Development of play skills
- Skill development
- General medical history and physical examination
- Baseline physical parameters
- Gross and fine motor coordination
- Family history
- Developmental disabilities/psychiatric illness
- Family coping/support
- Sibling adjustment
- Observational interview of child
- Mental status examination
- Relatedness
- Separation behavior

Ancillary tests/information
- Preschool/school report
- Psychological evaluation
- Cognitive testing using a nonverbal measure if indicated — e.g., Leiter International Performance Scale
- Measure of adaptive behavior — e.g., Vineland Adaptive Behavior Scale
- Speech/language evaluation
- Occupational therapy assessment ideally available for skill assessment
- Other consultations — e.g., Pediatrics, Neurology, Genetics and ancillary investigations.

Autism Spectrum Disorder

Genetic Consultation and Counselling in ASD Families

Based on the advances that we have seen in genetic research and the increased risk for individuals with specific genetic markers, genetic risk counselling has expanded from risk estimates based on epidemiological data and family history to estimates based on test results in specific individuals. The latter has the potential to single out a particular family member as the "carrier" and raises new ethical dilemmas, generating stigma and blame with conflict arising over test results (Gershon & Ailley-Rodriguez, 2013).

A careful diagnostic assessment is an important start to obtain a detailed family and medical history, confirm the diagnosis, and rule out associated conditions and known genetic syndromes with or without dysmorphic features (e.g., birth marks). This assessment is followed by a targeted screen for viral titres (e.g., rubella), metabolic screening (e.g., urine for organic acids and mucopolysaccharides, plasma lactate and amino acid levels), and DNA testing for fragile X in males. A third tier of screening includes chromosomal microarray studies for structural genomic and mitochondrial (mt) DNA problems, as well as biochemical (organic, amino acid and fatty acid levels) and mitochondrial function assays (pyruvate and lactate).

In the case of positive family history, a balanced approach to counselling would include:

1. Explanation of the relative risk for autism to family members in positive terms (e.g., a 19 out of 20 chance that a future child will not have autism rather than a 1 in 20 chance the child will).

2. The significantly increased risk for the offspring if both parents have definite cases of autism in the family.

3. The risk for offspring of non-affected siblings is probably less than 1 in 500.

4. The risk for lesser variant symptoms in siblings is in the region of 10-20% but it should be emphasized that these individuals generally become self-sufficient adults.

5. It is not the task of the counselor to make decisions for the family but rather to facilitate the best available risk analysis in an empathic clinical context. In the case of identification of specific genetic markers and genetic testing of family members, a psychotherapeutic approach may be needed to address personal and interpersonal tensions and conflicts that may arise.

The Child with ASD in the Context of the Family

High levels of stress exist for both mothers and fathers in families with a child with ASD. While both experience parenting stress generated by the child's diagnosis, it is mothers rather than fathers who suffer from depression. This depression correlates with their parenting distress (Wolf, Noh, Fisman, & Speechley, 1989).

In studies comparing the parents of children with PDD with parents who had a child with Down syndrome, both mothers and fathers of children with PDD described high levels of stress related to the decreased adaptability of their child (making parenting difficult because of the child's difficulty in adjusting to environmental change); increased demandingness (related to the frequency and severity of behavior problems); and decreased acceptability (perceiving their child as less attractive, less appropriate, and less intelligent than desired). Parents of children with Down syndrome experienced an extra burden only in their child's acceptability (Noh, Dumas, Wolf, & Fisman, 1989).

In addition to the stress generated by the child, the mothers (and not the fathers) experienced additional parental stress related to their own feelings of dysphoria, a sense of lack of competence in parenting, and feelings of poor health. There is a spill over into the marital relationship (Fisman, Wolf & Noh, 1989) with mothers experiencing lowered levels of marital intimacy, which relates to a lowered sense of spousal self-esteem and a lack of recreation time in the marriage.

There is also an impact on the emotional and behavioral adjustment of the unaffected siblings. In one study, it is the high level of parenting stress that was found to impact sibling adjustment (Fisman, Wolf, Ellison, & Freeman, 2000). In addition, those factors that are normally protective for children in families such as marital satisfaction, lack of parental depression, a cohesive family, and a warm, non-conflictual sibling relationship do not appear to be operative for siblings in these highly stressed families (Fisman et al., 1996). Because of the demands of the very difficult child with ASD, the sibling without a disability may feel neglected and his or her needs ignored. This is reflected in the tendency for unaffected siblings to externalize their distress with behavior problems at a younger age and to develop more internalizing symptoms (anxiety and depression) with the transition into puberty (Wolf, Fisman, & Ellison, 1998).

The question has been raised that there may be an increased rate of mood and anxiety disorders in the parents and siblings of children with autism apart from the stress factor (Smalley, McCracken, & Tanguay, 1995); however, none of the twin studies has confirmed this relationship and a family history study (Szatmari et al., 1995) did not find that the rates of psychiatric symptoms were increased in extended relatives compared with controls.

The impact of living with a child with PDD and the effect on the entire family system has implications for planning interventions. While parents and siblings need to become partners in treatment, this cannot be done without consideration of the needs of unaffected family members both for considerable formal as well as informal support.

Effective Intervention Strategies in ASD across the Lifespan

With the rejection of the final remnants of the self-blame hypothesis and the acceptance that these disorders are biologically based, the field of intervention has been able to move forward over the past few decades. The main goals for intervention at every phase of the life cycle are to optimize skill development and adaptation, especially communication and social skills, and to minimize interfering behaviors, particularly irritability, aggression, and self-harm. A range of biological, structured social and behavioral interventions has been developed. Treatment planning needs to take place in the context of the family system with an awareness of the need for social support to non-disabled family members and an appreciation of what is possible in the individual family context. Consideration must be given to effective educational and community interventions. With the transition to adulthood there is necessarily a shift from predominantly family to predominantly community-based supports.

Early Intervention and Applied Behavioral Analysis (ABA)

The application of the rules by which behavior is determined by environmental factors to improve socially important behaviors is referred to as applied behavioral analysis. Applying these principles in the early years with children who have PDD may alter their developmental trajectory.

Lovaas (1987) described dramatic improvements with his early intervention program. Harris and Handleman (1994) have described the factors that characterize **effective early intervention programs**. These include:

- Individualized comprehensive programming
- Assessment of the child's strengths and deficits
- Identification of contextual variables that affect the child's behavior
- Linking assessment findings to curriculum
- Favorable teacher to child ratios, including one-to-one in the early stages of programming and interaction with peers in the child with PDD's natural environment.

Overview of Intervention Approaches

Behavioral Interventions

Behavioral interventions can be divided into three broad categories: a) those that target antecedents to a particular behavior; b) those that consequence a particular behavior; and c) those that promote skill development. In all categories, the planned treatment intervention is based on a thorough functional analysis of behavior and skills.

Antecedent interventions are implemented **before** the expected target behaviors occur. These approaches may be useful across the life span in reducing problem behaviors. For example, environmental changes that reduce visual distractions can result in a decrease in self-stimulatory behavior in adolescents and adults with autism.

Consequence-based interventions are procedures that are implemented **as a result of** a problem behavior. Consequence-based interventions are most effectively used when combined in a "package" with antecedent and skill building interventions. See Table 5 for a description of consequence-based interventions.

Table 5:
Most Frequently Used Consequence-based Interventions

Interruption and Redirection	Physical prevention of an undesirable behavior and redirection to an alternative acceptable activity
Reinforcement-Based Procedures	Use of a response to a desirable behaviour to increase its future occurrence
Extinction Procedures	Withholding a response to reduce the occurrence of an undesirable behavior
Punishment Procedures	A response that decreases the future occurrence of an undesirable behavior

In using **consequence based interventions,** the reinforcer must be powerful enough to motivate the individual to carry out a targeted desirable behavior. Interviews with caregivers and teachers and observational techniques are necessary to identify reinforcers (Mason, McGee, Farmer-Dougan, & Risley, 1989). On occasion, cautious and judicious use of the identified problem behavior (e.g., self-stimulation) may be used for very brief periods to reinforce appropriate behavior. Extinction procedures are time consuming and do not, on their own, lead to alternative appropriate behavior development. They may result in a transient increase in the behavior.

Punishment procedures remain controversial, but, when used, they may be more effective with systematic variation over time (e.g., verbal reprimand, over-correction, and time out applied in a scheduled fashion to a behavior problem).

Skill acquisition is at the core of intervention for individuals with ASD. Skills not only improve functionality but also replace problem behaviors. Teaching new, adaptive skills is central to the development of successful educational programs. Skill acquisition programs fall into four main areas: language and communication; social skills; self-help and self-management skills; and prevocational/vocational skills.

The goals for **language and communication therapy** are to acquire socially meaningful speech and/or to develop functional communication skills that replace negative behavioral communication. These skills are best taught in naturalistic settings rather than in isolated environments, which has meant a shift from teaching rudimentary speech with reinforcement strategies unrelated to social communication to the reliance on inherent reinforcement in a social setting. For example, young children are taught with a variety of high interest toys and electronic devices, relying on the reinforcement of the toys and devices and the interaction between child and adult to stimulate communication. Similarly, adolescents can be taught the names of food items in the context of a functional activity such as meal preparation.

Functional communication training is also used for minimally verbal or nonverbal individuals. Gestures or signs can be used both for receptive purposes to supplement speech expressed by the caregiver and for expressive purposes by the individual with ASD to make meaningful requests (Carr & Kemp, 1989). Augmentative devices have become invaluable for people who lack verbal abilities (Schuler, Prizant, & Wetherby, 1997). At their simplest this is a picture, symbol, or word board to which the individual can point. Their most elaborate form is a hand held electronic device (a memo writer) that provides a printed message or functions as a voice synthesizer.

Social skills deficits are central to ASD. They range from total aloofness and absence of social engagement seen in some individuals with autistic disorder to a lack of social reciprocity and empathy for others in people with Asperger's disorder. **Social skills training** (see Table 6) can have a major impact in improving behavioral functioning across the lifespan for persons with ASD. This social skill development is a necessary component of any comprehensive intervention program. Much like functional communication, social skills are best taught in natural settings and in pairs or groups. Peer modeling is a useful strategy for teaching social skills. Classroom interventions using peer tutoring have been effective in improving social and academic skills of the child with ASD as well as of typically developing classmates (Kamps, Barbetta, Leonard, & Delquadri, 1994). In addition to modeling by peers without disabilities and by the group leader, social skills groups utilize role-play of social interactions and rehearsal of behaviors to be used in the community.

Table 6:
Components of a Social Skills Training Program

- Keeping appropriate physical distance
- Learning to initiate and terminate interactions
- Teaching flexibility in novel situations
- Voice modulation
- Recognizing and responding to emotions in others
- Understanding humor

Self-help skills training in the preschool and early school-age population and self-management skills training in the older child, adolescent and adult with PDD are designed to increase capacity for optimal independence. While these skills are acquired naturally in individuals without developmental disabilities, they must be taught painstakingly in persons with ASD. The focus for self-help skills training in the preschool child will be in the areas of feeding, toileting, grooming and dressing, as well as fine motor and gross motor coordination skills. In the older child and through to adulthood there is a shift to community awareness skills and introduction of self-management skills. The latter are behavioral strategies where persons take responsibility for their own behavior. Aids are generally used to help the individual self-monitor. Examples include pictorial or written schedules, which break tasks down into component parts

(Koegel, Koegel, Hurley, & Frea, 1992; Pierce & Shreibman, 1994). Both children and adults learn to administer their own contingent rewards and consequences.

Prevocational and vocational skills are a critical element in making the transition for ASD individuals from the educational system to the "real world." The opportunities to acquire these skills are best accomplished in a structured transition plan with clearly defined immediate and long-term goals coordinated by a case manager (Stowitzcheck, 1992). The entire transition plan needs to include leisure and living options in addition to an appropriate vocational plan. Prevocational skills training should begin in the educational curriculum with transportation training, money management training, and social skills appropriate for the workplace.

Pharmacotherapy

Most children with ASD do not significantly benefit from psychotropic medication, but the medications may be helpful for some individuals with ASD particularly where there is psychiatric comorbidity. They are best used in the context of a comprehensive treatment plan. There are two principles that guide the selection of a particular psychopharmalogic agent: The first relates to the neurochemical action of the recommended medication to a **neurotransmitter system** that may be disordered as was described under neurobiology of the ASD; the second guides medication choice by targeting the most interfering symptom(s). While the use of a single medication is preferable, sometimes it becomes necessary to combine agents to optimize the response to medication. While the "start low, go slow" aphorism applies generally in the use of psychotropic medication in children, this would be "lower and slower" in ASD. A summary follows of the main treatment strategies in ASD (Table 7).

Table 7:
Helpful Treatment Strategies in ASD

- Form a partnership with parent(s) and child
- First do no harm: avoid acute care hospitalization if possible
- Target a clear symptom if using medication
- Treat medical comorbidity (particularly if causing pain or affecting body function e.g. constipation, dental caries, ear infections, headaches, seizures
- Manage core symptoms with behaviour strategies
- Address communication and understand behaviour as communication
- Appreciate unrecognized changes in routine
- Identify sites of behaviour change e.g. home vs. school
- Maintain a healthy scepticism about miraculous cures
- Address psychosocial stress for the family and provide support and relief

Life Cycle Transitions

For the individual with an ASD and his or her family the negotiation of developmental transitions is accentuated and complicated. As we have discussed, the burden of care-taking frequently falls on the mother, but there is an impact on all family members. Life cycle transitions as they pertain to a family member with an ASD will be reviewed briefly with some suggestions for coping strategies.

The Crisis of Diagnosis

The diagnosis of an ASD is often associated with pain and grieving, although parents, particularly the primary caretaker parent, and sometimes other close family members and friends, know intuitively that there is something wrong prior to the official diagnosis.

When parents are in different phases of the grieving process, communication between them becomes difficult. This may occur where one parent is still at a stage of denial and disbelief whilst the diagnosis has been accepted by the other parent, who is then trying to cope with a sense of loss and hopelessness. At the time of diagnostic crisis there is need for a high level of social support to the family. If this is not available within the family social network, professional social work intervention is of paramount importance.

School Entry

School entry brings a set of challenges for parents with a child with an ASD. Families who have been fortunate enough to participate in intensive early intervention programs, may have difficulty accessing a similar level of intervention in a school system. With most children being included in regular classrooms, parents and professionals must advocate for sufficient special education resources to meet the child's needs. Particularly in the early school years, intensive programming often requiring 1:1 intervention, and computer assisted learning can be essential.

The **early school years** are often confusing for parents with children who have milder variants on the spectrum and are higher functioning (previously referred to as Asperger's disorder). The diagnosis may not be clear until the middle childhood years. Educators may interpret the child's social awkwardness, particularly their naïve tactless comments, as bad behavior. A diagnosis of ASD and appropriate advocacy by a well-trained professional is key to successful programming for these children.

Adolescence

Adolescence can be a difficult time for the person with an ASD and for his or her family (Ousley & Mesibov, 1991). Hormonal changes with arousal of sexual and aggressive impulses and the management of menstruation and masturbation can be challenging (Hellemans, Colson, Verbraeken, Vermeiren, & Deboutte, 2007). For lower functioning individuals with ASD, there is a wide gap between these inevitable hormonal changes and attendant impulses, coupled with the cognitive ability to understand and manage them.

For higher functioning adolescents, there is often an attempt to fit in with peers, and there may be poor social judgment and management of impulses. The intrinsic difficult with social skills associated with these disorders coupled with cognitive ability complicates the tasks of adolescence and may result in feelings of hopelessness and even suicidal thoughts. Awkward sexual expression such as inappropriate touching may create further difficulties for these youth. Academically, the increased demand for abstract conceptualizing accentuates the different learning needs of these young people (Rosenthal et al., 2013).

Special education approaches in the high school curriculum continue to be an essential component of the habilitative process for low, medium, and high functioning individuals with an ASD. Functional academics (i.e., language, reading, and math skills that enhance everyday function), along with the management of daily living routines, are most likely to achieve the highest possible level of adult independence.

Transition to Adulthood

Successful transition to adulthood is best achieved through planning and programming during the adolescent years. Issues of placement, capacity for independent living, vocational opportunities, and continued support services often absorb parental time and energy. The gap between intellectual ability and adaptive daily living skills particularly in the social area may mean that a high functioning individual becomes more comfortable in a vocational activity that may appear below his/her intellectual capability. With major curriculum adjustments and academic supports, a very high functioning person with ASD may be able to enter a postsecondary environment, but this is the exception rather than the rule. Most important is to find contentment and a "niche" within adult society.

Summary

This chapter has reviewed the diagnostic features of the autism spectrum disorders. Significant gains have been made in understanding the association with underlying identifiable disorders, particularly in the realm of genetics. The translation of newer findings to the challenges in clinical practice has been discussed. Issues of learning, communication, and vocational training have been explored. We have examined the vulnerabilities of these individuals and their potential effects, both negative and positive, on other family members. Discussion of day-to-day issues and the stresses of developmental transitions from childhood to adulthood provide an understanding of the life span trajectory for these individuals and their caregivers.

Resources

General resources

Answering Autism from A-Z
Karen J. Crystal
Publication Date: November 23, 2011
Karen J. Crystal is a mother and author, who has raised a son with autism from birth to adolescence. Karen describes the challenges of raising a child with autism through the early stages of diagnosis to the constant advocating for her son with

the educational system. *Answering Autism from A-Z* is written in a format for easy access to instant information by parents, caregivers, teachers and families on how to deal with autism on a daily basis.

Autism
Stuart Murray
Publication date: February 27, 2012
Autism is the first book to analyze the ways the ways in which autism is expressed in medical, historical and cultural narratives. The book presents a well rounded portrayal of the ways that autism is represented in the world at this time.

The Autism Answer Book: More Than 300 of the Top Questions Parents Ask
William Stillman
Publication Date: September 1, 2007
The Autism Answer Book provides clear and confident counsel and straightforward answers to pressing questions.covering such topics as: getting a diagnosis, social sensitivities, physical well-being, mental health, and school success. Written in an easy-to-read Q&A format, *The Autism Answer Book* helps parents understand and accept their child and develop a plan for success.

Autism Aspergers: Solving the Relationship Puzzle--A New Developmental Program that Opens the Door to Lifelong Social and Emotional Growth
Steven E. Gutstei
Publication date: January 1, 2000

Autism: Advancing on the Spectrum: From Inclusion in School to Participation in Life
Melissa Niemann
Publication date: April 29, 2011
Full of life lessons learned from the actual journey of a young woman with autism, this book is an inspiration for anyone who wants to make a difference in the life of an individual with on the autism spectrum.

The Autism Encyclopedia
John Neisworth Ph.D. (Editor), Pamela Wolfe Ph.D. (Editor)
Publication date: November 1, 2004
An A-Z reference on autism spectrum and pervasive developmental disorders, with 500+ comprehensive entries for parents and professionals.

Autism Spectrum Disorders: The Complete Guide
Chantal Sicile-Kira (Author), Temple Grandin (Foreword)
Publication date: August 31, 2004
Based on nearly two decades of personal and professional experiences with individuals and families affected by this growing epidemic, *Autism Spectrum Disorders* explains all aspects of the condition.

A History of Autism: Conversations with the Pioneers
Adam Feinstein
Publication date: June 2010

This unique book fully explores the history of autism from the first descriptions of autistic-type behavior to the present day.

Living Along the Autism Spectrum: What Does It Mean to Have Autism or Asperger's Syndrome?
Cathy Pratt, Ph.D.
Living Along the Autism Spectrum examines the perspectives of both a father and an individual on the spectrum. Topics range from family coping to employment. The DVD provides valuable insight into the range of emotions experienced in connection with an autism diagnosis and covers topics that can be used to generate important discussions.

Diagnosis/Early Intervention

An Early Start for Your Child with Autism,
Sally J. Rogers, Ph.D., Geraldine Dawson, Ph.D., and Laurie A. Vismara, Ph.D
Publication Date: May 21, 2012
In this book the authors translate the Early Start Denver Model approach into step-by-step strategies for parents and other caregivers. Their approach employs straightforward techniques that fit into family routines and are compatible with professionally delivered behavioral interventions for autism spectrum disorders. The goal is to promote learning, play, communication and social engagement through activities in the home and community.

Early Intervention and Autism2-Early Intervention and Autism
James Ball, Ed.D. BCBA
Publication Date: January 1 2008
This book will guide you through your child's early years by providing sound advice based on over twenty years of experience. In an easy-to-read, question-answer format, "Dr. Jim" explains "what makes your child tick", how to get the most out of early intervention services, and how to choose the most effective treatment options.

Bridging the Gap: An Early Childhood Curriculum for Children with Autism
B. Blaine Campbell
Publication Date: November 25, 2008
Drawing from the elements of Applied Behavioral Analysis therapy, *Bridging the Gap* uses essential skills and methods to allow children with Autism to transition into public school smoothly. This accessible curriculum uses ABA terminology and skills in a preschool schedule format. The lessons are designed to allow for a certain amount of flexibility, so that each element is appropriate for each student.

The First Year: Autism Spectrum Disorders: An Essential Guide for the Newly Diagnosed Child
Nancy D. Wiseman
Publication Date: 2009
The First Year: Autism Spectrum Disorders walks parents through a wide range of medical and lifestyle concerns, helping them navigate the healthcare, insurance, and educational systems and ensuring the best possible outcome for their child.

Therapeutic/Behavioral Interventions

Behavior Analysis for Lasting Change 3/E
G. Roy Mayer, Beth Sulzer-Azaroff, and Michele Wallace
This comprehensive introduction to the field of behavior analysis has been completely updated and references a vast number of scientifically-supported constructive solutions within many areas of human performance.

Relationship Development Intervention with Young Children: Social and Emotional Development Activities for Asperger Syndrome, Autism, PDD and NLD
Steven E. Gutstein, Rachelle K. Sheely
Publication Date: February, 2002
Designed for younger children, typically between the ages of two and eight, this comprehensive set of enjoyable activities emphasizes foundation skills such as social referencing, regulating behavior, conversational reciprocity and synchronized actions. The authors include many objectives to plan and evaluate a child's progress, each one related to a specific exercise.

Talking Is Hard for Me! Encouraging Communication in Children with Speech-Language Difficulties
Linda M. Reinert, M.S., CCC-SLP
Publication Date: 2013
This multilayered guide lets parents and caregivers team up with children to help them communicate.

Medical, Biomedical, Diet Interventions

Clinical Manual for the Treatment of Autism
Eric Hollander and Evdokia Anagnostou
Publication Date: 2007
The book describes, in a straightforward manner, how to diagnose autism, providing examples and guidelines for evaluation and testing of individuals of all ages and levels of functioning. It then evaluates the appropriate role of various medications for specific target symptoms and individuals: SSRIs and antidepressants, anticonvulsants and mood stabilizers, conventional and atypical antipsychotics, cholinesterase inhibitors, and stimulants and non-stimulants.

The PRT Pocket Guide: Pivotal Response Treatment for Autism Spectrum Disorders
Robert Koegel, PhD & Lynn Koegel, PhD
Publication Date: 2012
A great resource for educators, behavior specialists, early interventionists, SLPs, occupational therapists, and families, this reader-friendly pocket guide is the perfect introduction to PRT, the popular approach that uses natural learning opportunities to modify pivotal areas of behavior.

Social Skills/Other Interventions

Activity Schedules for Children With Autism, Second Edition: Teaching Independent Behavior
Lynn McClannahan & Patricia Krantz
Publication Date: 2010
An activity schedule is a set of pictures or words that cues a child to engage in a sequence of activities. When activity schedules are mastered, children are more self-directed and purposeful in their home, school, and leisure activities -- doing puzzles, interacting with classmates, and preparing food with minimal assistance from adults. In this book, parents and professionals will find detailed instructions and examples to help them develop activity schedules.

Creative Therapy for Children With Autism, ADD, and Aspergers
Janet Tubbs
Publication Date: 2007
Over thirty years ago, Janet Tubbs began using art, music, and movement to reach children with low self-esteem and behavioral problems. Believing that unconventional children required unconventional therapies, she then applied her program to children with autism, ADD/ADHD, and Asperger's syndrome. Her innovative methods not only worked, but actually defied the experts. In this book, Tubbs has put together a powerful tool to help parents, therapists, and teachers work with their children.

A Picture's Worth: PECS and Other Visual Communication Strategies in Autism
Andy Bondy, Ph.D. & Lori Frost, M.S., CCC-SLP
Publication Date: 2001
This book examines the value of non-verbal communication strategies for children with autism, and presents the Picture Exchange Communication System (PECS) in detail. PECS is a communication system that allows a child to use a picture (or series of pictures) to express his needs and desires without a prompt or cue from another person.

Road to Independence: Independence Skills *Training for Special Needs Children*
Brenda M. Batts
Publication Date: 2004
Brenda Batts, Behavior Consultant, and mother of Alex, a son who has autism, shares her behavior management and potty training techniques through her book, *Road to Independence*. She has compiled over 12 years experience in the rearing of her son and through behavior training for thousands of special needs clients (Autism, PDD, Aspergers, ADHD, Down syndrome, fragile X, etc.). The central focus of this writing is to help you empower your child to become more independent.

Autism Spectrum Disorder

Adolescents/Young Adults

Adolescents on the Autism Spectrum: A Parent's Guide to the Cognitive, Social, Physical, and Transition Needs of Teenagers with Autism Spectrum Disorders
Chantal Sicile-Kira
Publication Date: 2006
A complete guide to the cognitive, emotional, social, and physical needs of pre-teens and teenagers with autistic disorders, ranging from relatively mild Asperger's syndrome to more severe functional impairment.

A Full Life with Autism: From Learning to Forming Relationships to Achieving Independence
Chantal Sicile-Kira and Jeremy Sicile-Kira, foreword by Temple Grandin
Publication Date: 2012
A guide for helping children who have autism lead meaningful and independent lives as they reach adulthood.

The Girls' Guide to Growing Up: Choices & Changes in the Tween Years
Terri Couwenhoven, MS
Publication Date: 2011
This appealing and easy-to-follow guide for girls with intellectual disabilities is an introduction to the physical and emotional changes they'll encounter during puberty. Written on a third-grade reading level for preteens or young teenaged girls to read by themselves or with a parent, it's filled with age-appropriate facts, realistic illustrations and photos, icons, and a Q&A.

Growing Up on the Spectrum: A Guide to Life, Love, and Learning for Teens and Young Adults with Autism and Aspergers,
Lynn Kern Koegel, PhD, and Claire LaZebnick
Publication Date: 2010
Addressing universal parental concerns, from first crushes and a changing body to how to succeed in college and beyond, Growing Up on the Spectrum is a beacon of hope and wisdom for parents, therapists, and educators alike.

Aspergers Syndrome

Aspergers Syndrome Guide for Teens and Young Adults
Craig Kendall
Publication Date: 2009
The book offers solutions for some of a teen's most difficult problems such as: inability to have friends and develop deep meaningful relationships; spending too much time alone and spending too much time on the computer; low self esteem; being bullied at school; getting in trouble with the law; wanting to date but failing; failure at getting or keeping a job; inability to take care of themselves.

Aspergers and Girls
Featuring Tony Attwood and Temple Grandin, plus 7 more experts
Publication Date: 2006
This book describes the unique challenges of women and girls with Aspergers syndrome with the candid narratives written by the indomitable women who have lived them. You'll also hear from experts who discuss whether "Aspie girls" are slipping under the radar, undiagnosed; why many AS women feel like a minority within a minority (outnumbered by men 4:1); practical solutions that school systems can implement for girls; social tips for teenage girls, navigating puberty, the transition to work or university, and the importance of careers.

For Professionals

Asperger Syndrome in Adulthood: A Comprehensive Guide for Clinicians
Kevin P. Stoddart, Lillian Burke, Robert King
Publication Date: 2012
This book is one of the only guides to Aspergers syndrome (AS) as it manifests itself in adults. It integrates research and clinical experience to provide mental health professionals with a comprehensive discussion of AS in adulthood, covering issues of diagnosis as well as co-morbid psychiatric conditions, psychosocial issues, and various types of interventions—from psychotherapy to psychopharmacology. It also discusses basic diagnostic criteria, controversies about the disorder, and possible interventions and treatments for dealing with the disorder.

Asperkids: An Insiders's Guide to Loving, Understanding and Teaching Children with Asperger Syndrome
Jennifer Cook O'Toole
Publication Date: 2012
The author discusses theory of mind, the necessity for concrete forms of communication, and ways to inspire imagination through sensorial experiences. In particular she explores the untapped power of special interests, explaining how to harness these interests to encourage academic, social, and emotional growth.

Managing Anxiety in People with Autism: A Treatment Guide for Parents, Teachers and Mental Health Professionals
Anne M. Chalfant, PsyD
Publication Date: 2011
Managing Anxiety explains a range of different types of strategies that can help manage and treat anxiety at school, home, and in clinical settings and takes into consideration the different roles people play in a child's or adult's life: parent, sibling, teacher, etc. Readers learn about ways to modify behavior and/or the environment to indirectly reduce anxiety, as well as interventions, such as medication or psychotherapy, which deal with symptoms directly

More Than Hope: For Young Children On the Autism Spectrum: A Step-by-Step Guide to Everyday Intervention
Tanya Paparella, PhD, with Laurence Lavelle, PhD

Publication Date: 2012
This book takes each significant area of development and explains why children with autism learn differently. It then provides step-by-step intervention strategies to develop communication, social interaction, and normal behavior.

Siblings of Children with Autism: A Guide for Parents and Professionals
Sandra L. Harris and Beth A. Glasberg
Publication Date: 2012
This revised and updated edition takes a fresh look at what it's like to grow up as the brother or sister of a child with autism; it covers the basics of sibling relationships at all ages and describes how autism can affect these dynamics. Parents get important advice about balancing responsibilities for each child, encouraging their kids to share feelings, explaining autism to other children, and initiating play and interaction between siblings.

For Parents

Activity Schedules for Children with Autism: Teaching Independent Behavior
Lynn E. McClanahan, PhD & Patricia J. Krantz, PhD
Publication Date: 1999
Activity schedules are simple, yet revolutionary teaching tools that enable children with autism to accomplish activities with greatly reduced adult supervision. An activity schedule is a set of pictures or words that cues a child to engage in a sequence of activities.

Autism in the Family: Caring and Coping Together
Robert A. Naseef, PhD
Publication Date: 2013
A warm, down-to-earth, and practical guide for parents and an enlightening read for the professionals who work with them. This book will be a valuable companion as families love and support their child with autism.

Autism Spectrum Disorders: What Every Parent Needs to Know
American Academy of Pediatrics
Publication Date: 2012
This book helps parents understand how ASDs are defined and diagnosed and provides information on the most current types of behavioral and developmental therapies. It also helps parents understand what they can do to help promote a smooth transition from adolescence through the teen years and into adulthood.

Chaos to Calm: Discovering Solutions to the Everyday Problems of Living with Autism
Martha Gabler
Publication Date: 2013
Chaos to Calm describes how Martha Gabler discovered that effective solutions really did exist for the overwhelming behavior problems of her own son with profoundly, severe nonverbal autism.

Hope for Families of Children on the Autistic Spectrum
Lynda T. Young
Publication Date: 2011
Hope for Families of Children on the Autism Spectrum looks at the family as a whole, making every attempt to include all members in the experience of special needs children. It discusses everything from doctor and dental visits to play times with friends, explains how to handle crisis, and how to recognize signs of frustration and excitement.

Living Well with Mitochondrial Disease: A Handbook for Patients, Parents and Families
Cristy Balcells, RN, MSN
Publication Date: 2013
Living Well with Mitochondrial Disease helps make sense of mitochondrial disease (Mito), an overwhelming and complex group of diagnoses that has grown exponentially in recent years. This guide is the first book about Mito written for patients and their families. It helps readers understand how the mitochondria work (they are the powerhouse of the cell, providing energy for the entire body), how people with mitochondrial defects are diagnosed and treated, and how to live well when you, your child, or someone you love is struggling with disabling symptoms.

Making Sense of Autistic Spectrum Disorders: Creating the Brightest Future for Your Child with the Best Treatment Options
James Coplan, MD
Publication Date: 2010
In this authoritative and empowering book, the author gives caregivers of children on the autistic spectrum the knowledge they need to navigate the complex maze of symptoms, diagnoses, tests, and treatment options that await them.

More than Hope: for Young Children on the Autism Spectrum: A Step-by-Step Guide to Everyday Intervention
Tanya Paparella, PhD, with Laurence Lavelle, PhD
Publication Date: 2012
More Than Hope, for Young Children on the Autism Spectrum describes powerful intervention strategies to change the areas of early child development most impacted by autism

More than a Mom: Living a Full And Balanced Life When Your Child Has Special Needs (Mom's Choice Awards Recipient)
Heather Fawcett, and Amy Baskin
Publication Date: 2006
More than a Mom addresses the universal concerns and questions of all mothers, coupled with the added intensity of raising children with disabilities.

Parent Survival Manual: A Guide to Crisis Resolution in Autism and Related Developmental Disorders
Eric Schopler
Publication Date: 1995

This practical guide offers effective solutions to various behavior problems such as aggression, communication, perseveration, play and leisure, eating and sleeping, and toileting and hygiene.

Parenting on the Autism Spectrum: A Survival Guide- 2nd ed.
Lynn Adams, PhD
Publication date: 2013
Parents of children with an autism spectrum disorder want to be proactive. This book, now in its second edition, offers a collection of practical, real-world information and insights to help parents do just that: plan for their child's needs. The book combines current research and literature reviews with the experiences gleaned by the author as she has worked with families impacted by ASD for the past twenty years.

Connor's Gift: Embracing Autism in this New Age
Tracie Carlos
Publication Date: 2011
Conner's Gift introduces the world to a very special boy and the family who love him. He is at once funny, charming, silly, sweet, and can also be a challenge that most would choose to avoid. And that is what makes *Connor's Gift* an outstanding read.

For Siblings

All About My Brother
Sarah Peralta
Publication Date: 2002
This is an invaluable contribution to helping typically developing children understand that a child with autism is a child first, and is someone interesting to know. Sarah gives insight into the sibling relationship in a way only a child can do it. The book is heart-warming and introspective and the writing style makes it appropriate for children and adults alike.

Living with a Brother or Sister with Special Needs: A Book for Sibs
Donald Meyer and Patricia Vedasy
Publication Date: 1996
Living with a Brother or Sister with Special Needs focuses on the intensity of emotions that brothers and sisters experience when they have a sibling with special needs, and the hard questions they ask: What caused my sibling's disability? Could my own child have a disability as well? What will happen to my brother or sister if my parents die? Written for young readers, the book discusses specific disabilities in easy to understand terms. It talks about the good and not-so-good parts of having a brother or sister who has special needs and offers suggestions for how to make life easier for everyone in the family.

My Little Brother Is a Little Different - An Autism Story
Tammy Parker Cox
Publication Date: 1996
My Little Brother Is a Little Different is a short and real life story about the loving interaction between a big sister and her little brother who has autism. Whether you know someone who has autism or not, this book will surely charm you.

The Other Kid: A Draw It Out Guidebook for Kids Dealing with a Special Needs Sibling
Lorraine Donlon
Publication Date: 2011
Parents and sibling support group leaders can use this workbook as a tool to help children express all their wonders and worries. The book allows the children to read, think, draw, and discuss their feelings in a way that reassures them that their feelings are normal and acceptable.

The Sibling Slam Book: What It's REALLY Like to Have a Brother or Sister with Special Needs
Don Meyer & David Gallagher
Publication Date: 2005
The Sibling Slam Book doesn't slam in the traditional sense of the word. The tone and point-of-view of the answers are all over the map. Some answers are assuredly positive, a few are strikingly negative, but most reflect the complex and conflicted mix of emotions that come with the territory. It is a book that parents, friends, and counselors can feel confident recommending to any teenager with a brother or sister with a disability.

What's Wrong with Alex? A Story for Siblings and Friends of Children Diagnosed with Autism
Sonseeahray Hodge Scott
Publication Date: 2011
Johnny can't wait for his little brother to come home so he can play with him. But soon things start not going according to his plan as his little brother, Alex is not meeting his childhood milestones. *What's Wrong with Alex?* helps explain to young children what Autism is like in a language they understand

Internet Resources

Centre for the Study of Autism www.autism.com

Autism Society of Ontario
www.autismsociety.on.ca

Geneva Centre for Autism www.autism.net

Kerry's Place Autism Services, Aurora, Ontario k.p.autismservices@ci.on.ca

References

American Psychiatric Association (APA) (1980). *Diagnostic and statistical manual of mental disorders, 3rd edition*. Washington, DC: Author.

American Psychiatric Association (APA) (1987). *Diagnostic and statistical manual of mental disorders, 3rd edition revised*. Washington, DC: Author.

American Psychiatric Association (APA) (1994). *Diagnostic and statistical manual of mental disorders, 4th edition*. Washington, DC: Author.

American Psychiatric Association. (2013). *Diagnostic and statistical manual of mental disorders,* (DSM-5). American Psychiatric Pub.

Bailey, A., Le Couteur, A., Gottesman I., Bolton P., Simonoff E., Yuzda E., & Rutter, M. (1995). Autism as a strongly genetic disorder: Evidence from a British twin study. *Psychological Medicine, 25,* 63-77.

Bailey, A., Phillips, W., & Rutter, M. (1996). Autism: Toward an integration of clinical, genetic, neuropsychological, and neurobiological perspectives. *Journal of Child Psychology and Psychiatry, 37,* 89-126.

Baron-Cohen, S. (1989). The autistic child's theory of mind: A case of specific developmental delay. *Journal of Child Psychology and Psychiatry, 30,* 285-297.

Barthelemy, C., Bruneau, N., & Conet-Eymard, J. M. (1988). Urinary free and conjugated catecholamines and metabolites in autistic children. *Journal of Autism and Developmental Disorders, 18,* 583-591.

Ben Bashat, D., Kronfeld-Duenias, V., Zachor, D.A., Ekstein, P.M., Hendler, T., Tarrasch, R… Sira, L. B. (2007). Accelerated maturation of white matter in young children with autism: A high b value DWI study. *Neuroimage, 37,* 40–47.

Bishop, D.V.M. (1989). Asperger's syndrome and semantic-pragmatic disorder: Where are the boundaries? *British Journal of Communication, 24,* 107-121.

Bolton, P., Macdonald, H., Pickles, A., Rios P., Goode, S., Crowson, M.,.. Rutter, M. (1994) A case-control family history study of autism. *Journal of Child Psychology & Psychiatry, 35,* 877-900.

Brook, S. I., & Bowler, D. M. (1992). Autism by another name? Semantic and pragmatic impairments in children. *Journal of Autism and Developmental Disorders, 22,* 61-81.

Butler, M. G., Youngs, E. L., Roberts, J. L., & Hellings, J. A. (2012). Assessment and treatment in autism spectrum disorders: A focus on genetics and psychiatry. *Autism Research and Treatment,* 242537.

Cantor, D. S., Thatcher, R. W., Hrybyk, M., & Kaye, H. (1986). Computerized EEG analyses of autistic children. *Journal of Autism and Developmental Disorders, 16,* 169-187.

Cantwell, D., Rutter, M., & Baker, L. (1978). Family factors. In M. Rutter & E. Schopler (Eds.), *Autism: A reappraisal of concepts and treatment* (pp. 269-296). New York: Plenum.

Carr, E. G., & Kemp, D. C. (1989). Functional equivalence of autistic leading and communicative, pointing: Analysis and treatment. *Journal of Autism and Developmental Disorders, 19*, 561-578.

Centers for Disease Control and Prevention. (2014). Prevalence of Autism Spectrum Disorder Among Children Aged 8 Years — Autism and Developmental Disabilities Monitoring Network, 11 Sites, United States, 2010. Retrieved from http://www.cdc.gov/mmwr/preview/mmwrhtml/ss6302a1.htm?s_cid=ss6302a1_w

Chandana S. R., Behen M. E., Juhasz C., Muzik, O., Rothermel, R.D., Mangner, T.J. ... Chugani, D.C. (2005). Significance of abnormalities in developmental trajectory and asymmetry of cortical serotonin synthesis in autism. *International Journal of Devevelopmental Neuroscience, 23*, 171–182.

Chugani, D. C. (2012). Neuroimaging and neurochemistry of autism. *Pediatric Clinics of North America, 59*(1), 63-73.

Creak, M. (1963). Schizophrenic syndrome in childhood: Further progress of a working party. *Developmental Medical Child Neurology, 6*, 530-535.

Ecker, C., Spooren, W., & Murphy, D. G. (2013). Translational approaches to the biology of autism: False dawn or a new era? *Molecular Psychiatry, 18*(4), 435-442.

Ernst M., Zamatkin A. J., Matochik, J. A., Pascualvaca, D., & Cohen, R.M. (1997). Low medial prefrontal dopaminergic activity in autistic children. *Lancet, 350*(9078), 638.

Fisman, S. N., Wolf, L. C., Ellison, D., & Freeman, T. (2000). A longitudinal study of siblings of children with chronic disabilities. *Canadian Journal of Psychiatry, 45*, 369-375.

Fisman, S. N., Wolf, L. C., Ellison, D., Gillis, B., Freeman, T., & Szatmari, P. (1996). Risk and protective factors affecting the adjustment of siblings of children with chronic disabilities. *Journal of American Academy of Child and Adolescent Psychiatry, 35*, 1532-1541.

Fisman, S. N., Wolf, L. C., & Noh, S. (1989). Marital intimacy in parents of exceptional children. *Canadian Journal of Psychiatry, 34*, 519-525.

Folstein, S., & Rutter, N. (1977). Infantile autism: A genetic study of 21 twin pairs. *Journal of Child Psychology and Psychiatry, 18*, 297-321.

Fombonne E. (2005). Epidemiology of autistic disorder and other pervasive developmental disorders. *Journal of Clinical Psychiatry, 66*(10), 3-8.

Gershon E.S. & Alliey-Rodriguez N. (2013). New ethical issues for genetic counseling in common mental disorders. *American Journal of Psychiatry, 170*(9), 968-976.

Gillberg, C., Bjure, J., Uvebrant, P., & Vestergren, E. (1993). SPECT (Single Photon Emission Tomography) in 31 children and adolescents with autism and autistic like conditions. *European Child and Adolescent Psychiatry, 2*, 50-59.

Gillberg, C., & Svennerholm, L. (1987). CSF monoamines in autistic syndromes and other pervasive developmental disorders of early childhood. *British Journal of Psychiatry, 151*, 89-94.

Grafodatskaya, D., Chung, B., Szatmari, P., & Weksberg, R. (2010). Autism spectrum disorders and epigenetics. *Journal of the American Academy of Child & Adolescent Psychiatry, 49*(8), 794-809.

Gupta A.R., & State M.W. (2007). Recent advances in the genetics of autism. *Biological Psychiatry, 61*(4), 429-437.

Hameury, L., Roux, S., Barthelemy, C., Adrien, J. L., Desombre, H., Sauvage, D., et al. (1995) Quantified multidimensional assessment of autism and other pervasive developmental disorders. Application for bioclinical research. *European Child and Adolescent Psychiatry, 4*, 123-135.

Harris, S. L., & Handleman, J. S. (Eds). (1994). Preschool education programs for children with autism. Austin, TX: Pro-ED.

Harfterkamp, M., van de Loo-Neus, G., Minderaam R.B., van der Gaag, R.J., Escobar, R., Schacht, A… Hoekstra, P.J. (2012). A randomized double-blind study of atomoxetine versus placebo for attention-deficit/hyperactivity disorder symptoms in children with autism spectrum disorder. *Journal of the American Academy of Child and Adolescent Psychiatry, 51*(7), 733-741.

Hellemans, H., Colson, K., Verbraeken, C., Vermeiren, R., & Deboutte, D. (2007). Sexual behavior in high-functioing male adolescents and young adults with autism spectrum disorder. *Journal of Autism and Developmental Disorders, 37*(2), 260-269.

Horder, J., & Murphy, D. G. (2012). Recent advances in neuroimaging in autism. *Neuropsychiatry, 2*(3), 221-229.

Jones, M. B., & Szatmari, P. (1988). Stoppage rules and genetic studies of autism. *Journal of Autism and Developmental Disorders, 20*, 241-248.

Just, M.A., Cherkassky, V.L., Keller, T.A., Minshew, N.J. (2004). Cortical activation and synchronization during sentence comprehension in high-functioning autism: evidence of underconnectivity. *Brain 127*, 1811–1821.

Kamps, D. M., Barbetta, P. M., Leonard, B. R., & Delquadri, J. (1994). Classwide peer tutoring: An integration strategy to improve reading skills and promote peer interaction among students with autism and general education peers. *Journal of Applied Behavior Analysis, 27*, 49-61.

Kanner, L. (1943). Autistic disturbances of affective contact. *Nervous Child, 2*, 217-250.

Kim Y.S & Leventhal B.L. (2015). Genetic epidemiology and insights into interactive genetic and environmental effects in Autism Spectrum Disorders. *Biological Psychiatry, 77*,66-74.

Koegel, L. K., Koegel, R. L., Hurley, C., & Frea, W.D. (1992). Improving social skills and disruptive behavior in children with autism through self-management. *Journal of Applied Behavior Analysis, 25,* 341-353.

Kolvin, I. (1971). Studies in the childhood psychosis. Diagnostic criteria and classification. *British Journal of Psychiatry, 118,* 381-384.

Leiter, R. G. (1948). *Leiter international performance scale.* Chicago, IL: Stoelting.

Leventhal, B. L., Cook, E. H. Jr., Morford, M., Ravitz, A., & Freedman, D. X. (1990). Relationships of whole blood serotonin and plasma norepinephrine within families. *Journal of Autism and Developmental Disorders, 20,* 499-511.

Lord, C., Rutter, M., Goode, S., Heemsberger, J., Jordan, H., Mawhood, L., & Schoppler, E. (1989). Autism diagnostic observation schedule: a standardized observation of communicative and social behavior. *Journal of Autism and Developmental Disorders, 19,* 185-212.

Lord, C., Rutter, M., & Le Couteur, A. (1994). Autism Diagnostic Interview-revised. A revised version of a diagnostic interview for caregivers of individuals with possible pervasive developmental disorders. *Journal of Autism and Developmental Disorders, 24,* 659-685.

Lotter,V.(1966) Epidemiology of autistic conditions in young children. *Social Psychiatry, 1*(3) 124-135.

Lounds, T. J., Dove D., Veenstra-VanderWeele, J., Sathe, N., McPheeters, M.L., Jerome, R.N., & Warren, Z. (2012). Interventions for adolescent and young adults with autism spectrum disorders. *Comparative Effectiveness Reviews(65).* Rochville, MD: Agency for Healthcare Research and Quality,

Lovaas, O. I. (1987). Behavioral treatment and normal educational and intellectual functioning in young autistic children. *Journal of Consulting and Clinical Psychology, 55,* 3-9.

Martineau, J., Barthelemy, C., Jouve, J., Muh, J. P., & Lelord, G. (1992). Monoamines (serotonin and catecholamines) and their derivatives in infantile autism: Age-related changes and drug effects. *Developmental Medical Child Neurology, 34,* 595-603.

Mason, S. S., McGee, G. G., Farmer-Dougan, V., & Risley, T.R. (1989). A practical strategy for ongoing reinforcer assessment. *Journal of Applied Behavior Analysis, 22,* 171-179.

McPheeters, M. L., Warren, Z., Sathe, N., Bruzek, J. L., Krishnaswami, S., Jerome, R. N., & Veenstra-Vanderwelle, J. (2011). *Pediatrics,* 127(5): e1312-e1321.

Morrison, J. (2014). *DSM-5 made easy: A clinician's guide to diagnosis.* New York, NY: Guilford Press.

Nakamura K., Sekine Y., Ouchi Y., Tsujii, M., Yoshikawa, E., Futatsubashi, M... Mori, N. (2010). Brain serotonin and dopamine transporter bindings in adults with high-functioning autism. *Archives of General Psychiatry,* 67(1), 59–68.

Noh, S., Dumas, J. E., Wolf, L. D., & Fisman, S. N. (1989). Delineating sources of stress in parents of exceptional children. *Family Relations, 38*, 456-461.

Ousley, O.Y. & Mesibov, G.B. (1991). Sexual attitudes and knowledge of high functioning adolescents and adults with autism. *Journal of Autism and Developmental Disorders, 21*(4), 471-481.

Ozonoff, S., & McEvoy, E. E. (1994). A longitudinal study of executive dysfunction and theory of mind development in autism. *Development and Psychopathology, 6*, 415-431.

Panksepp, J., & Sahley, T. L. (1987). Possible brain opioid involvement in disrupted social intent and language development in autism. In E. Schopler & G. B. Mesibov (Eds.), *Neurobiological issues in autism* (pp. 357-372). New York: Plenum Press.

Pickles, A., Bolton, P., Macdonald, H., Bailey, A., Le Couteur A, Sim, C. H., & Rutter, M. (1995). Latent-class analysis of recurrence risks for complex phenotypes with selection and measurement error: A twin and family history study of autism. *American Journal of Medical Genetics, 57*, 717-726.

Pierce, K., & Shreibman, L. (1994). Teaching daily living skills to children with autism in unsupervised settings through pictorial self-management. *Journal of Applied Behavior Analysis, 27*, 471-481.

Piven, J., Arndt, S., Bailey, J., Havercamp, S., Andreasen, N. C., & Palmer, P. (1995). An MRI study of brain size in autism. *American Journal of Psychiatry, 152*, 1145-1149.

Piven, J., Saliba, K., Bailey, J. & Arndt, S. (1997). An MRI study of autism: The cerebellum revisited. *Neurology, 49*, 546-551.

Piven, J., Wzorek, M., Landa, R., Lainhart, J., Bolton, P., Chase, G.A., & Folstein, S. (1994). Personality characteristics of the parents of autistic individuals. *Psychological Medicine, 24*, 783-795.

Ritvo, E.R., Jorde, L.B, Mason-Brothers, A., Freeman, B.J., Pingree, C., Jones, M.B… Mo, A. (1989). The UCLA-University of Utah epidemiologic survey of autism: Recurrence risk estimates and genetic counseling. *American Journal of Psychiatry, 146*(8), 1032-1036.

Ritvo, E. R., Spence, M. A., Freeman, B. J., Mason-Brothers, A., Mo, A., & Marazita, M. I. (1985). Evidence for autosomal recessive inheritance in 46 families with multiple incidences of autism. *American Journal of Psychiatry, 142*, 187-192.

Rosenthal, M., Wallace, G.L., Lawson, R., Wills, M.C., Dixon, E., Yerys, B.E., & Kenworthy, L. (2013). Impairments in real-world executive function increase from childhood to adolescence in autism spectrum disorders. *Neuropsychology, 27*(1), 13-18.

Rossignol, D.A. & Frye, R.E. (2012). Mitochondrial dysfunction in autism spectrum disorders: A systematic review and meta-analysis. *Molecular Psychiatry, 17*(3), 290-314.

Schaefer G. B. & Mendelsohn N. J. (2008). Clinical genetics evaluation in identifying the etiology of autism spectrum disorders. *Genetics in Medicine, 10*(4), 301–305.

Schaefer, G. B., Starr, L., Pickering, D., Skar, G., Dehaai, K., & Sanger, W. G. (2010). Array comparative genomic hybridization findings in a cohort referred for an autism evaluation. *Journal of Child Neurology, 25*(12), 1498–1503.

Schuler, A. L., Prizant, B. M., & Wetherby, A. M. (1997). Enhancing language and communication development: Prelinguistic approaches. In D. Cohen & F. Volkmar (Eds), *Handbook of autism and pervasive developmental disorders* (2nd ed.) (pp. 539-571). New York: John Wiley & Sons, Inc.

Sebat J., Lakshmi B., D. Malhotra D., Troge, J., Lese-Martin, C., Walsh, T... Wigler, M. (2007). Strong association of de novo copy number mutations with autism, *Science, 316*(5823), 445–449.

Semrud-Clikeman, M., & Hynd, G. W. (1990). Right hemispheric dysfunction in nonverbal learning disabilities: Social, academic, and adaptive functioning in adults and children. *Psychological Bulletin, 197,* 196-209.

Smalley, S. L., Asarnow, R. F., & Spence, M. A. (1988). Autism and genetics: A decade of research. *Archives of General Psychiatry, 45,* 953-961.

Smalley, S. L., McCracken, J., & Tanguay, P. (1995). Autism, affective disorders, and social phobia. *American Journal of Medical Genetics, 60,* 19-26.

Sparrow, S. S., Balla, D. & Cicchetti, D. V. (1984). *Vineland Adaptive Behavior Scales* (expanded form). Circle Pines, MN: American Guidance Service.

Steffenburg, S., Gillberg, C., Hellgren, L., Andersson, L., Gillberg, I. C., Jakobsson, G., & Bryson, S. E. (1989). A twin study of autism in Denmark, Finland, Iceland, Norway, and Sweden. *Journal of Child Psychology and Psychiatry, 30,* 405-416.

Stowitscheck, J. J. (1992). Policy and planning in transition programs at the state agency level. In F.R. Rusch, L. DeStefano, L. Chadsey-Rusch, A. Phelps, & E. Syzmanski (Eds), *Transition from school to adult life: Models, linkages, and policy* (pp. 519-536). Sycamore, IL: Sycamore.

Szatmari, P., Jones, M. B., Fisman, S., Tuff, L., Bartolucci, G., Mahoney, W. J., & Bryson, S. E. (1995). Parents and collateral relatives of children with pervasive developmental disorders: A family history study. *American Journal of Medical Genetics, 60,* 282-289.

Szatmari, P., Jones, M. B., Tuff, L., Bartolucci, G., Fisman, S., & Mahoney W. (1993). Lack of cognitive impairment in first-degree relatives of children with pervasive developmental disorders. *Journal of American Academy of Child and Adolescent Psychiatry, 32,* 1264-1273.

Szelazek, J. T., Williamson, P. C., Fisman, S., Steele, M., Gati, J. S., Densmore, R. S... Ellison, D. (2000). Regional brain functioning during verbal fluency tasks in subjects with Asperger's Disorder. Published abstract in conference proceedings *Beyond 2000: Healthy tomorrows for children and youth*. Canadian Academy of Child Psychiatry/Canadian Paediatric Society/Canadian Institute of Child Health. Ottawa, ON.

Travers, B. G., Adluru, N., Ennis, C., Trompdo, P. M., Destiche, D., Doran, S. & Alexander, A.L. (2012). Diffusion tensor imaging in autism spectrum disorder: A review. *Autism Research, 5,* 289–313.

Vissers, M.E., Cohen, M.X., & Geurts, H.M. (2012). Brain connectivity and high functioning autism: A promising path of research that needs refined models, methodological convergence, and stronger behavioral links. *Neuroscience & Biobehavioral Reviews, 36*(1), 604-625.

Volkmar, F. R., Cicchetti, D. V., Bregman, J., & Cohen, D. J. (1992). Three diagnostic systems for autism: DSM-III, DSM-IV, and ICD-10. *Journal of Autism and Developmental Disorders, 22,* 483-492.

Wing, L. (1981). Asperger's syndrome. A clinical account. *Psychological Medicine, 11,*115-129.

Wing, L. (1986). Letter: Clarification of Asperger's syndrome. *Journal of Autism and Developmental Disorders, 16,* 513-515.

Wing, L., & Gould, J. (1979). Severe impairments of social interaction and associated abnormalities in children. Epidemiology and classification. *Journal of Autism and Developmental Disorders, 9,* 11-29.

Wolf, L. C., Fisman, S. N., & Ellison, D. (1998). Effect of differential parental treatment in sibling dyads with one disabled child: A longitudinal perspective. *Journal of American Academy of Child and Adolescent Psychiatry, 37,* 1317-1325.

Wolff, J. J., & Piven, J. (2013). On the emergence of autism: Neuroimaging findings from birth to preschool. *Neuropsychiatry, 3*(2), 209-222.

Wolf, L. C., Noh, S., Fisman, S. N., & Speechley, M. (1989). Psychological effects of parenting stress on parents of autistic children. *Journal of Autism and Developmental Disorders, 19,* 157-166.

Xiao-Mian S., Jing Y., Chongxuna Z., Min L., & Hui-Xing D. (2005). Study of 99mTc-TRODAT-1 imaging on human brain with children autism by single photon emission computed tomography. Conference Proceedings IEEE *Engineering in Medicine and Biology Society, 5,* 5328–5330.

Zilbovicius, M., Garreau, B., Samson, Y., Remy, P., Barthelemy, C., Syrota, A., & Lelord, G. (1995). Delayed maturation of the frontal cortex in childhood autism. *American Journal of Psychiatry, 152,* 248-252.

Demysifying Syndromes II

Chapter 7

22q11.2 deletion syndrome

Chelsea Lowther, Erik Boot, Kerry Boyd, and Anne S. Bassett

Introduction

22q11.2 deletion syndrome (22q11.2DS) is the most common microdeletion syndrome in humans (Bassett et al., 2011; Kaminsky et al., 2011; McDonald-McGinn & Sullivan, 2011). As the name implies, 22q11.2DS is caused by a small missing piece of genetic material on chromosome 22 (Figure 1). 22q11.2DS is a multi-system disorder, meaning that several body systems are affected, including but not limited to the cardiovascular system (heart and blood vessels), endocrine system (hormones), and central nervous system (brain). The most common feature of 22q11.2DS is developmental delay and/or intellectual disability. (Bassett et al., 2011; Swillen et al., 1999; van Amelsvoort et al., 2004). Individuals with 22q11.2DS often manifest a wide range of clinical symptoms of variable severity, ranging from congenital anomalies (birth defects) to psychiatric illnesses later in life. As a result of this *variable expression*, many individuals with the 22q11.2 deletion go undiagnosed (Liu et al., 2014). Timely recognition of 22q11.2DS can assist in genetic counseling (the process by which affected individuals and/or relatives are advised of the nature and consequences of 22q11.2DS), identifying associated health issues and alerting patients and families about treatment options (Costain, Chow, Ray, & Bassett, 2012; Fung et al., 2015).

Figure 1: The 22q11.2 deletion

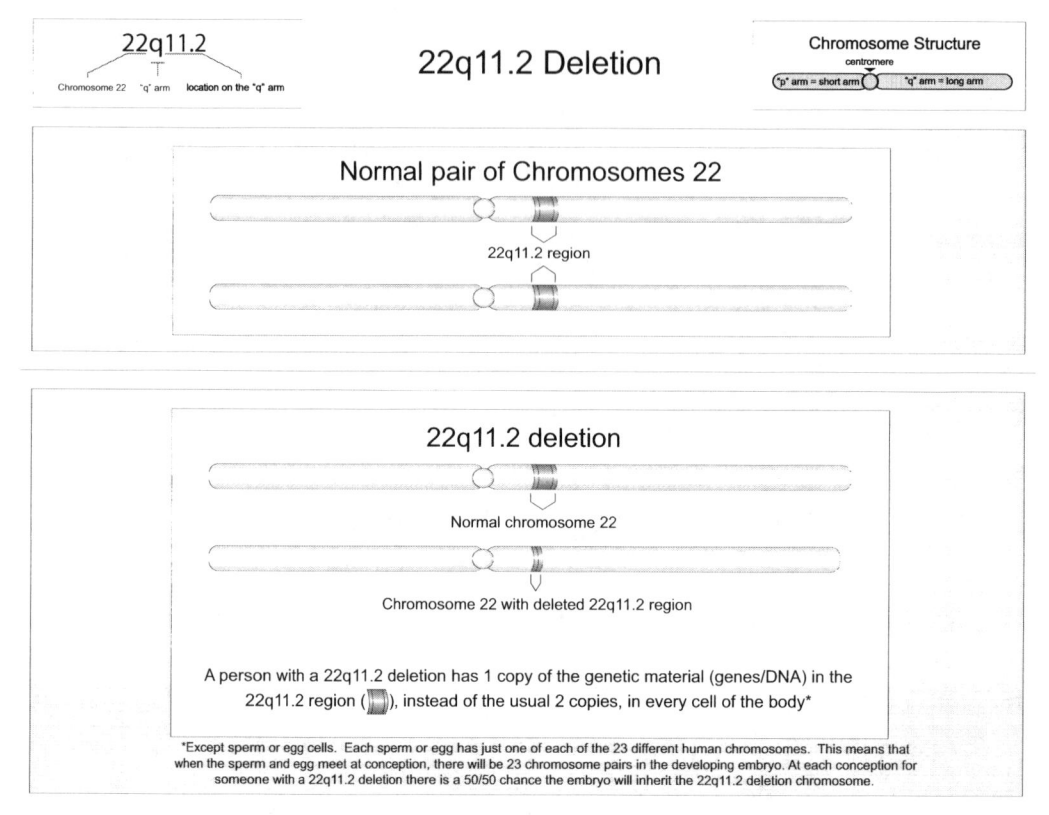

This chapter will outline key information on 22q11.2DS including history of the syndrome's identification, information on the underlying genetics, description of the clinical symptoms and features from infancy to adulthood, and case examples describing the clinical challenges of individuals with 22q11.2DS. The goal of this chapter is to provide readers, including caregivers, nurses, educators, social workers, and mental health care professionals with up-to-date information about 22q11.2DS in order to better serve and care for individuals with this unique genetic condition.

The 22q11.2 Deletion

22q11.2DS is the most common microdeletion syndrome in humans, with an estimated prevalence of 1 in 2,000-4,000 live births (Bassett et al., 2011; Goodship, Cross, LiLing, & Wren, 1998), although this prevalence rate is likely to be an underestimation. Routine newborn screening for 22q11.2DS is currently unavailable; therefore the true live birth prevalence of 22q11.2DS in the general population remains unknown (McDonald-McGinn & Sullivan, 2011). In the largest prenatal study to date the prevalence of the typical 22q11.2 deletion was found to be 1 in 347 among all pregnancies referred for prenatal testing (Costain, McDonald-MGinn, & Bassett, 2013; Wapner et al., 2012). This study also found that even when pregnancies with congenital defects (physical abnormalities existing at birth) such as heart

22q11.2 deletion syndrome

defects were removed, the prevalence of the typical 22q11.2 deletion was 1 in 1,022 (Costain et al., 2013; Wapner et al., 2012).

Long before genetic technologies were capable of detecting the 22q11.2 deletion underlying 22q11.2DS, physicians around the world described unrelated groups of individuals with similar clinical characteristics known as a "syndrome." As a result of the variable expression of 22q11.2DS, multiple names were given to the same genetic condition. For example, DiGeoge syndrome (DGS) was named after pediatric endocrinologist Dr. Angelo DiGeorge in the early 1960's after he characterized a group of infants with low serum calcium levels, recurrent infections secondary to problems with the thymus gland, heart defects, and palatal anomalies. In the late 1970's, a speech pathologist, Robert Shprintzen, reported several individuals with velopharyngeal incompetence, heart defects, learning disabilities, and similar facial features, which he termed Velocardiofacial syndrome (VCFS) (Shprintzen et al., 1978). It was not until the early 1990's that researchers began to notice common features among these syndromes and set out to identify a potential underlying genetic cause.

The name given to this genetic condition historically depended on the medical specialty or type of clinical service evaluating the individual. The discovery of the 22q11.2 deletion helped unify these seemingly unrelated syndromes and provided a single underlying cause (Lindsay et al., 1995; Scambler et al., 1992). Unfortunately, many individuals continue to use various names when referring to affected individuals with 22q11.2DS, which challenges the ability to communicate across medical specialties, complicates a researcher's ability to identify relevant papers in the literature, and often confuses health care professionals, affected individuals, their family members, and others. The International 22q11.2 Foundation Inc. (http://www.22q.org/) has begun the *Same Name Campaign* in an effort to establish the use of consistent terminology across the world. Experts in the field agree that 22q11.2 deletion syndrome (22q11.2DS) should be the single term used, as it accurately depicts the syndrome's underlying cause.

Over 90% of individuals identified to have the 22q11.2 deletion are the first in their family to have this genetic change (Edelmann, Pandita, & Morrow, 1999). Thus, for the majority of people the 22q11.2 deletion represents a new or spontaneous change (i.e., not found in either parent). The deletion is believed to occur before conception when the egg and sperm are forming. It is important for families to know that the 22q11.2 deletion is not the result of anything that happened during pregnancy, labor/delivery, or after birth. In the remaining 10% of cases the 22q11.2 deletion is inherited from a parent (Delio et al., 2013; McDonald-McGinn & Sullivan, 2011). Maternal age does not appear to be a risk factor for 22q11.2DS (Delio et al., 2013).

The 22q11.2 deletion can now best be detected using a standard genetic test called a microarray, which can detect deletions and duplications across the entire genome in a single test. The typical 22q11.2 deletion is too small to be detected by older cytogenetic tests such as karyotype. Individuals with unexplained developmental delay/intellectual disability, autism spectrum disorders, and/or multiple congenital abnormalities are all recommended to have microarray as a first-tier clinical diagnostic test (Miller et al., 2010).

22q11.2 deletions arise because the 22q11.2 region has several long stretches of almost identical genetic sequence (called segmental duplications), which make the region prone to errors by non-allelic homologous recombination (NAHR; Stankiewicz & Lupski, 2002). During sexual cell division, homologous chromosomes (e.g., pair of chromosomes you inherit from your mother and father) exchange genetic material, allowing new combinations and increased genetic diversity in offspring. NAHR is the process by which unequal exchange of genetic material occurs between such chromosomes, leading to deletions and/or duplications. This mechanism is thought to be responsible for other genomic disorders such as Williams syndrome, Prader-Willi syndrome, Angelman syndrome, and Smith Magenis syndrome. The typical 22q11.2 deletion is roughly 2.5 million base pairs (2.5 Mb) in size (Bassett et al., 2011; Edelmann et al., 1999). Smaller deletions within the 22q11.2 region do occur, however less frequently (Rump et al., 2014; Weksberg et al., 2007). The typical 22q11.2 deletion contains over 40 genes (segments of DNA that provide instructions for making proteins). There is only one copy of these genes in the deleted region, instead of the normal two copies (Figure 1). In other words the "dosage" of these genes is less than normal. Several of these genes are known to have important functions during early development and later in life. Nevertheless, much remains to be discovered with respect to how the 22q11.2 deletion leads to the clinical features of 22q11.2DS.

Clinical features of 22q11.2DS

This section will introduce the collection of features associated with 22q11.2DS from infancy to adulthood. It is important to note that there is a great deal of variability among individuals with 22q11.2DS, even within families. Parents identified to have 22q11.2DS after identification of their affected child tend to have milder clinical features (McDonald-McGinn et al., 2001). The features can also vary depending on the age of the individual (Bassett et al., 2011; Fung et al., 2015). In the absence of newborn screening in combination with longitudinal follow up studies, the entire spectrum of clinical manifestations associated with 22q11.2DS remains unknown. The increasing success of pediatric cardiac surgery since the 1960s has increased the life expectancy of individuals with 22q11.2DS and others born with heart defects and has therefore facilitated the identification of new later onset conditions (Carotti et al., 2008; Fung et al., 2015).

Facial and Other Minor Physical Features

Physical features typically described in 22q11.2DS include: a long, narrow face, narrow eye openings, broad nasal bridge, prominent tubular nose with a protuberant nasal tip, a small, open mouth, and slender hands with thin, tapered fingers. Small ears are also common in 22q11.2DS, sometimes with an overfold at the top (Liu et al., 2014; Monteiro et al., 2013). These facial features, however, are often subtle, vary from person to person, and may or may not be present, especially in non-Caucasian individuals (Liu et al., 2014; Monteiro et al., 2013). In many cases even experts cannot identify individuals with 22q11.2DS based on facial features alone.

Cardiovascular Issues

About 40% of individuals with 22q11.2DS are born with a congenital heart defect (Bassett et al., 2005; Bretelle et al., 2010). Severe congenital heart defects block oxygen from circulating around the body and cause the skin to appear "blue," especially around the mouth, hands, and feet (sometimes called blue baby syndrome). These serious heart defects are usually diagnosed and surgically repaired during infancy, but milder heart defects may escape medical attention. Therefore, all individuals with a 22q11.2 deletion should be evaluated (e.g., with an echocardiogram) for heart defects at diagnosis (Bassett et al., 2011; Fung et al., 2015). Most individuals with a major congenital heart defect will require lifelong follow up. Other vascular issues associated with 22q11.DS can include malposition of arteries and varicose veins (Bassett et al., 2011; Fung et al., 2015).

Endocrinology Issues

Hypocalcemia (low blood calcium levels) occurs in ~80% of 22q11.2DS cases at some point in life (Cheung, George, Andrade, et al., 2014). Hypocalcemia in 22q11.2DS is thought to be caused by inadequate levels of parathyroid hormone, which regulates the level of calcium absorbed by the body (Cuneo et al., 1996). Magnesium is also known to regulate parathyroid hormone and may also be found to be low (hypomagnesemia) in 22q11.2DS (Cheung, George, Costain, et al., 2014). The clinical presentation of hypocalcemia varies widely, from asymptomatic to life-threatening. Brain development and/or functionality may be affected (Cheung, George, Andrade, et al., 2014), and milder symptoms include fatigue and emotional irritability; however, hypocalcemia may also predispose the individual to abnormal involuntary movements of any sort (e.g., tremors, seizures, serious irregular heartbeats) and osteopenia/osteoporosis (Bilezikian et al., 2011; Cheung, George, Andrade, et al., 2014). Hypocalcemia may arise in the newborn period and appear to resolve, but can emerge again at any age. It is, therefore, recommended that ionized calcium and parathyroid hormone levels be regularly monitored in 22q11.2DS, especially during times of high biological stress such as surgery, pregnancy, and acute illness (Bassett et al., 2011; Fung et al., 2015). Hypothyroidism (too little thyroid hormone) is found in about 30% of individuals with 22q11.DS and hyperthyroidism (too much thyroid hormone) in about 5%. Therefore, periodic monitoring of thyroid function in 22q11.2DS using standard blood tests is also recommended (Bassett et al., 2011; Fung et al., 2015).

Palate and Velopharyngeal Insufficiency

There are a number of conditions that may affect the roof of the mouth (palate) in 22q11.2DS (McDonald-McGinn & Sullivan, 2011). Typical palatal defects of 22q11.2DS include submucosal cleft palate (hole in the roof of the mouth that is covered by skin). This birth defect can be challenging to identify during infancy and can lead to hypernasal speech, feeding/swallowing difficulties, and middle ear disease if left unrepaired. Velopharyngeal insufficiency (VPI; when the muscles that coordinate the soft palate and the throat do not work properly) is the most common palatal anomaly of 22q11.2DS. VPI can also lead to hypernasal cry/speech, difficulties with sucking/feeding, and regurgitation of milk/food through the nose (nasal regurgitation). Overt cleft palate and/or cleft palate are rare in 22q11.2DS (Bassett et al., 2011; Fung et al., 2015).

Gastrointestinal Issues

Swallowing problems (dysphagia), vomiting, and gagging are frequently seen in children with 22q11.2DS and may lead to poor weight gain (Digilio et al., 2001). Swallowing problems may persist into adulthood. Other common 22q11.2DS related problems that involve the gastrointestinal tract include gastro-esophageal reflux disease (GERD; stomach contents coming back up the esophagus), delayed stomach emptying, gallstones, and constipation (Eicher et al., 2000; Gerdes, Solot, Wang, McDonald-McGinn, & Zackai, 2001). Routine treatments, such proton pump inhibitors for GERD, for these conditions appear to be successful (Bassett et al., 2011).

Immunology Issues

The immune system's ability to fight infectious disease is compromised in a proportion of children with 22q11.2DS (McDonald-McGinn & Sullivan, 2011). The frequency of upper respiratory infections is increased and infections tend to last longer than expected. Luckily, most children do not develop life-threatening infections. Immunological evaluation is recommended when 22q11.2DS is diagnosed and before providing live vaccines (Bassett et al., 2011). Relatively little is known about immunologic problems in adults with 22q11.2DS; however, immunological evaluation and follow-up for those with recurrent infections is recommended (Bjork, Oskarsdottir, Andersson, & Friman, 2012). In adults, the focus is more on the emergence of autoimmune conditions such as hypothyroidism, hypoparathyroidism, and arthritis.

Neuromuscular/Musculoskeletal Abnormalities

Approximately 45% of individuals with 22q11.2DS have problems with their spine (Bassett et al., 2011), including scoliosis (curvature of the spine of various degrees) and/or abnormalities of the upper spine at the neck (Hamidi et al., 2014). The clinical consequences of neck abnormalities are unknown. Other less common abnormalities include abnormal number (too many or too few) ribs (Bassett et al., 2011). A musculoskeletal examination should be considered at diagnosis (Bassett et al., 2011; Fung et al., 2015).

Sensory Problems

Children and adults with 22q11.2DS may experience sensory problems that involve the ears, nose, and/or eyes. Hearing impairments are found in approximately 40% of children and adults with 22q11.2DS (Bassett et al., 2011; Persson, Friman, Oskarsdottir, & Jonsson, 2012; Vieira et al., 2014). Impaired ability to smell is also common in 22q11.2DS and often goes undetected (Romanos et al., 2011). It is important to identify smell abnormalities because affected individuals may not be able to detect dangerous smells such as toxic fumes, smoke, and spoiled foods. Eye abnormalities are also common and include trouble focusing, far-sightedness, problems with eye alignment, and other eye problems (Casteels, Casaer, Gewillig, Swillen, & Devriendt, 2008).

Hematology

Blood disorders occur at an increased rate in 22q11.2DS compared to the general population. Examples of blood disorders include low blood count (anemia) and low platelet count (cells that help stop bleeding) (Bassett et al., 2011; McDonald-McGinn & Sullivan, 2011). The latter may lead to bleeding problems and should be monitored pre- and post-surgery (Bassett et al., 2011).

Dental Problems

Individuals with 22q11.2DS are at an increased risk for multiple dental problems including abnormal development of teeth, enamel disturbances, and cavities (Bassett et al., 2011; Fung et al., 2015; Nordgarden et al., 2012).

Sexuality and Reproductive Issues

As with any adolescent or adult, romantic partnerships, sexual activity, and pregnancy are important aspects of adult life for individuals with 22q11.2DS. However, impaired decision making in 22q11.2DS may increase the likelihood of high-risk sexual activity (Costain, Chow, Silversides, & Bassett, 2011). Developmentally appropriate sexual education and routine reproductive health care should be provided as indicated, which would include contraceptive counselling for men and women, information on routine Pap tests, and education on risks, symptoms, and routine testing for sexually transmitted infections. A recent study showed that individuals, especially males, with 22q11.2DS have fewer offspring (reduced reproductive fitness) compared to their siblings without 22q11.2DS (Costain et al., 2011); however, women with 22q11.2DS without intellectual disability or schizophrenia had similar number of offspring to their unaffected sisters (Costain et al., 2011). Many health conditions common to 22q11.2DS, including endocrine, cardiovascular, and psychiatric illnesses, may pose risks for the mother and/or fetus. Therefore, high-risk antepartum care should be considered for pregnancies that involved mothers and/or fetuses with 22q11.2DS

Cognitive and Adaptive Functioning

The majority (~80%) of young children with 22q11.2DS are developmentally delayed and take longer to reach developmental milestones such as crawling, walking, and talking (Roizen et al., 2007; Swillen et al., 1997). Children often have below average language development and may require speech therapy (Gerdes et al., 2001). School aged children may be found to have borderline to mild, or rarely, moderate intellectual disability; few cases have been identified to have severe to profound intellectual disability (Antshel, Fremont, & Kates, 2008; Chow, Watson, Young, & Bassett, 2006; Swillen et al., 1997; Swillen et al., 1999; van Amelsvoort et al., 2004). Expressive and receptive language deficits are also common (Moss et al.,

1999; Swillen et al., 1999). Cognitive decline is observed in a proportion (~30%) of children and adolescents, therefore periodic neuropsychological testing is recommended to reassess strengths and weaknesses over time (Duijff et al., 2012; Duijff et al., 2013; Vorstman et al., 2015).

The majority of adults with 22q11.2DS have an intelligence quotient (IQ) in the borderline (IQ 70-84) or mild intellectual disability range (IQ 55-69). Some children and adults demonstrate a markedly lower performance IQ score compared to verbal IQ score, consistent with a non-verbal learning disorder (Rourke et al., 2002; Swillen et al., 1999). Research suggests adults with 22q11.2DS and a normal full scale IQ test score (>85) may still have deficits in social judgement and/or arithmetic skills that can make tasks such as managing money and paying bills difficult (De Smedt, Swillen, Verschaffel, & Ghesquiere, 2009). The majority of adults with 22q11.DS studied have trouble carrying out the tasks required for independent living (Butcher et al., 2012). Few studies as yet have extensively studied the cognitive and adaptive functioning profile in older adults with 22q11.2DS; however, a recent study demonstrated a significant decline in IQ before the onset of psychosis in individuals with 22q11.2DS (Vorstman et al., 2015).

The key to improving cognitive and educational outcomes in 22q11.2DS is early detection. Most children and adults with 22q11.2DS will have some form of cognitive deficit, including borderline-moderate intellectual disability and/or specific learning disabilities, especially in math (Bassett et al., 2011; Fung et al., 2015; Swillen et al., 1999). However, because the 22q11.2DS phenotype is highly variable, children entering preschool should undergo a full neuropsychological assessment to determine individual strengths and weaknesses. Interventions and educational plans should be individually tailored to each individual with 22q11.2DS. Cognitive and adaptive functioning may change across the lifespan, especially with the onset of psychiatric and/or neurologic disorders therefore periodic follow-up assessments are recommended.

Several considerations regarding cognitive and adaptive functioning must be taken into account once individuals with 22q11.2DS reach adulthood. For example, low intellectual functioning and/or major psychiatric disorders such as schizophrenia may compromise decision-making capabilities, particularly with respect to medical procedures, financial choices and complex life decisions (Fung, 2015). Where appropriate, a power of attorney or legal guardianship should be considered. As a result of medical and/or psychiatric conditions, affected individuals may experience increased fatigue and/or stress related responses. Therefore, accommodations for the post-secondary school and/or the workplace environment, including modified course load, part-time employment, increased emphasis on rote memorization, or increased breaks, may be required (Fung et al., 2015). Other related strategies to improve functioning may include keeping a structured routine to increase predictability and decrease anxiety, use of verbal reminders to overcome auditory learning deficits, and providing simple, written and/or verbal instructions for various tasks such as household chores and taking medication (Fung et al., 2015).

Case Study #1

David was born following an uncomplicated full-term pregnancy and delivery in the early 1990's. He was noted in the delivery room to have a right-sided cleft lip and palate and soon afterwards was found to have a heart murmur that was subsequently diagnosed as a ventricular septal defect (hole in the wall that separates the two lower chambers of the heart). His cleft lip was repaired when he was 4 months of age and palate at 1 year. Around that time, he was noted to be delayed in his motor milestones and was referred to the local infant development program. Assessment at 15 months of age indicated mild delays in language and motor skills. He was a cheerful and energetic infant who enjoyed social play. David's vocalization consisted primarily of vowel sounds, and he was not yet walking or picking up small objects. He continued to make steady progress during the preschool years, although he continued to show significant delays in speech, sound, and language development. His general health was good, although he did have recurrent ear infections, some feeding difficulties, and was slow to gain weight.

David was initially seen by a clinical geneticist at 18 months of age in 1992. At that time he was noted to have distinctive facial features including protuberant ears with simplified helices (outer ear structure), broad nasal bridge, and a slightly flattened facial profile (see photograph taken at 4 years of age). Routine analysis of his chromosomes (karyotype) was reported to be normal. He was reassessed at the age of 5 years and noted to have persistent developmental delay as well as difficulty keeping up academically with his kindergarten peers. His height and weight also continued to be near the lower end of the growth curves despite average adult height of both parents. The diagnosis of 22q11.2DS was later confirmed by FISH testing. This test had not been commercially available in 1992 when David was initially assessed by the geneticist. Further investigations including abdominal ultrasound, measurement of serum calcium, and immune factors were all within normal limits.

Despite improvements in language skills, David's repertoire of speech sounds remained quite limited. David's speech became increasingly hypernasal, causing difficulty in making himself understood (e.g., poor intelligibility of his speech). Assessment of his velopharyngeal function (ability to coordinate muscles of the palate) showed abnormalities. Surgical intervention at the age of 7 years helped reduce the hypernasal tone of David's speech and improved his intelligibility.

David has continued to experience difficulties at school. He has required a modified academic program although he remains included in regular stream with the support of an educational aide. Assessment at age 7 years indicated that David's overall intellectual abilities were at the 1st percentile. There was a significant discrepancy between his verbal reasoning skills and visual spatial reasoning skills, consistent with a mild intellectual disability and nonverbal learning disorder. He also exhibited significant difficulties with concentration, organizational skills, and impulse control. He was very distractible, had difficulty waiting his turn, and needed reminders to follow basic safety rules (e.g., running out into the street to retrieve a ball). At the age of 8 years, formal assessment using standardized measures was consistent with a diagnosis of Attention Deficit Hyperactivity Disorder. He showed a positive response to stimulant medication and remained on a low dose of that medication with some improvement in attention and behavior at school.

Neurodevelopmental and Mental Health Disorders

Childhood onset conditions such as autism spectrum disorder and attention deficit hyperactivity disorder (mainly inattentive type) are present at increased rates in children with 22q11.2DS, with symptoms often persisting into adulthood (Schneider et al., 2014). High rates of anxiety disorders are also identified in individuals with 22q11.2DS onset in both childhood or later in life (Fung et al., 2015; Schneider et al., 2014).

About one in four adults with 22q11.2DS have schizophrenia, characterized by negative symptoms (problems with motivation, social withdrawal), positive symptoms (psychotic symptoms: hallucinations, delusions, and/or disorder of thought form), and disorganized behavior (Bassett & Chow, 2008). This prevalence represents an approximately twenty-fold increased risk of schizophrenia over the general population risk of about 1% (Bassett & Chow, 2008; Bassett, Scherer, & Brzustowicz, 2010; Fung et al., 2010). 22q11.2DS represents the first clinically recognizable genetic subtype of schizophrenia, identified in roughly 1 in 100 of all individuals diagnosed with this illness (Bassett et al., 2003). The symptoms of schizophrenia in 22q11.2DS are very similar to those with schizophrenia in the general population, apart from lower mean IQ (Chow et al., 2006). Caregivers of individuals with 22q11.2DS should be vigilant in looking for changes in thinking, emotions, and/or behavior and seek out appropriate professionals (e.g., psychiatrist) when necessary (Bassett et al., 2011; Fung et al., 2015).

Neurological Issues

Individuals with 22q11.2DS are at an increased risk for seizures and epilepsy. The prevalence of epilepsy in 22q11.2DS is between 5-7%, significantly higher than in the general population (0.5-1%) (Bassett et al., 2005; Kao et al., 2004). Seizures of all types are observed, including generalized, focal, and myoclonic (Fung et al., 2015). Single and recurrent seizures are common across the lifespan and may be related to hypocalcaemia and/or hypomagnesemia or other metabolic abnormalities of 22q11.2DS (Cheung, George, Andrade, et al., 2014; Ryan et al., 1997). Recent research suggests that adults with 22q11.2DS may be at an increased risk for early onset (<50 years) Parkinson's disease (Booij, van Amelsvoort, & Boot, 2010; Butcher et al., 2013; Zaleski et al., 2009). Other studies suggest that adults with 22q11.2DS may be more prone to (neurological) side-effects of medications, such as antipsychotics and that they are at increased risk for movement abnormalities (Boot et al., 2015; Butcher et al., 2013). Therefore, physicians should be alert to treatable neurologic conditions, and periodic neurologic assessments should be considered, especially in adults presenting with changes in motor functioning (Boot et al., 2015; Fung et al., 2015).

Premature Mortality

Individuals with 22q11.2DS who survive into adulthood are at an increased risk for early death (Bassett et al., 2009). In one study of 102 adults with 22q11.2DS, survival rates to ages 40 and 50 were 89.9 and 73.9%, respectively (Bassett et al., 2009). The causes of death reported were sudden, unexpected death (most common),

22q11.2 deletion syndrome

heart failure, stroke, suicide, and complications after surgery. More studies are needed to more fully understand the earlier demise by many decades in 22q11.2DS compared to unaffected siblings and general population expectations.

Case Study #2

Sandy was born in the 1970's. She was delivered by caesarean section with fetal distress at 42 week's gestation. Shortly after birth she was noted to have a high pitched, harsh sound when she breathed in and feeding difficulties (gagging, coughing during feeds). Her parents were concerned that something was wrong but were offered no explanation. She was treated with an antibiotic for the cough. At age 2 and ½ she was assessed by a speech pathologist. Although she was speaking in sentences, she was barely intelligible because of the "air escaping through her nose" known as hypernasal speech. A submucous cleft palate was identified, and she subsequently had surgery to repair the defect.

Sandy was enrolled in a preschool and then entered the public school system. She disliked school and the teasing she received about her speech. There had been an effort to keep her in a regular classroom with a reduced workload, but this setting still created increasing frustration and an awareness that she could not keep up with others. When she was age 10, her parents were made aware of her significant academic difficulties and were witnessing a change in Sandy's emotional state. Sandy had become highly anxious, and her distress was associated with vomiting, which persisted over several years. Gastrointestinal workups could find no organic cause for the vomiting.

Sandy's parents recall that the start of high school was "too much for her." Over several years they noted an increase in bizarre and aggressive behavior to the point where Sandy had become unmanageable at home. She became distressed and consumed by fears that strangers were staring at her and "doing things" to her. She complained of hearing voices telling her what to do. She had difficulties elaborating on these experiences. Instead, she would often explode into outbursts of yelling or bouts of vomiting while attempting to recount these experiences.

While she was on a psychiatric ward of a university hospital, she received two brain scans that were both normal. She was treated with traditional antipsychotic medication, a behavior program, and family interventions. In 1985 at the age of 15 years, a genetics consult was obtained, and it was concluded that there was no obvious genetic basis to explain Sandy's problems. She was discharged from the psychiatric ward to an adolescent unit affiliated with the hospital and eventually went to live in a series of group homes.

Ten years later at age 25 years, Sandy was referred to an interdisciplinary team for individuals with dual diagnosis (developmental delay and/or intellectual disability and behavior problems). Sandy had ongoing problems with the unshakeable belief that strangers were watching/influencing her, episodes of uncontrollable agitation, and poor response to caregivers support measures. The team re-referred the family to genetics in 1995. There was no family history of developmental delay, major medical conditions, or psychiatric problems. On examination, her height was "on par" with family members. Apart from Sandy's hypernasal speech, her most striking physical features were: almond shaped eyes, flat cheekbones, prominent nasal tip, and slender, tapered fingers. A FISH test was positive for 22q11.2DS, and as is the case with 90% of individuals with 22q11.2DS, her parents were found to be negative for the deletion.

Once a genetic diagnosis was made and the syndrome explained by a genetic counsellor, the family expressed an enormous sense of relief at "finally having an answer." They had felt helpless and blamed but now felt like they "have it on paper... it's not our fault." The clinical service providers reviewed the medical concerns and proceeded with additional investigations for conditions known to be associated with 22q11.2DS. The parents were further assured by additional medical/neurological evaluations, which did not reveal additional problems. In light of the 22q11.2DS diagnosis and its association with schizophrenia, the psychiatric team discussed alternatives to treatment of psychotic symptoms. Sandy showed a marked improvement in thought processes and preoccupation with paranoid thoughts over a 1 year period after changing the antipsychotic medication. A serotonin reuptake inhibitor (SSRI) treatment for persistent anxiety was also started, and Sandy subsequently experienced a reduction in vomiting.

The family and group home worked with the team's psychologist, speech pathologist, and behavior therapist to identify Sandy's areas of strength and weaknesses. Neuropsychological assessment placed her in the mild range of intellectual disability. Sandy's verbal IQ was much higher than her performance IQ and adaptive skills measures. Sandy's areas of strength included simple focused attention and rote verbal memory. The team and caregivers were able to formulate suitable approaches for day-to-day interactions (e.g., use of slow rate of speech and short, simple phrases), enhancing adaptive skills (e.g., step-by-step diagrams, supportive coaching/cueing, modeling, and repetition), learning style in special education classroom (e.g., computer used with good effect and enthusiasm), and ways to avoid or deal with stressful situations (e.g., outings with a suitable "coach," a quiet place to retreat if necessary). She also became an eager participant in social skills and anger management groups. With a multi-modal intervention and integrated care approach Sandy's parents stress that they are now able to see their daughter for who she is -- "a unique person with a personality all her own who wants to know that she is loved."

Clinical Management and Genetic Counselling for 2211.2qDS

Early detection of 22q11.2DS is critical for informing future care and improving long term health outcomes. An extensive medical workup should be completed once an individual is identified to have 22q11.2DS (Table 1; Bassett et al., 2011; Fung et al., 2015). Developmental assessments and neurocognitive testing are essential to determining the educational assistance and other services, such as early childhood programs, that could maximize developmental outcomes. Educators should be vigilant for learning difficulties, especially in math. A significant minority of individuals with 22q11.2DS are diagnosed with a non-verbal learning disorder; therefore children may require additional help with visuo-spatial skills. Individuals with 22q11.2DS may face a wide range of medical and/or psychiatric challenges in their lifetime, or few problems. Treatment for various medical and/or psychiatric illnesses should follow standard guidelines with special attention being paid to potential underlying contributory conditions (Bassett et al., 2011; Fung et al., 2015). For example, affected individuals experiencing seizures should have ionized calcium and magnesium levels checked. Caregivers and physicians should be vigilant for emerging medical and/or psychiatric symptoms. Anticipatory care, including screening and monitoring for 22q11.2DS-associated clinical features allows for timely intervention (Bassett et al., 2011). Importantly, standard treatments, in the context of the multi-system nature of 22q11.2DS, appear to be effective for related problems (Bassett et al., 2011; Fung et al., 2015).

Table 1:
Summary of Recommended Medical Workup Once a 22q11.2DS Diagnosis Is Established (Bassett et al., 2011; Fung et al., 2015)

- Physical examination
- Developmental history
- Medical, surgical, and psychiatric history
- Family history
- Genetic counseling for the affected individual and family
- 22q11.2 deletion testing (see below) for parents
- Annual blood work: complete blood work including platelets, ionized calcium, parathyroid hormone, and thyroid stimulating hormone (TSH)
- Other investigations: echocardiogram, abdominal/renal ultrasound, brain MRI
- Referrals made as needed

All individuals identified to have 22q11.2DS and immediate family members should receive genetic counselling by a trained genetic counsellor, medical geneticist or other experienced medical specialist. Although inherited 22q11.2 deletions are rare, parents of affected individuals should be tested for the 22q11.2 deletion. If the 22q11.2 deletion is identified to be inherited, then additional relatives should be tested as indicated. As the knowledge of 22q11.2DS increases, periodic follow up genetic counselling sessions should be scheduled accordingly. Affected individuals should be counselled on the 50% risk of transmitting the 22q11.2 deletion at each pregnancy and highlight that it is not currently possible to predict the range or severity of clinical manifestations in the affected offspring. The complex multi-system nature of 22q11.2DS suggests that multiple specialists may be involved in the care of a single affected individual. Affected individuals should be referred to a clinic specializing in 22q11.2DS in order to receive coordinated multi-disciplinary care (Bassett et al., 2011; Fung et al., 2015).

Conclusion

22q11.2DS is a rare genetic condition that involves the loss of genetic material on the long arm of one of the two chromosomes 22. In over 90% of cases, the 22q11.2 deletion is a new or spontaneous change and in the remaining about 10% of cases the deletion was inherited from a parent. 22q11.2DS is a highly variable multi-system disorder that is markedly under recognized, especially in adults. Affected individuals may be diagnosed in infancy or childhood due to a congenital heart defect, palatal anomaly, other birth defects, or developmental delay. In adulthood, diagnosis may become possible as a relative of an affected individual. Clinical genetic testing for 22q11.2DS has been available since 1992-1994 and can be performed using a small blood sample. Microarray is now the genetic test of choice recommended for all individuals with intellectual disability, autism spectrum disorder, and/or multiple congenital anomalies (Miller et al., 2010). Early detection of 22q11.2DS is crucial for informing genetic counselling and anticipatory care. Regardless of the age of diagnosis, identification of 22q11.2DS can lead to early interventions and significantly improve clinical management and long term outcomes.

Resources

Dalglish Hearts and Minds Clinic (22q11.2DS clinic for adults)
Toronto General Hospital
Norman Urquhart Building, 8th Floor
200 Elizabeth Street
Toronto, ON M5G 2C4

22q and You Center
The Clinical Genetics Center
The Children's Hospital of Philadelphia
34th street and Civic Center Boulevard
Philadelphia, PA 19104
Website: www.chop.edu/centers-programs/22q-and-you-center

22q Foundation
Website: www.22q.org

Online Mendelian Inheritance of Man (OMIM)
Website: http://www.ncbi.nlm.nih.gov/omim

NCBI Genes and Disease
Website: www.ncbi.nlm.nih.gov/disease/DGS.html

GeneReviews
Website: www.ncbi.nlm.nih.gov/books/NBK1116

References

Antshel, K. M., Fremont, W., & Kates, W. R. (2008). The neurocognitive phenotype in velo-cardio-facial syndrome: a developmental perspective. *Developmental Disability Research Review, 14*(1), 43-51.

Bassett, A. S., & Chow, E. W. (2008). Schizophrenia and 22q11.2 deletion syndrome. *Current Psychiatry Reports, 10*(2), 148-157.

Bassett, A. S., Chow, E. W., AbdelMalik, P., Gheorghiu, M., Husted, J., & Weksberg, R. (2003). The schizophrenia phenotype in 22q11 deletion syndrome. *American Journal Psychiatry, 160*(9), 1580-1586.

Bassett, A. S., Chow, E. W., Husted, J., Hodgkinson, K. A., Oechslin, E., Harris, L., & Silversides, C. (2009). Premature death in adults with 22q11.2 deletion syndrome. *Journal of Medical Genetics, 46*(5), 324-330.

Bassett, A. S., Chow, E. W., Husted, J., Weksberg, R., Caluseriu, O., Webb, G. D., & Gatzoulis, M. A. (2005). Clinical features of 78 adults with 22q11 Deletion Syndrome. *American Journal of Medical Genetics Part A, 138*(4), 307-313.

Bassett, A. S., McDonald-McGinn, D. M., Devriendt, K., Digilio, M. C., Goldenberg, P., Habel, A.,. . . Eliez, S. (2011). Practical guidelines for managing patients with 22q11.2 deletion syndrome. *Pediatrics, 159*(2), 332-339 e331.

Bassett, A. S., Scherer, S. W., & Brzustowicz, L. M. (2010). Copy number variations in schizophrenia: critical review and new perspectives on concepts of genetics and disease. *American Journal of Psychiatry, 167*(8), 899-914.

Bilezikian, J. P., Khan, A., Potts Jr, J. T., Brandi, M. L., Clarke, B. L., Shoback, D., … Sanders, J. (2011). Hypoparathyroidism in the adult: Epidemiology, diagnosis, pathophysiology, target-organ involvement, treatment, and challenges for future research. *Journal of Bone & Mineral Research, 26 (10)*, 2317-2337.

Bjork, A. H., Oskarsdottir, S., Andersson, B. A., & Friman, V. (2012). Antibody deficiency in adults with 22q11.2 deletion syndrome. *American Journal of Medical Genetics Part A. 158A*(8), 1934-1940.

Booij, J., van Amelsvoort, T., & Boot, E. (2010). Co-occurrence of early-onset Parkinson disease and 22q11.2 deletion syndrome: Potential role for dopamine transporter imaging. *American Journal of Medical Genetics Part A, 152A*(11), 2937-2938.

Boot, E., Butcher, N. J., van Amelsvoort, T., Lang, A. E., Marras, C., Pondal, M., … Bassett, A. S. (2015). Movement abnormalities in adults with 22q11.2 deletion syndrome *American Journal of Medical Genetics Part A*, 167(3):639-45.

Bretelle, F., Beyer, L., Pellissier, M. C., Missirian, C., Sigaudy, S., Gamerre, M., … Philip, N. (2010). Prenatal and postnatal diagnosis of 22q11.2 deletion syndrome. *Euro J Med Genet, 53*(6), 367-370. doi: 10.1016/j.ejmg.2010.07.008

Butcher, N., Chow, E., Costain, G., Karas, D., Ho, A., & Bassett, A. (2012). Functional outcomes of adults with 22q11.2 deletion syndrome. *Genetic Medicine, 14*(10), 836-843.

Butcher, N., Kiehl, T., Hazrati, L., Chow, E., Rogaeva, E., Lang, A., & Bassett, A. (2013). Association between early-onset Parkinson disease and 22q11.2 deletion syndrome: Identification of a novel genetic form of Parkinson disease and its clinical implications. *JAMA Neurol, (70)*, 1359-1366.

Carotti, A., Digilio, M. C., Piacentini, G., Saffirio, C., Di Donato, R. M., & Marino, B. (2008). Cardiac defects and results of cardiac surgery in 22q11.2 deletion syndrome. *Developmental Disability Research Review, 14*(1), 35-42.

Casteels, I., Casaer, P., Gewillig, M., Swillen, A., & Devriendt, K. (2008). Ocular findings in children with a microdeletion in chromosome 22q11.2. *European Journal of Pediatrics, 167*(7), 751-755.

Cheung, E. N., George, S. R., Andrade, D. M., Chow, E. W., Silversides, C. K., & Bassett, A. S. (2014). Neonatal hypocalcemia, neonatal seizures, and intellectual disability in 22q11.2 deletion syndrome. *Genetic Medicine, 16*(1), 40-44.

Cheung, E. N., George, S. R., Costain, G. A., Andrade, D. M., Chow, E. W., Silversides, C. K., & Bassett, A. S. (2014). Prevalence of hypocalcemia and its associated features in 22q11.2 deletion syndrome. *Clinical Endocrinology, 81*(2), 190-196.

Chow, E. W., Watson, M., Young, D. A., & Bassett, A. S. (2006). Neurocognitive profile in 22q11 deletion syndrome and schizophrenia. *Schizophrenia Research, 87*(1-3), 270-278.

Costain, G., Chow, E. W., Ray, P. N., & Bassett, A. S. (2012). Caregiver and adult patient perspectives on the importance of a diagnosis of 22q11.2 deletion syndrome. *Journal of Intellectual Disability Research, 56*(6), 641-651.

Costain, G., Chow, E. W., Silversides, C. K., & Bassett, A. S. (2011). Sex differences in reproductive fitness contribute to preferential maternal transmission of 22q11.2 deletions. *Journal of Medical Genetics, 48*(12), 819-824.

Costain, G., McDonald-McGinn, D. M., & Bassett, A. S. (2013). Prenatal genetic testing with chromosomal microarray analysis identifies major risk variants for schizophrenia and other later-onset disorders. *American Journal of Psychiatry, 170*(12), 1498.

Cuneo, B. F., Langman, C. B., Ilbawi, M. N., Ramakrishnan, V., Cutilletta, A., & Driscoll, D. A. (1996). Latent hypoparathyroidism in children with conotruncal cardiac defects. *Circulation, 93*(9), 1702-1708.

De Smedt, B., Swillen, A., Verschaffel, L., & Ghesquiere, P. (2009). Mathematical learning disabilities in children with 22q11.2 deletion syndrome: a review. *Developmental Disability Research Review, 15*(1), 4-10.

Delio, M., Guo, T., McDonald-McGinn, D. M., Zackai, E., Herman, S., Kaminetzky, M., . . . Morrow, B. E. (2013). Enhanced maternal origin of the 22q11.2 deletion in velocardiofacial and DiGeorge syndromes. *American Journal of Human Genetics, 92*(3), 439-447.

Digilio, M. C., Marino, B., Cappa, M., Cambiaso, P., Giannotti, A., & Dallapiccola, B. (2001). Auxological evaluation in patients with DiGeorge/velocardiofacial syndrome (deletion 22q11.2 syndrome). *Genetic Medicine, 3*(1), 30-33.

Duijff, S. N., Klaassen, P. W., de Veye, H. F., Beemer, F. A., Sinnema, G., & Vorstman, J. A. (2012). Cognitive development in children with 22q11.2 deletion syndrome. *British Journal of Psychiatry, 200*(6), 462-468.

Duijff, S. N., Klaassen, P. W., Swanenburg de Veye, H. F., Beemer, F. A., Sinnema, G., & Vorstman, J. A. (2013). Cognitive and behavioral trajectories in 22q11DS from childhood into adolescence: a prospective 6-year follow-up study. *Research in Developmental Disabilities, 34*(9), 2937-2945.

Edelmann, L., Pandita, R. K., & Morrow, B. E. (1999). Low-copy repeats mediate the common 3-Mb deletion in patients with velo-cardio-facial syndrome. *American Journal of Human Genetics, 64*(4), 1076-1086.

Eicher, P. S., McDonald-Mcginn, D. M., Fox, C. A., Driscoll, D. A., Emanuel, B. S., & Zackai, E. H. (2000). Dysphagia in children with a 22q11.2 deletion: unusual pattern found on modified barium swallow. *Journal of Pediatrics, 137*(2), 158-164.

Fung, W. L., Butcher, N. J., Costain, G., Andrade, D. M., Boot, E., Chow, E. W., . . . Bassett, A. S. (2015). Practical guidelines for managing adults with 22q11.2 deletion syndrome. *Genetic Medicine, Epub: Jan 9th 2015*.

Fung, W. L., McEvilly, R., Fong, J., Silversides, C., Chow, E., & Bassett, A. (2010). Elevated prevalence of generalized anxiety disorder in adults with 22q11.2 deletion syndrome. *American Journal of Psychiatry, 167*(8), 998.

Gerdes, M., Solot, C., Wang, P. P., McDonald-McGinn, D. M., & Zackai, E. H. (2001). Taking advantage of early diagnosis: preschool children with the 22q11.2 deletion. *Genetic Medicine, 3*(1), 40-44.

Goodship, J., Cross, I., LiLing, J., & Wren, C. (1998). A population study of chromosome 22q11 deletions in infancy. *Archives of Disease in Childhood, 79*(4), 348-351.

Hamidi, M., Nabi, S., Husein, M., Mohamed, M. E., Tay, K. Y., & McKillop, S. (2014). Cervical spine abnormalities in 22q11.2 deletion syndrome. *Cleft Palate-Craniofacial Journal, 51*(2), 230-233.

Kaminsky, E. B., Kaul, V., Paschall, J., Church, D. M., Bunke, B., Kunig, D., . . . Martin, C. L. (2011). An evidence-based approach to establish the functional and clinical significance of copy number variants in intellectual and developmental disabilities. *Genetic Medicine, 13*(9), 777-784.

Kao, A., Mariani, J., McDonald-McGinn, D. M., Maisenbacher, M. K., Brooks-Kayal, A. R., Zackai, E. H., & Lynch, D. R. (2004). Increased prevalence of unprovoked seizures in patients with a 22q11.2 deletion. *American Journal of Medical Genetics Part A, 129*, 29-34.

Lindsay, E. A., Greenberg, F., Shaffer, L. G., Shapira, S. K., Scambler, P. J., & Baldini, A. (1995). Submicroscopic deletions at 22q11.2: variability of the clinical picture and delineation of a commonly deleted region. *American Journal of Medical Genetics, 56*(2), 191-197.

Liu, A. P., Chow, P. C., Lee, P. P., Mok, G. T., Tang, W. F., Lau, E. T., . . . Chung, B. H. (2014). Under-recognition of 22q11.2 deletion in adult Chinese patients with conotruncal anomalies: Implications in transitional care. *European Journal of Medical Genetics, 57*(6), 306-311.

McDonald-McGinn, D., & Sullivan, K. (2011). Chromosome 22q11.2 deletion syndrome (DiGeorge syndrome/velocardiofacial syndrome). *Medicine (Baltimore), 90*(1), 1-18.

McDonald-McGinn, D. M., Tonnesen, M. K., Laufer-Cahana, A., Finucane, B., Driscoll, D. A., Emanuel, B. S., & Zackai, E. H. (2001). Phenotype of the 22q11.2 deletion in individuals identified through an affected relative: cast a wide FISHing net! *Genetic Medicine, 3*(1), 23-29.

Miller, D. T., Adam, M. P., Aradhya, S., Biesecker, L. G., Brothman, A. R., Carter, N. P., . . . Ledbetter, D. H. (2010). Consensus statement: chromosomal microarray is a first-tier clinical diagnostic test for individuals with developmental disabilities or congenital anomalies. *American Journal of Human Genetics, 86*(5), 749-764.

Monteiro, F. P., Vieira, T. P., Sgardioli, I. C., Molck, M. C., Damiano, A. P., Souza, J., . . . Gil-da-Silva-Lopes, V. L. (2013). Defining new guidelines for screening the 22q11.2 deletion based on a clinical and dysmorphologic evaluation of 194 individuals and review of the literature. *European Journal of Pediatrics, 172*(7), 927-945.

Moss, E. M., Batshaw, M. L., Solot, C. B., Gerdes, M., McDonald-McGinn, D. M., Driscoll, D. A., . . . Wang, P. P. (1999). Psychoeducational profile of the 22q11.2 microdeletion: A complex pattern. *Journal of Pediatrics, 134*(2), 193-198.

Nordgarden, H., Lima, K., Skogedal, N., Folling, I., Storhaug, K., & Abrahamsen, T. G. (2012). Dental developmental disturbances in 50 individuals with the 22q11.2 deletion syndrome; relation to medical conditions? *Acta Odontol Scandanavia, 70*(3), 194-201.

Persson, C., Friman, V., Oskarsdottir, S., & Jonsson, R. (2012). Speech and hearing in adults with 22q11.2 deletion syndrome. *American Journal of Medical Genetics Part A, 158 A (12)*, 3071-3079.

Roizen, N. J., Antshel, K. M., Fremont, W., AbdulSabur, N., Higgins, A. M., Shprintzen, R. J., & Kates, W. R. (2007). 22q11.2DS deletion syndrome: developmental milestones in infants and toddlers. *Journal of Developmental & Behavioral Pediatrics, 28*(2), 119-124.

Romanos, M., Schecklmann, M., Kraus, K., Fallgatter, A. J., Warnke, A., Lesch, K. P., & Gerlach, M. (2011). Olfactory deficits in deletion syndrome 22q11.2. *Schizophrenia Research, 129*(2-3), 220-221.

Rourke, B. P., Ahmad, S. A., Collins, D. W., Hayman-Abello, B. A., Hayman-Abello, S. E., & Warriner, E. M. (2002). Child clinical/pediatric neuropsychology: Some recent advances. *Annual Reviews in Psychology, 53*, 309-339.

Rump, P., de Leeuw, N., van Essen, A. J., Verschuuren-Bemelmans, C. C., Veenstra-Knol, H. E., Swinkels, M. E., . . . van Ravenswaaij-Arts, C. M. (2014). Central 22q11.2 deletions. *American Journal of Medical Genetics Part A, 164A*(11), 2707-2723.

Ryan, A. K., Goodship, J. A., Wilson, D. I., Philip, N., Levy, A., Seidel, H., . . . Scambler, P.J. (1997). Spectrum of clinical features associated with interstitial chromosome 22q11 deletions: a European collaborative study. *Journal of Medical Genetics, 34*(10), 798-804.

Scambler, P. J., Kelly, D., Lindsay, E., Williamson, R., Goldberg, R., Shprintzen, R., . . . Burn, J. (1992). Velo-cardio-facial syndrome associated with chromosome 22 deletions encompassing the DiGeorge locus. *Lancet, 339*(8802), 1138-1139.

Schneider, M., Debbané, M., Bassett, A. S., Chow, E. W. C., Fung, W. L. A., Van den Bree, M. B. M., . . .Eliez, S. (2014). Psychiatric disorders from childhood to adulthood in 22q11.2 deletion syndrome: results from the International Consortium on Brain and Behavior in 22q11.2 Deletion Syndrome. *American Journal of Psychiatry, 171*(6), 627-639.

Shprintzen, R. J., Goldberg, R. B., Lewin, M. L., Sidoti, E. J., Berkman, M. D., Argamaso, R. V., & Young, D. (1978). A new syndrome involving cleft palate, cardiac anomalies, typical facies, and learning disabilities: velo-cardio-facial syndrome. *Cleft Palate Journal, 15*(1), 56-62.

Stankiewicz, P., & Lupski, J. R. (2002). Genome architecture, rearrangements and genomic disorders. *Trends Genetics, 18*(2), 74-82.

Swillen, A., Devriendt, K., Legius, E., Eyskens, B., Dumoulin, M., Gewillig, M., & Fryns, J. P. (1997). Intelligence and psychosocial adjustment in velocardiofacial syndrome: a study of 37 children and adolescents with VCFS. *Journal of Medical Genetics, 34*(6), 453-458.

Swillen, A., Vandeputte, L., Cracco, J., Maes, B., Ghesquiere, P., Devriendt, K., & Fryns, J. P. (1999). Neuropsychological, learning and psychosocial profile of primary school aged children with the velo-cardio-facial syndrome (22q11 deletion): evidence for a nonverbal learning disability? *Child Neuropsychology, 5*(4), 230-241.

van Amelsvoort, T., Henry, J., Morris, R., Owen, M., Linszen, D., Murphy, K., & Murphy, D. (2004). Cognitive deficits associated with schizophrenia in velo-cardio-facial syndrome. *Schizophrenia Research, 70*(2-3), 223-232.

Vieira, T. P., Monteiro, F. P., Sgardioli, I. C., Souza, J., Fett-Conte, A. C., Monlleo, I. L., . . . Gil-da-Silva-Lopes, V. L. (2014). Clinical Features in Patients With 22q11.2 Deletion Syndrome Ascertained by Palatal Abnormalities. *Cleft Palate Craniofacial Journal*.

Vorstman, J. A., Breetvelt, E., Duijff, S. N., Jalbrzikowsk, M., Vogels, A., Swillen, A., . . .Bassett, A.S. (2015). A decline in verbal intelligence precedes the onset of psychosis in patients with the 22q11.2 deletion syndrome. *Journal of the American Medical Association in Psychiatry, Feb 25, 2015* [Epub ahead of print].

Wapner, R. J., Martin, C. L., Levy, B., Ballif, B. C., Eng, C. M., Zachary, J. M., . . . Jackson, L. (2012). Chromosomal microarray versus karyotyping for prenatal diagnosis. *New England Journal of Medicine, 367*(23), 2175-2184.

Weksberg, R., Stachon, A. C., Squire, J. A., Moldovan, L., Bayani, J., Meyn, S., . . . Bassett, A. S. (2007). Molecular characterization of deletion breakpoints in adults with 22q11 deletion syndrome. *Human Genetics, 120*, 837-845.

Zaleski, C., Bassett, A. S., Tam, K., Shugar, A. L., Chow, E. W., & McPherson, E. (2009). The co-occurrence of early onset Parkinson disease and 22q11.2 deletion syndrome. *American Journal of Medical Genetics Part A, 149A*(3), 525-528.

CHAPTER 8

Angelman Syndrome

Jane Summers

Introduction

In 1965, Dr. Harry Angelman published a case study about three unrelated children who displayed a strong resemblance to each other. All three children had severe intellectual disability, seizure disorder, ataxic or jerky movements, lack of speech development and frequent bouts of laughter (Angelman, 1965). The cause of what came to be known as Angelman syndrome (or AS) remained unknown until 1987, when a microdeletion was discovered on the long arm of chromosome 15 (bands q11-q13) in several individuals with the characteristic clinical features (Kaplan et al., 1987; Magenis, Brown, Lacy, Budden, & LaFranchi, 1987). A maternal origin for the deletion was discovered soon after (Knoll et al., 1989; Williams et al., 1990); the cause of AS was traced to a disruption of the maternal copy of the UBE3A gene in 1997 (Kishino, Lalande, & Wagstaff, 1997).

This chapter begins by providing a review of the genetic aspects of AS, followed by an overview of the main diagnostic and clinical features. Afterward, the physical, neurodevelopmental, and behavioral characteristics of individuals with AS are described in greater detail. Intervention studies that address core and associated features of AS are discussed, then implications for therapy and parent support are highlighted.

Prevalence

The prevalence of AS is estimated to be approximately 1/12,000- 1/24,000 live births (Mertz et al., 2013; Petersen, Brondum-Nielsen, Hansen, & Wulff 1995). Among individuals with intellectual disability and seizure disorder, however, the prevalence may be higher (Clayton-Smith, 1995), including adults with severe disability who live in long-term care facilities and who may have been overlooked (Buckley, Dinno, & Weber, 1998; Jacobsen et al., 1998). There are accounts of siblings having AS (Fisher, Burn, Alexander, & Gardner-Medwin, 1987; Willems, Dijkstra, Brouwer, & Smit, 1987). AS has been reported among different racial groups and in various countries around the world (Williams, Angelman et al., 1995).

Genetic Aspects of AS

Deficiency of the imprinted, maternally expressed UBE3A (ubiquitin protein ligase 3A) gene and the E6-AP protein it produces are linked to the cause of AS (Dagli, Buiting & Williams, 2011). E6-AP is involved in a biochemical pathway that results in the breakdown of proteins that accumulate in the cytoplasm of cells in the body (Lombroso, 2000). Normally, the maternal copy of this gene is primarily active in neurons, while the paternal copy is almost completely repressed or "switched off" through a phenomenon known as genomic imprinting (Rougeulle, Glatt, & Lalande, 1997). By contrast, both copies of the gene are active in the other organs and tissues in the body (Chamberlain & Lalande, 2010). Thus, the neurological features of AS are thought to be related to changes in neuronal structure and function (Mabb, Judson, Zylka, & Philpot, 2011; Mardirossian, Rampon, Salvert, Fort, & Sarda, 2009; Williams, Driscoll, & Dagli, 2010) which are a result of the significant reduction of UBE-3A protein expression throughout multiple brain regions due to loss of function of the maternal copy of the gene (Daily, Smith & Weeber, 2012).

There are several mechanisms that lead to deficient expression of the maternally imprinted copy of the UBE-3A gene. The most common mechanism is related to a large random or spontaneous deletion of maternal origin in the AS/PWS region of chromosome 15 (q11.2-q13). This deletion is very large when viewed at a molecular level (consisting of about 4 million base pairs) and results in the loss of several genes, including the critical UBE-3A gene as well as a pigment gene and a cluster of genes that are implicated in seizure disorders (Jiang, Lev-Lehman, Bressler, Tsai, & Beaudet, 1999). Deletion cases account for approximately 75% of all individuals with AS (Buiting et al., 2015). In a second group of individuals, a small point mutation has been detected in the maternally inherited UBE3A gene itself, comprising about 5-10% of cases. AS can also be caused by paternal uniparental disomy (UPD), in which both copies of chromosome 15 are inherited from the father, accounting for only about 1-2% of cases. In a fourth group of individuals, there is no maternal deletion of 15q11-q13, and copies of chromosome 15 are inherited from both parents. The maternal chromosome 15, however, carries a paternal imprint due to a defect in an imprinting control center. Consequently, the maternal copy of the UBE-3A gene functions like the paternal copy and is virtually silenced in the brain. Imprinting defects occur in about 3% of individuals with AS. In the remaining group of individuals (about 10-15%), it is not possible to detect any molecular abnormalities of 15q11-q13. For them, a tentative diagnosis of AS is made on the basis of clinical history and features. There is the possibility that some as yet undiscovered mechanism is responsible for their AS, as well as the chance they have been diagnosed incorrectly because a different condition has given rise to clinical features that resemble the AS phenotype ("Angelman-like syndromes"), such as Pitt-Hopkins or Christianson syndrome (Tan, Bird, Thibert & Williams, 2014). It should be noted that the percentages of individuals who fall into the different molecular categories may vary slightly from study to study.

Molecular Testing

If an individual is suspected of having AS, guidelines that were established for molecular testing and analysis should be followed (Ramsden, Clayton-Smith, Birch, & Buiting, 2010). Analysis of methylation patterns within 15q11-q13 can detect a paternal imprint that can be caused by a deletion, UPD or imprinting center defect; however, subsequent testing is required (FISH, microsatellite analysis, and polymorphic DNA markers) to establish the specific underlying mechanism. In cases where the methylation pattern in 15q11-q13 is normal, mutation analysis of UBE3A is undertaken.

Why Is It Important to Know About the Genetic Mechanism?

There are at least two reasons why it is important to know about the underlying cause of AS in an individual. The first is that the risk of recurrence differs according to the mechanism that causes the syndrome (Dagli et al., 2011). The lowest risk of recurrence (<1%) is found in deletion or UPD cases. A much higher risk of recurrence (up to 50%) can happen when mutations in the UBE-3A gene or imprinting center are inherited from the mother. An increased risk of recurrence is also present if AS is caused by an inherited chromosomal translocation. In cases where there are no molecular abnormalities, the recurrence risk is unknown but theoretically could be as high as 50%. Given this complex picture, it is easy to see why families need access to genetic counseling by professionals who are well acquainted with the rapidly evolving knowledge in regard to the genetics of AS.

The second reason why it is important to know about the underlying genetic mechanism is related to the finding of phenotypic differences among individuals with different etiologies for their AS. Individuals with AS that is caused by a deletion of 15q11-q13 have the most pronounced or classical physical and neurobehavioral abnormalities (Gentile et al., 2010; Smith et al., 1996), while nondeletion cases that are caused by UPD or involve mutations in the UBE-3A gene or imprinting center typically have a somewhat less severe phenotype (Bottani et al., 1994; Moncla, Mazlac, Livet, et al.,1999a; Moncla, Malzac, Voelckel, et al., 1999b). Moncla et al. (1999b) have proposed ordering the molecular classes on a gradient of clinical severity (from most severe to least severe), such that deletion cases > UBE-3A mutations > imprinting defects and/or UPD cases. Advances in knowledge have resulted in a growing recognition that the clinical features of AS may be more heterogeneous than once thought. Thus, identification of a broader spectrum of AS features has important implications for diagnosis, prognosis and treatment.

Clinical and Diagnostic Features of AS

Consensus criteria have been published to assist in the evaluation and diagnosis of AS (Williams, Angelman et al. 1995, Williams et al., 2006). The main clinical features of AS have been divided into three categories: features that are consistently present (100% of cases), frequent features (more than 80% of cases), and associated features (between 20-80% of cases). Universal features of AS are: (1) intellectual disability (functionally severe range); (2) movement or balance disorder, which may present as unsteadiness or jerky movements; (3) absent or minimal expressive speech abilities along with better developed receptive language and non-verbal communication skills; and (4) "behavioral uniqueness" as manifested by any combination of excitable personality, apparently happy demeanor, frequent laughing or smiling, and hypermotoric behavior.

Abnormal electroencephalography (EEG) results are virtually universal in AS and are not dependent on seizure status. EEG patterns are also distinctive for the syndrome (Clayton-Smith, 2010) and can help with the diagnosis of AS in children who have not yet experienced seizures (Tan et al., 2011; Williams et al., 2006) or can be used to exclude the diagnosis of AS and prompt the search for other conditions that are genetically distinct but share overlapping clinical features (Tan et al., 2011; Tan et al., 2014).

Associated features in AS are more variable in their expression and frequency and include a range of craniofacial and oro-motor characteristics, such as a prominent jaw, wide mouth and wide-spaced teeth, protruding tongue, and wide-based gait. Sleep abnormalities and abnormal food-related behavior such as increased appetite and excessive food seeking may also occur.

Neurodevelopmental and Behavioral Characteristics

Cognitive and Learning Characteristics

Investigations into the neurodevelopmental profile of individuals with AS have focused primarily on children. Using standardized psychometric measures, researchers have found that children with AS demonstrate severe impairments in cognitive and adaptive functioning, with a generally greater ability to perform concrete tasks that require less language (Gentile et al., 2010; Williams et al., 2006). Children with AS show a forward progression in skill development for the most part but learn at a much slower rate than typically developing children and eventually reach a point (around 24-30 months) at which their skill development starts to plateau (Williams et al., 2006). The most severe delays and restricted range of skills are typically found among children with the genetic deletion versus those from non-deletion groups (Gentile et al., 2010; Mertz, Thaulov et al., 2014; Varela, Kok, Otto, & Koiffmann, 2004). The notable exception is in the area of spoken language, with severe deficits being present irrespective of children's molecular subtype (Gentile et al., 2010; Mertz, Thaulov et al., 2014). In terms of adaptive functioning, children typically display relative strengths in socialization and relative weaknesses in motor skills (Peters, Goddard-Finegold et al., 2004). Children with the genetic deletion have lower adaptive skills in relation to language and motor functioning than children from non-deletion groups, whereas daily living and socialization scores are comparable for both groups (Gentile et al., 2010). Brun Gasca et al. (2010) reported that individuals with AS are able to function relatively well (compared to communication skills) on personal life skills tasks that have a high functional value for them (e.g., locating items of personal value around the home).

Children with AS who also have a comorbid diagnosis of autism have more severe impairments in cognitive and adaptive functioning and develop more slowly than children with AS alone (Peters, Beadet, Madduri & Bacino, 2004). Interestingly, many children with AS who meet the diagnostic criteria for autism have larger genetic deletions (Sahoo et al., 2006), raising the possibility that genes in addition to UBE3A impact children's learning and development (Peters, Horowitz, Barbieri-Welge, Lounds Taylor, & Hundley, 2012). More information about AS and autism is provided later in the chapter.

Language and Communication

The virtual absence of spoken language is one of the most frequently cited characteristics of AS and has a significant impact on individuals' day-to-day functioning. Speech deficits are present across all genetic subtypes and are greater in magnitude than would be expected based on the level of intellectual functioning alone (Gentile et al., 2010). Speech deficits are also significantly greater in individuals with AS than those from other syndrome groups (fragile X, Prader-Willi, Smith-Magenis, Lowe, Cri du Chat and Cornelia de Lange; Arron, Oliver, Moss, Berg, & Burbridge, 2011). Individuals with non-deletion forms of AS may be able to produce a range of consonant and 2-syllable sounds as well as a small number (up to 7) of words (Mertz, Thaulov et al., 2014) whereas greater impairments in expressive nonverbal communication skills are found among those with the genetic deletion, more severe intellectual disability, epilepsy, and/or who take anticonvulsant medication (Didden, Korzilius, Duker & Curfs, 2004). Nonverbal forms of communication that are used by individuals with AS include reaching, pointing, touching, eye contact, head nods and shakes, manipulating other people's hands, and using natural gestures (Jolleff & Ryan, 1993; Penner, Johnston, Faircloth, Irish, & Williams, 1993). Manual signs are used less frequently than gestures (Jolleff & Ryan, 1993) and can be difficult to understand because of the presence of motor impairments (Calculator, 2002; Jolleff, Emmerson, Ryan, & McConachie, 2006).

In addition to *how* individuals with AS communicate, there are differences in *what* they communicate about (communicative function). Many individuals with AS engage in communicative acts for basic purposes such as indicating their needs and preferences and requesting attention from others but less so for more advanced functions such as requesting information, commenting, or imitating speech or gestures (Didden et al., 2009). Requesting skills may be on a par with other individuals who are functioning at a similar developmental level but are less well developed for naming objects or activities and imitating others (Didden, Korzilius, Duker, & Curfs, 2004). Receptive language skills are significantly better developed than expressive language skills in most individuals with AS (Gentile et al., 2010;

Jolleff et al., 2006; Mertz, Thaulov et al., 2014; Summers & Szatmari, 2009) and may be sufficient for them to comprehend simple instructions (Jolleff & Ryan, 1993), as well as identify common objects (Summers, 2012a; Zingale et al., 2012). While the cause of their severe communication impairment is largely unknown and may be ultimately traced to lack of UBE3A protein expression (Gentile et al., 2010; Mertz, Thaulov et al., 2014), there is also emerging evidence of abnormalities in the formation and function of neural pathways in brain regions that are responsible for language, cognitive, and social development in individuals with AS (Peters et al., 2011; Wilson et al. 2011). Pre-linguistic factors such as lack of joint attention, referential eye gaze, and imitation skills may also play a role in the communication impairments found in AS (Summers & Impey, 2011).

Because spoken language is not a viable option for individuals with AS, they must usually rely on alternative and augmentative (AAC) systems as their main means of communication. Gestures, signs, vocalizations, and physical manipulation of others are examples of unaided approaches, while aided systems may involve technology and can include the use of photographs, picture communication symbols, and speech generating devices. The results of a recent parent survey (Calculator, 2013) indicated that many children with AS use a total communication method that consists of a combination of unaided and aided approaches. Mobile technologies such as the iPad are rapidly becoming the single most common electronic AAC device being used by individuals with AS, alone or in conjunction with other devices (Calculator, 2014). Reasons underlying children's adoption or continued use of aided approaches (specifically, electronic devices) included relative ease of use and gaining access to preferred items and social attention, whereas failure to use devices was related to lack of understanding about how to use the device and preferring easier methods to communicate. Parents placed the greatest significance on children's ability to make choices and express their wants and needs, followed by the ability to communicate with a range of partners, to share their feelings and experiences with others, to learn functional skills and to initiate and maintain conversations (Calculator & Black, 2010). The most effective usage of devices will likely be achieved when their features are intentionally matched with the skill profile and learning needs of specific individuals with AS and the range of environments in which they communicate.

Behavioral Characteristics

As noted earlier (Williams, Angelman et al., 1995, Williams et al., 2006), universal features of AS consist of intellectual disability (functionally severe range), movement or balance disorder, and absent or minimal expressive speech. "Behavioral uniqueness" rounds out this list, referring to a combination of exuberant, happy demeanor; frequent laughter; excitable personality; and hypermotoric behavior (Williams et al., 2006). When considered together, these features denote a distinctive clinical profile (Williams, 2010). Additional information regarding the behavioral characteristics of individuals with AS has been gathered from literature reviews, case studies, parent and caregiver surveys, and direct observations (Table 1).

Table 1.
Studies on the Behavioral Phenotype of AS

Study	Details of Study	Findings
Summers et al. (1995)	-parents of 11 children with AS (mean age 5.4 years) completed a modified version of the Child Behavior Checklist (CBCL) -additional analysis of behavioral data from 34 studies (108 cases) was also conducted	-behavioral concerns identified from published studies included hyperactivity/restlessness, feeding problems as infant, attention deficits, aggression, repetitive or stereotyped behavior, chewing or mouthing hands/objects, sleep problems, tantrums and noncompliance -parental concerns from the CBCL included attention deficits, aggressive behavior, mouthing objects and sleep problems
Summers & Feldman (1999)	-parents of 27 children and young adults with AS (mean age 9.08 years) completed the Aberrant Behavior Checklist (ABC) -comparison groups consisted of individuals receiving service from a behavior management clinic and a community sample	-ABC scores for participants in the AS group were lower on irritability and lethargy/social withdrawal subscales than both comparison groups as well as on items that measured temper tantrums and outbursts
Clarke & Marston (2000)	-caregivers of 73 individuals with del+ AS (mean age 11.0 years) completed the Aberrant Behavior Checklist (ABC), Reiss Screen for Maladaptive Behavior (for those over 12 years), and open-ended questions -ABC results were compared to groups of individuals with ID who resided in institutions and community settings as well as other syndrome groups (Prader-Willi, Cri du Chat and Smith-Magenis)	-individuals in the AS group scored lower on lethargy and inappropriate speech subscales from the ABC than those from the community sample -Reiss Screen results – sleep problems were relatively common, signs of severe mental illness were not reported -other issues that were identified by >50% of caregivers included fascination with water and eating problems (such as overeating or narrow range of food preferences) -problems with hyperactivity tended to diminish over time
Walz & Benson (2002)	-caregivers of 68 individuals with AS (mean age 10.07 years) completed the parent form of the Nisonger Child Behavior Rating Form (CBRF) -comparison groups consisted of Down, Prader Willi, and ID with mixed etiologies	-individuals with AS were rated as more likely to engage in hand flapping than other groups -mouthing and pica
Berry et al. (2005)	-subset of questions from the Developmental Behaviour Checklist (DBC) were administered to caregivers of 91 individuals with AS (mean age 13.6 years) -comparison group was derived from a population based registry of individuals with ID	-individuals with AS were significantly more likely than those in the comparison group to display problems with chewing or mouthing objects or parts of body, eating non-food items, food fads/excessive eating, sleep disturbance, hyperactivity, and hand flapping -AS group significantly less likely to display poor attention span and impulsivity
Horsler & Oliver (2006a)	-analysis of 64 studies that provided information on behavioral functioning in 734 cases (ranging in age from 2 months – 75 years) of AS	-problems reported included feeding problems in infancy, sleep disturbance, restlessness/short attention span, and excessive mouthing and chewing

Walz & Baranek (2006)	-parents of 340 children and young adults with AS (mean age 10.98 years) completed the Sensory Experiences Questionnaire -normative sample consisted of typically developing children between the ages of 3-6 years	-sensory seeking behavior such as frequently putting objects in mouth and flapping arms or hands repeatedly was reported in approximately 75% of the total sample -sensory avoidant behavior (distress during grooming routine) was found in 64% of the total sample -sensory abnormalities may persist over time -preschool children with AS showed greater sensory abnormalities than children in the normative sample
Didden et al. (2006)	-modified version of the Choice Assessment Scale (CAS) was completed by caregivers of 105 individuals with AS, ranging in age from 1-45 years -purpose was to identify preferred, possibly reinforcing items and activities in individuals with AS	-individuals with AS were rated as having a stronger preference for water-related than non-water related items
Didden et al. (2008)	-modified version of CAS was administered to caregivers of 27 individuals with AS (mean age 16.2 years) -comparison group was composed of individuals with Down syndrome and non-syndromal intellectual disability	-individuals with AS were rated as having a stronger preference for water-related items than individuals from both comparison groups
Tan et al. (2011)	-information was gathered regarding behavioral characteristics of 92 children with AS (ages 5-60 months) who participated in the Angelman Syndrome Natural History study	-mouthing, short attention span, sleep problems, and fascination with water were found
Arron et al. (2011)	-variety of questionnaires were administered to caregivers of 104 individuals with AS (mean age 13.4 years) -comparison groups consisted of non-specific ID along with syndrome groups (Fragile X, Prader-Willi, Smith-Magenis, Lowe, Cri du Chat, Cornelia de Lange)	-"base rate" of behavior problems was established for individuals with non-specific ID -aggression was present in 73% of AS group, which was three times more likely than comparison group -those showing aggression were more socially connected and likely to behave impulsively -SIB was present in 45% of AS group, no difference from comparison group -possibility that aggression is socially motivated
Larson et al. (2015)	-structured questions administered during a telephone survey of 110 caregivers of adolescents and adults with AS (mean age 24.3 years)	-behavior problems identified by caregivers included aggression (pulling others' hair, hitting), yelling/screaming, dropping to the floor, hugging too tightly or hugging strangers, biting, chewing clothing or items

Some of these studies (Larson, Shinnick, Shaaya, Thiele, & Thibert, 2015; Summers, Allison, Lynch, & Sandler, 1995; Tan et al., 2011) used a within-syndrome approach to obtain data on the range and prevalence of particular behaviors among individuals with AS. The remaining studies compared individuals with AS to those with non-specific intellectual disabilities ("diverse or mixed etiologies") and/or individuals with other genetic syndromes, thus yielding information about a possible behavioral phenotype of AS (Dykens, 1995). These comparison studies provide an indication of which behaviors may be more common (e.g., aggression, sleep problems, preference for water-related activities, chewing or mouthing objects or parts of body, excessive eating) or less common (e.g., irritability and social withdrawal, poor attention span) among individuals with AS, relative to individuals without the syndrome.

Table 2.
Studies on Impact of Social and Environmental Influences on the Behavior of Individuals with AS

Study	Details of Study	Findings
Oliver, Demetriades & Hall (2002)	-3 children with AS, ages 7-17 years -conditions — continual praise by adult; adult physical proximity but no interaction; adult involved in instructional tasks; adult not present in room -evaluated duration of laughing and smiling	-duration of laughing and smiling highest in continual praise condition, intermediate level during no interaction and instructional task, lowest when adult not present
Horsler & Oliver (2006b)	-13 children with AS, ages 4-11 years -evaluated duration of laughing and smiling under 2 conditions — social interaction (adult eye contact, physical and verbal interaction, animated facial expression) and restricted social interaction (adult verbal attention but no eye contact, no animated facial expression)	-duration of laughing and smiling higher in social interaction condition than restricted social interaction condition -possibility that children's behavior may evoke a social response from adult
Oliver et al. (2007)	-13 children with AS, ages 4-17 years -observed at school -comparison group — children matched for age, gender, ability level -3 conditions — unstructured activities, receiving 1:1 attention from adult, sharing adult attention with other children -evaluated laughing, smiling, physical contact	-children with AS smiled more often than children in comparison group in all 3 conditions, showed increased tendency to initiate physical contact in social situations -children with AS more likely to initiate smiling than children in comparison group -adult was more likely to smile and make eye contact with children with AS than comparison group -social contact may be an especially powerful reinforcer for children with AS
Strachan et al. (2009)	-7 children with AS, ages 5-11 years -observed at school -3 conditions — high attention, low attention, participation in challenging task -evaluated social behavior (laughing, smiling, crying, frowning, physical initiation) and aggression	-laughing and smiling varied across conditions and were more likely to occur during high attention -aggressive behavior occurred for most children under a variety of conditions and at low rates

Mount et al. (2011)	-11 children with AS, ages 3-18.5 years -studied impact of contextual factors (familiarity of adult, eye contact by adult, talking by adult) on child's behavior (laughing, smiling, looking toward adult's face, attempting to touch adult)	-children were more likely to approach their mother than a female stranger when mother was looking at them, but not when mother wasn't making eye contact -looked at adults even if no interaction was occurring -duration of laughing, smiling and eye contact were not influenced by familiarity of adult -social attention is a powerful potential reward for children with AS

Another line of behavioral research has sought to study the impact of social and environmental influences on prosocial behavior in children with AS (see Table 2 for details of related studies). A common feature of these studies is that aspects of the social environment are systematically manipulated and the resulting impact on children's behavior (e.g., laughing, smiling, looking at or making physical approaches toward an adult) is measured. Some of the experimental conditions approximate real-life situations, such as when an adult is providing continuous attention, is paying attention to another child or is placing demands on the child with AS. In general, the duration of children's laughing and smiling is in proportion to the amount (e.g., continuous versus intermittent) and quality (e.g., direct eye contact and animated facial expression versus no eye contact minimal engagement) of social attention being provided by an adult. Children with AS may be particularly desirous of and responsive to social attention from adults, including those with whom they have an established relationship. Moreover, adults are particularly likely to respond in a positive manner to displays of social interest by children with AS. A strong possibility that emerges from this line of research is that children with AS may find adult attention to be particularly rewarding but lack more conventional communication skills to access it. Problematic approach behavior may fill this void, functioning as a way to both obtain and maintain adult social attention. A cautionary note is that while social attention could be used as an incentive for learning adaptive behavior, it can also function as an inadvertent reward for challenging behavior such as grabbing or hair pulling.

Physical and Mental Health Issues in AS

Physical Health and Medical Conditions

In general, the major health-related issues faced by individuals with AS are in relation to their seizure disorder and musculoskeletal problems. Epilepsy is a frequent feature (occurring in 80-95% of the AS population) and is often diagnosed by the age of 3 years (Tan et al., 2011).

Many individuals experience multiple types of seizures and take more than one anticonvulsant to control their seizure activity (Thibert et al., 2009; Thibert, Larson, Hsieh, Raby, & Thiele, 2013). The medical management of seizures is an ongoing issue and the process is apt to be very active at times, particularly when seizures first emerge or become more difficult to manage. Anticonvulsant medication may cause unpleasant side effects such as fatigue, lethargy, and irritability and can further add to cognitive impairment (Thibert et al., 2009). However, such treatment is essential from the standpoint of controlling seizure activity. Dietary interventions (e.g., ketogenic diet or low glycemic index diet treatment) show some promise for treating seizures (Thibert et al., 2009, 2012). Seizures may be associated with increased health risks such as aspiration and choking as well as injuries caused by falls. Abnormal bone mineral density due to prolonged treatment with antiepileptic drugs combined with limited mobility may be problematic for a subset of individuals with AS (Coppola et al., 2007), and the possibility of recurrent bone fractures does exist (Rusinska, Dzonek, & Chlebna-Sokol, 2013).

Sleep problems are very prevalent in AS, affecting upwards of 80-90% of the population (Summers et al., 1995; Williams et al., 1995, 2006). Common sleep problems include difficulty initiating sleep, early wakening, fragmented sleep, snoring and sleep apnea (Anderson et al., 2008). Sleep difficulties may be related to the presence of epilepsy, as well as seizure type (Conant, Thibert & Thiele, 2009). Poor nighttime sleep in children and adolescents with AS may be associated with insomnia and daytime sleepiness (Goldman, Bichell, Surdyka, & Malow, 2012), which could have a negative impact on their learning and behavior (Bruni et al., 2004). Family functioning can be adversely impacted by the sleep problems experienced by the individual with AS to the point that parents may feel fatigued or even depressed by the situation (Didden, Korzilius, Smits, & Curfs, 2004).

Orthopedic problems can also have a major impact on the quality of life of individuals with AS. Treatment options may consist of exercise, adaptive walking devices and bracing and/or surgery for scoliosis. Physiotherapy can be very important during various periods in time to assist the child with AS to learn to walk, encourage the adolescent with AS to remain active to prevent excessive weight gain and maintain a full range of motion, and to help the adult with AS to stay mobile as long as possible to guard against future joint and spine problems (Buckley et al., 1998; Clayton-Smith, 2001). Individuals with scoliosis may be at heightened risk for cardiorespiratory problems (Buntinx et al., 1995). Fortunately, many individuals with AS are able to enjoy physical activities such as horseback riding, swimming, and riding an adapted bicycle (Larson et al., 2015) which may improve their physical outcomes and provide opportunities for social inclusion.

Other medical problems that have been reported among some individuals with AS include ocular/vision problems (particularly strabismus) and hearing difficulties caused by ear infections (Clayton-Smith, 1993; Zori et al., 1992) as well as reflux and gastrointestinal difficulties (Clayton-Smith, 1993; Larson et al., 2015). Obesity is an area of interest due to its potential health-related consequences as well as its overlap with the clinical features of Prader Willi syndrome. Mertz, Christensen, Vogel, Hertz, and Ostergaard (2014) found that children with UPD in their study who were 2 years of age and older were more prone to display a strong and persistent drive to access food than same-age children with a deletion or gene mutation. Larson et al. (2015) reported that approximately one-third of their sample of adolescents and adults were overweight to obese, possibly due in part to difficulties self-regulating their food intake and/or a reduced sense of fullness after eating. Individuals with hypopigmentation are at risk of sunburn and protective measures such as sunscreen should be taken when going outside (Williams, Zori et al., 1995).

Common reasons for individuals being admitted to hospital include treatment for seizures as well as gastrointestinal and respiratory problems, and the need for dental work (Thomson, Glasson, & Bittles, 2006). Individuals with AS may be at particular risk for accidental injury or even death. Some of the factors that may have a bearing on this issue include their lack of awareness of potential hazards or dangers; characteristically high levels of activity, combined with a short attention span and impulsivity; and a tendency to engage in particular behaviors (e.g., mouthing or swallowing non-food items or involvement in water-related activities). As a result, constant and close supervision, along with hazard-proofing the environment, are required to maintain their safety. A compelling reminder of the need for constant vigilance was provided by a report of drowning as an accidental cause of death in a 9-year-old boy with AS (Ishmael, Begleiter, & Butler, 2002). The child had managed to escape unnoticed into the backyard and was found floating in a shallow wading pool. There was the possibility that he had suffered a seizure while in the pool. Another risk factor may be poor communication skills. Herbst and Byard (2012) reported on the sudden death of a 5-year-old boy with AS due to acute upper airway obstruction caused by enlarged tonsils as a result of a viral infection. Detection of significant swallowing problems in this case may have been hampered by the presence of mouthing and drooling and the child's inability to verbalize physical symptoms.

Mental Health Problems

It stands to reason that individuals with AS can experience mental health problems, just like anyone else. Risk factors may include a family history of mental illness and exposure to traumatic or stressful life events. However, it is very difficult to make an accurate psychiatric diagnosis in individuals with severe intellectual disability and minimal expressive language skills. Before attempting to diagnose a possible mental health problem, it is important to first rule out other causes for behavioral changes or expressions of distress, such as the presence of physical and medical conditions or a mismatch between individuals' needs and the characteristics and demands of their environment. On this note, Berg, Arron, Burbridge, Moss, and Oliver (2007) found a correlation between caregiver reported health problems and signs of lowered mood, interest, and pleasure among individuals with genetic syndromes who lack verbal skills, including those with Angelman syndrome. In general, evidence for a mental health problem should be gathered from multiple sources, including a thorough review of medical, developmental, and behavioral information and interviews of knowledgeable informants. Behavioral equivalents for mental health symptoms can be obtained from direct observation of the individual with AS in different environments and completion of questionnaires and checklists that have demonstrated utility for the AS population (Berry, Leitner, Clarke, & Einfeld, 2005; Clarke & Marston, 2000; Summers & Feldman, 1999).

Wink (2012) outlined an approach for identifying possible signs of a mental health problem in an individual with AS that is based on a consideration of the following factors: (a) changes in behavior, such as loss of interest in preferred activities or avoiding people or places; (b) changes in energy level, such as inability to sit still or moving more slowly; (c) changes in appetite, such as increased or decreased food intake; (d) changes in mood, such as looking anxious or worried or showing increased irritability; and (e) changes in sleep, such as sleeping more or less than usual. Knowledge regarding the core symptoms of AS is important in order to evaluate the significance of behavioral changes. For instance, individuals' outwardly happy demeanor may overshadow bouts of crying or sadness (Laan, den Boer, Hennekam, Renier, & Brouwer, 1996) as well as underlying problems with fear and anxiety (Pelc, Cheron, & Dan, 2008). According to caregiver reports, adolescents and adults with AS may be more likely to show signs of anxiety than signs of depression (Larson et al., 2015). Caregiver surveys reveal usage of psychotropic medication (primarily antidepressants and anxiolytics, antipsychotics and stimulants) by approximately 4-12% of individuals with AS (Larson et al., 2015; Peters, 2010).

The social, communication, and behavioral impairments found among individuals with AS often overlap with features of autism spectrum disorder (ASD) and are likely related to some extent to their low mental age (Trillingsgaard & Ostergaard, 2004; Williams, 2010). The proportion of children (since adults have not been typically studied) with AS who meet diagnostic criteria for ASD varies widely across studies, depending upon the nature and scope of the study (e.g., ascertainment of incidence, characterization of study sample, description of AS phenotype) as well as the range of genetic subtypes included and diagnostic criteria used. Estimates of ASD range from 50-100% in groups of children studied (Bonati et al., 2007; Peters, Beaudet et al., 2004; Sahoo et al., 2007; Steffenburg, Gillberg, Steffenburg & Kyllerman, 1996; Summers, 2012a; Trillingsgaard & Ostergaard, 2004). Children with AS who meet diagnostic criteria for ASD and those with idiopathic ASD bear some similarities to each other, such as showing deficits in joint attention and the use of gestural communication. However, children with AS and ASD generally show greater social interest and responsiveness than children with ASD. They may also display fewer repetitive behaviors that are negatively correlated with scores on an autism screening tool, a finding that could be due to low developmental level (Walz, 2007). For some children with AS, an outwardly excitable and exuberant personality may overshadow a lack of social understanding and underlying social communication problems (Bonati et al., 2007; Oliver et al., 2007).

In general, children with AS and features of ASD are more likely to have significant cognitive impairments, show less social engagement, and learn more slowly than children with AS who do not receive a diagnosis of ASD. Children with the genetic deletion, and possibly those with larger deletions (Class I deletions), are more likely to show features of ASD, while children with non-deletion forms of AS are less likely to do so. Moreover, intellectual disability alone is not responsible for the features of autism in AS, because improvements (albeit small) in aspects of cognitive functioning over time are not accompanied by reductions in symptoms

Demysifying Syndromes II

of AS (Mertz, Thaulov et al., 2014; Peters et al., 2012). It has been speculated that the AS critical region contains autism susceptibility genes (Bonati et al., 2007).

Natural History of AS

A number of larger-scale studies have helped to inform our understanding of the characteristics of AS at different ages and stages (see Table 3 for specific details).

Table 3.
Natural History of AS[a]

Age	Characteristics
Infancy and early childhood	<ul><li>feeding problems</li><li>jerky movements, poor muscle tone</li><li>abnormal EEG pattern</li><li>seizures (by age 3) very common in children with deletion</li><li>developmental delays</li><li>absent or delayed babbling</li><li>happy disposition</li><li>physical growth parameters may start to slow down</li><li>sleep problems nearly universal</li></ul>
Middle childhood	<ul><li>seizures may develop later (by age 5-6) in children with UPD and imprinting defects</li><li>seizures tend to become milder and easier to control over time</li><li>facial features may evolve (prominent jaw, wide mouth and widely spaced teeth)</li><li>most will be walking by age 5</li><li>hyperactivity and reduced attention span are very noticeable</li><li>sleep disturbance may worsen</li><li>severe expressive speech delays; somewhat better receptive language</li><li>increased weight gain possible</li><li>obesity may occur in children with UPD/imprinting defects</li></ul>
Adolescence	<ul><li>puberty is normal but onset may be delayed</li><li>seizure picture may improve</li><li>weight gain and obesity may occur</li><li>mobility may decline in individuals with severe ataxia or those with weight gain</li><li>scoliosis may develop during adolescent growth spurt or worsen</li><li>sleep may improve</li></ul>

Adulthood	• generally healthy but life expectancy unknown • biggest issues are seizures and reductions in mobility with associated skeletal problems • seizures may recur • quieter and calmer, improved attention span • poor sleep is still an issue but often improved over childhood • variability in self-care skills but supervision still needed • gastrointestinal issues are common • obesity can be a major concern • majority are able to walk independently • many are able to participate in physical activities such as swimming and riding an adapted bike • music is enjoyed and can be a motivator

[a] Compiled from Buckley, Dinno & Weber (1998); Clayton-Smith (1993, 2001); Laan et al. (1996); Larson et al. (2015); Sandanam et al. (1997); Tan et al. (2011); Williams (2010); Williams, Zori et al. (1995); Zori et al. (1992)

The earliest signs of AS are non-specific, including feeding problems (related to weak suck and swallow, tongue thrusting, regurgitation, reflux) and poor weight gain, hypotonia, and jerky limb movements (Fryburg, Breg, & Lindren, 1991; Van Lierde, Atza, Giardino, & Viani, 1990; Yamada & Volpe, 1990). Reduced cooing and babbling may be noted, and seizures may develop before one year of age in a percentage of infants. Parents typically seek a medical evaluation in response to one or more of these concerns (Zori et al., 1992), and a diagnosis of failure-to-thrive, cerebral palsy, or global developmental delay may be given. Prader-Willi may be mistakenly diagnosed on the basis of developmental delay, feeding problems and hypotonia, but the dissimilarity of the two syndromes becomes more obvious over time.

Generally, the course of development in children with AS is typified by severely limited but forward progression in skills. While most children with AS do eventually learn to walk, the timing of when this occurs is influenced by the extent of their gait and movement disorder. Children with more severe balance and coordination problems learn to walk later and display movement patterns that are characteristic of AS (e.g., wide-based stance, arms held up and hands pointing forward and down). Many but not all children have light-colored hair, skin, and eyes. Seizure disorder is usually evident in most by 5 years of age. For many children, seizures are difficult to control initially, and different medications may be tried until optimal control is achieved. During the early-to-mid school years, skill development and behavior management issues seem to take center stage. Problems with children's reduced levels of sleep, high levels of motor activity, and extremely short attention span may place inordinately high demands on caregivers to provide constant supervision and assistance with activities of daily living. While these factors may combine to make this a particularly challenging period of time, the situation may be offset by children's sociability and pleasant disposition.

Adolescence may bring some improvements, but along with it new challenges. Seizures may become more infrequent in some adolescents with AS to the point where medication is no longer needed. Reductions in levels of motor activity and improvements in attention span have been noted (Clayton-Smith, 2001), along with increased levels of sleep. Skills continue to develop and the process may be assisted by an improved ability to concentrate. Puberty often occurs at the typical time, and females with AS are capable of procreation (Lossie & Driscoll, 1999). Masturbation may become an issue but individuals can be directed to engage in this behavior in private. However, individuals with AS are very vulnerable to sexual exploitation due to their low level of intellectual functioning and sociable nature, and they, therefore, require close supervision (Clayton-Smith, 2001). Weight gain may become an issue during adolescence and may be related to reductions in mobility and level of motor activity. Scoliosis may become evident during a period of rapid growth during the teenage years.

Most adults with AS are generally healthy and do not appear to have a reduced lifespan. Their happy disposition is still obvious, but they can and do show signs of sadness as well. Improvements in attention span and a reduction in hyperactivity have been noted in many individuals. There is no evidence of regression in skills and ongoing instruction in communication and self-care skills remains indicated. The major issues during this period continue to be related to seizures and problems with ambulation. Most adults with AS continue to experience seizures; however, the seizure type and frequency is variable. For some individuals, seizures can recommence after a relatively quiet period during adolescence and can be difficult to bring under control. Mobility tends to deteriorate with age, in association with scoliosis and movement disorder. Some adults with AS require wheelchairs for safety reasons and to make it easier to care for their needs (Buckley et al., 1998).

Interventions to Improve Individuals' Functioning

At the present time, neuroscientists are actively pursuing ways to restore UBE3A to normal levels in the brain by unsilencing the paternal allele to ameliorate or eliminate symptoms of the syndrome (Huang et al., 2012; Philpot, Thompson, Franco & Williams, 2011). The prospect of developing gene therapies for individuals with AS, while exciting, may be some time away. Current therapies are supportive rather than curative in nature and are geared toward controlling or reducing symptoms that arise from physical, neurological, cognitive, and behavioral features associated with AS. Recognizing and treating conditions that cause pain and discomfort, managing seizures, minimizing side effects of medication, providing social attention judiciously to increase desirable behavior, and improving the quality of individuals' sleep may optimize their physical and emotional health and reduce the occurrence of challenging behavior (Summers, 2012b; Summers, Taylor-Weir & Kako, 2014). An important focus for education is on improving individuals' ability to communicate and teaching skills that can improve their personal and social competence (Leyser & Kirk, 2011). Specific parental priorities for educational and therapeutic programming include teaching communication, recreational, self-care, motor and academic skills as well as addressing challenging behavior (such as sleep and eating problems, aggression, and non-compliance) (Radstaake, Didden et al., 2014). See Table 4 for details of intervention studies.

Table 4.
Intervention Studies

Study	Primary Intervention Targets	Details	Findings
Summers et al. (1992)	-sleep problems	-9 year old child with AS -treatment elements included restricting his sleep during the day, restricting his access to fluids during the evening, administering medication prior to bedtime, establishing a consistent bedtime, redirecting him back to bed with minimal attention if he got up during the night	-child's night sleep improved dramatically following implementation of treatment package -night sleep declined non-significantly following removal of medication and under parents' administration of program
Didden et al. (2001)	-daytime continence	-6 children and adolescents with AS, ranging from 6-19 years -modified Azrin and Foxx toileting program -initial phase of toilet training— children were prompted to use toilet regularly and were rewarded for successful voids -consequences were used for toileting accidents -second phase encouraged independent use of toilet and staying drier for longer periods; rewards shifted from tangible to social	-significant increases were found in mean number of correct voids in toilet per day across participants after initiation of training -gains were maintained up to 2.5 years later -reduction in mean number of toileting accidents across participants from training to maintenance phase
Calculator (2002)	-parent skills for teaching gestural communication	-9 children with AS, ages 3-10 years and their parents - parents were taught to recognize children's natural use of gestures and teach and reinforce their use of enhanced natural gestures (intentional gestures that could be understood by anyone)	-parents expressed positive views toward the training program and became more familiar with children's gestures -by parent report — children tended to learn slowly and some had difficulty initiating gestures
Summers & Hall (2008)	-parent skills for implementing ABA teaching procedures	-4 children with AS ages 4-9 years and their mothers -mothers read an ABA instructional manual and attempted to teach a new skill to their children afterward -ABA teaching procedures outlined in manual consisted of setting up materials and environment, ensuring child was attentive, implementing discrete teaching trials, using appropriate prompts, and reinforcing correct responding	-overall improvement in mothers' correct implementation of ABA teaching procedures after exposure to the instructional manual -individual differences found in their ability to implement procedures

Summers & Szatmari (2009)	-basic language and learning skills	-3 children with AS, ages 3-6 years -all received 2-3 ABA-based teaching sessions for 1 year -skills targeted for intervention included fine and gross motor imitation, motor imitation using objects, requesting (using sign and picture exchange), following receptive instructions, visual matching and self-help	-all 3 children mastered some elements of an exchange-based communication system -2 mastered following some one-step instructions and imitating motor actions -1 mastered visual matching to sample
Summers (2012a)	-cognitive, adaptive and language functioning	-treatment group - 3 children from previous study + one 9-year-old -comparison group — children matched on age, gender, and molecular subtype -treatment group received 2-3 ABA-based teaching sessions for 1 year	-evidence of improved receptive language, motor, and visual discrimination abilities among children in the treatment group relative to the control group after 1 year of intervention
Radstaake et al. (2012)	-challenging behavior	-4 children with AS, ages 5-18 years -after the function of their challenging behavior was identified, they underwent functional communication training -taught a functionally equivalent communicative behavior (exchange of picture or object) that allowed them to access reinforcement, prior to the challenging behavior occurring ("precursor" stage)	-independent communicative response (picture or object exchange) was accompanied by reduction of challenging behavior for all 4 children -effects were maintained over 3-5 month period
Radstaake et al. (2013)	-challenging behavior	-3 children with AS, ages 6-15 years -functional analysis of challenging behavior was undertaken -functional communication training was initiated to teach a functionally equivalent replacement behavior (using an object or speech generating device) when potential precursor behavior was observed	-challenging and replacement behaviors were shown to be functionally equivalent -all 3 children learned to use the replacement behavior and reductions in the occurrence of challenging behavior were found
Allen et al. (2013)	-sleep problems	-5 children with AS, ages 2-11 years -behavioral treatment package consisted of modifications to the sleep environment, maintaining a consistent sleep-wake schedule and minimizing parental attention for disruptive bedtime behaviors	-disruptive bedtime behavior decreased and improved ability to fall asleep independently occurred across children -gains were maintained at up to 3 month follow up -improvements in behavior during the day were noted
Radstaake et al. (2014a)	-daytime continence	-7 children and adults with AS, ages 6-25 years -elements of toilet training program included restricting responses in bathroom to behaviors that were associated with using the toilet, providing reinforcement for successful voids and consequences for accidents	-increases in number of correct voids in the toilet occurred for all participants following initiation of training -rate of accidents and maintenance of toileting gains after 3-18 months varied across participants

Isla & Fortea (2015)	-communication skills	-4-year-old child with AS and her mother -mother was taught to implement Hanen "More Than Words" (MTW) program -individual and group intervention took place over an 11-week period	-increases in child's ability to "fill in" sounds and movements in social games and to integrate vocalizations, eye gaze and gesture during communicative acts were noted -parent expressed positive views toward intervention and incorporated new skills into everyday contexts

Family Issues

The benefits of intervention are obvious for individuals with AS but may also have a positive impact on family members. Parents are a continuous and guiding force in the lives of their children and play a pivotal role in their ongoing learning and development. Mothers and fathers of children with AS who display challenging behavior may experience higher levels of anxiety and stress than parents of children with autism or other genetic disorders associated with severe intellectual disability (Griffith et al., 2011). Wullfaert, Scholte, and Van Bercklaer-Onnes (2010) reported higher levels of stress among mothers of children with AS compared to mothers of children with Prader-Willi syndrome. While maternal stress levels of the former group were not found to be related to the level of children's challenging behavior, the investigators speculated that child characteristics such as communication impairments or low developmental level may have been contributing factors. The high levels of parental support that are required by children with AS may result in less time and attention being given to the other children in the family, while the siblings themselves may have difficulty connecting with their brother or sister with AS who has severe cognitive and communication deficits and end up taking on a more active role with them (Love, Richters, Didden, Korzilius, & Machalicek, 2012). Families should be able to access services and supports in their own right to help them cope with the physical, emotional, and financial demands that may arise when caring for the child or adult with AS.

Summary

This chapter has provided a review of the genetic and clinical features of Angelman syndrome. Intervention studies that address core and associated features of AS were discussed and implications for therapy and parent support were highlighted. The goal of providing "help for today, hope for tomorrow" may be realized through combining behavioral and educational interventions with emerging biomedical treatments and in doing so may offer new opportunities for improving the quality of life for individuals with AS and their families.

Resources

Canadian Angelman Syndrome Society
P.O. Box 37
Priddis, Alberta T0L 1W0
Phone 403 931-2415
Fax 403 931-4237
www.angelmancanada.org

Angelman Syndrome Foundation
75 Executive Drive, Suite 327
Aurora, IL 60504
Phone 630 978-4245
Fax 630 978-7408
www.angelman.org

Angelman Behavior Modules
www.angelmanbehaviors.org
Modules on:
- Aggression as communicative behavior
- Social and environmental influences on aggressive behavior
- Cognitive issues and sensory impairments
- Mental health influences on aggressive behavior
- Neurologic and medical influences on aggressive behavior

References

Allen, K.D., Kuhn, B.R., DeHaai, K.A., & Wallace, D.P. (2013). Evaluation of a behavioral treatment package to reduce sleep problems in children with Angelman syndrome. *Research in Developmental Disabilities, 34*, 676-686.

Anderson, B., Pilsworth, S., Jamieson, S., Ray, J., Shneerson, J. M., & Lennox, G. G. (2008). Sleep disturbance in adults with Angelman syndrome. *Sleep and Biological Rhythms, 6*, 95-101.

Angelman, H. (1965). 'Puppet' children: A report on three cases. *Developmental Medicine and Child Neurology, 7*, 681-688.

Arron, K., Oliver, C., Moss, J., Berg, K., & Burbidge, C. (2011). The prevalence and phenomenology of self-injurious and aggressive behaviour in genetic syndromes. *Journal of Intellectual Disability Research, 55*, 109-120.

Berg, K., Arron, K., Burbidge, C., Moss, J., & Oliver, C. (2007). Carer-reported contemporary health problems in people with severe and profound intellectual disability and genetic syndromes. *Journal of Policy and Practice in Intellectual Disabilities, 4*(2), 120-128.

Berry, R. J., Leitner, R. P., Clarke, A. R., & Einfeld, S. L. (2005). Behavioral aspects of Angelman syndrome: A case control study. *American Journal of Medical Genetics, 132*, 8-12.

Bonati, M.T., Russo, S., Finelli, P., Valsecchi, M.R., Cogliati, F., Cavalleri, F.... Larizza, L. (2007). Evaluation of autism traits in Angelman syndrome: a resource to unfold autism genes. *Neurogenetics, 8,* 169-178.

Bottani, A., Robinson, W. P., DeLozier-Blanchet, D. D., Engel, E., Morris, M. A., Schmitt, B., ... Schinzel, A. (1994). Angelman syndrome due to paternal uniparental disomy of chromosome 15: A milder phenotype? *American Journal of Medical Genetics, 51,* 35-40.

Brun Gasca, C., Obiols, J.E., Bonillo, A., Artigas, J., Lorente, I., Gabau, E....Turk, J. (2010). Adaptive behaviour in Angelman syndrome: its profile and relationship to age. *Journal of Intellectual Disability Research, 54,* 1024-1029.

Bruni, O., Ferri, R., D'Agostino, G., Miano, S., Roccella, M., & Elia, M. (2004). Sleep disturbances in Angelman syndrome: a questionnaire study. *Brain & Development, 26,* 233-240.

Buckley, R. H., Dinno, N., & Weber, P. (1998). Angelman syndrome: Are the estimates too low? *American Journal of Medical Genetics, 80,* 385-390.

Buiting, K., Clayton-Smith, J., Driscoll, D.J., Gillessen-Kaesbach, G., Knanber, D., Schwinger, E.,...Horsthemke, B. (2015). Clinical utility card for: Angelman syndrome. *European Journal of Human Genetics, 23,* e1-e3.

Buntinx, I. M., Hennekam, C. M., Broumer, O. F., Stroink, H., Beuten, J., Mangelschots, K., & Fryns, J. P. (1995). Clinical profile of Angelman syndrome at different ages. *American Journal of Medical Genetics, 56,* 176-183.

Calculator, S. N. (2002). Use of enhanced natural gestures to foster interactions between children with Angelman syndrome and their parents. *American Journal of Speech-Language Pathology, 11,* 340-355.

Calculator, S.N. (2013). Use and acceptance of AAC systems by children with Angelman syndrome. *Journal of Applied Research in Intellectual Disabilities, 26,* 557-567.

Calculator, S.N. (2014). Parents' perceptions of communication patterns and effectiveness of use of augmentative and alternative communication systems by their children with Angelman syndrome. *American Journal of Speech-Language Pathology, 23,* 562-573.

Calculator, S. N., & Black, T. (2010). Parents' priorities for AAC and related instruction for their children with Angelman syndrome. *Augmentative and Alternative Communication, 26,* 30-40.

Chamberlain, S.J., & Lalande, M. (2010). Angelman syndrome, a genomic imprinting disorder of the brain. *Journal of Neuroscience, 30*(3), 9958-9963.

Clarke, D. J., & Marston, G. (2000). Problem behaviors associated with 15q- Angelman syndrome. *American Journal on Mental Retardation, 105,* 25-31.

Clayton-Smith, J. (1993). Clinical research on Angelman syndrome in the United Kingdom: Observations on 82 affected individuals. *American Journal of Medical Genetics, 46,* 12-15.

Clayton-Smith, J. (1995). On the prevalence of Angelman syndrome. *American Journal of Medical Genetics, 59*, 403-404.

Clayton-Smith, J. (2001). Angelman syndrome: evolution of the phenotype in adolescents and adults. *Developmental Medicine and Child Neurology, 43*, 476-480.

Clayton-Smith, J. (2010). Angelman syndrome. *Journal of Pediatric Neurology, 8*, 97-99.

Conant, K. D., Thibert, R. L., & Thiele, E. A. (2009). Epilepsy and the sleep-wake patterns found in Angelman syndrome. *Epilepsia, 50*, 2497-2500.

Coppola, G., Verrotti, A., Mainolfi, C., Auricchio, G., Fortunato, D., Operto, F., & Pascotto, A. (2007). Bone mineral density in Angelman syndrome. *Pediatric Neurology, 37*(6), 411-416.

Dagli, A., Buiting, K., & Williams, C.A. (2011). Molecular and clinical aspects of Angelman syndrome. *Molecular Syndromology, 2*, 100-112.

Daily, J., Smith, A.G., & Weeber, E.J. (2012). Spatial and temporal silencing of the human maternal UBE3A gene. *European Journal of Paediatric Neurology, 16*, 587-591.

Didden, R., Korzilius, H., Duker, P., & Curfs, L. M. G. (2004). Communicative functioning in individuals with Angelman syndrome: a comparative study. *Disability and Rehabilitation, 26*, 1263-1267.

Didden, R., Korzilius, H., Kamphuis, A., Sturmey, P., Lancioni, G., & Curfs, L. M. G. (2006). Preferences in individuals with Angelman syndrome assessed by a modified choice assessment scale. *Journal of Intellectual Disability Research, 50*(1), 54-60.

Didden, R., Korzilius, H., Smits, M. G., & Curfs, L. M. G. (2004). Sleep problems in individuals with Angelman syndrome. *American Journal on Mental Retardation, 109*, 275-284.

Didden, R., Korzilius, H., Sturmey, P., Lancioni, G., & Curfs, L. M. G. (2008). Preference for water-related items in Angelman syndrome, Down syndrome and non-specific intellectual disability. *Journal of Intellectual & Developmental Disability, 33*(1), 59-64.

Didden, R., Sigafoos, J., Korzilius, H., Baas, A., Lancioni, G. E., O'Reilly, M. F., & Curfs, L. M. G. (2009). Form and function of communicative behaviours in individuals with Angelman syndrome. *Journal of Applied Research in Intellectual Disabilities, 22*, 526-537.

Didden, R., Sikkema, S. P. E., Bosman, I. T. M., Duker, P. C., & Curfs, L. M. G. (2001). Use of a modified Azrin-Foxx toilet training procedure with individuals with Angelman syndrome. *Journal of Applied Research in Intellectual Disabilities, 14*, 64-70.

Dykens, E. M. (1995). Measuring behavioral phenotypes: Provocations from the "new genetics." *American Journal of Mental Retardation, 99*, 522-532.

Fisher, J. A., Burn, J., Alexander, F. W., & Gardner-Medwin, D. (1987). Angelman (happy puppet) syndrome in a girl and her brother. *Journal of Medical Genetics, 24,* 294-298.

Fryburg, J. S., Breg, W. R., & Lindgren, V. (1991). Diagnosis of Angelman syndrome in infants. *American Journal of Medical Genetics, 38,* 58-64.

Gentile, J. K., Tan, W., Horowitz, L. T., Bacino, C. A., Skinner, S. A., Barbieri-Welge, R., ... Peters, S. U. (2010). A neurodevelopmental survey of Angelman syndrome with genotype-phenotype correlations. *Journal of Developmental & Behavioral Pediatrics, 31*(7), 592-601.

Goldman, S. E., Bichell, T. J., Surdyka, K., & Malow, B. A. (2012). Sleep in children and adolescents with Angelman syndrome: association with parent sleep and stress. *Journal of Intellectual Disability Research, 56,* 600-608.

Griffith, G.M., Hastings, R.P., Oliver, C., Howlin, P., Moss, J., Petty, J., & Tunnicliffe, P. (2011). Psychological well-being in parents with Angelman, Cornelia de Lange and Cri du Chat syndromes. *Journal of Intellectual Disability Research, 55*(4), 397-410.

Hersbt, J., & Byard, R.W. (2012). Sudden death and Angelman syndrome. *Journal of Forensic Sciences, 57*(1), 257-259.

Horsler, K., & Oliver, C. (2006a). The behavioural phenotype of Angelman syndrome. *Journal of Intellectual Disability Research, 50,* 33-53.

Horsler, K., & Oliver, C. (2006b). Environmental influences on the behavioral phenotype of Angelman syndrome. *American Journal on Mental Retardation, 111*(5), 311-321.

Huang, H.S., Allen, J.A., Mabb, A.M., King, I.F., Miriyala, J., Taylor-Blake, B., ... Philpot, B.D. (2012). Topoisomerase inhibitors unsilence the dormant allele of UBE3A in neurons. *Nature Jan 12, 481,* 185-189.

Ishmael, H. A., Begleiter, M. L., & Butler, M. G. (2002). Drowning as a cause of death in Angelman syndrome. *American Journal on Mental Retardation, 107,* 69-70.

Isla, M., & Fortea, I.B. (2015). Parent-implemented Hanen program more than words in Angelman syndrome: A case study. *Child Language Teaching and Therapy,* 1-17.

Jacobsen, J., King, B. H., Leventhal, B. L., Christian, S. L., Ledbetter, D. H., & Cook, E. H. (1998). Molecular screening for proximal 15q abnormalities in a mentally retarded population. *Journal of Medical Genetics, 35,* 534-538.

Jiang, Y. H., Lev-Lehman, E., Bressler, J., Tsai, T. F., & Beadet, A. (1999). Genetics of Angelman syndrome. *American Journal of Human Genetics, 65,* 1-6.

Jolleff, N., Emmerson, F., Ryan, M., & McConachie, H. (2006). Communication skills in Angelman syndrome: Matching phenotype to genotype. *Advances in Speech-Language Pathology, 8*(1), 28-33.

Jolleff, N., & Ryan, M. M. (1993). Communication development in Angelman's syndrome. *Archives of Disease in Childhood, 69,* 148-150.

Kaplan, L. C., Wharton, R., Elias, E., Mandell, F., Donlon, T., & Latt, S. A. (1987). Clinical heterogeneity associated with deletions in the long arm of chromosome 15: Report of 3 new cases and their possible genetic significance. *American Journal of Medical Genetics, 28,* 45-53.

Kishino, T., Lalande, M., & Wagstaff, J. (1997). UBE3A/E6-AP mutations cause Angelman syndrome. *Nature Genetics, 15,* 70-73.

Knoll, J. H. M., Nicholls, R. D., Magenis, R. E., Graham, J. M., Lalande, M., & Latt, S. A. (1989). Angelman and Prader-Willi syndromes share a common chromosome 15 deletion but differ in the parental origin of the deletion. *American Journal of Medical Genetics, 32,* 285-290.

Laan, L. A. E. M., den Boer, A., Hennekam, R. C. M., Renier, W. O., & Brouwer, O. F. (1996). Angelman syndrome in adulthood. *American Journal of Medical Genetics, 66,* 356-360.

Larson, A.M., Shinnick, J.E., Shaaya, E.A., Thiele, E.A., & Thibert, R.L. (2015). Angelman syndrome in adulthood. *American Journal of Medical Genetics Part A, 167*(2), 331-344.

Leyser, Y. & Kirk, R. (2011). Parents' perspectives on inclusion and the schooling of students with Angelman syndrome: suggestions for educators. *International Journal of Special Education, 26*(2), 1-13.

Lombroso, P. J. (2000). Genetics of childhood disorders: XVI. Angelman syndrome: A failure to process. *Journal of the American Academy of Child and Adolescent Psychiatry, 39,* 931-933.

Lossie, A. C., & Driscoll, D. J. (1999). Transmission of Angelman syndrome by an affected mother. *Genetics in Medicine, 1,* 262-266.

Love, V., Richters, L., Didden, R., Korzilius, H., & Machalicek, W. (2012). Sibling relationships in individuals with Angelman syndrome: A comparative study. *Development Rehabilitation, 15*(2), 84-90.

Mabb, A.M., Judson, M.C., Zylka, M.J., & Philpot, B.D. (2011). Angelman syndrome: insights into genomic imprinting and neurodevelopmental phenotypes. *Trends in Neurosciences, 34*(6), 293-303.

Magenis, R. E., Brown, M. G., Lacy, D. A., Budden, S., & LaFranchi. S. (1987). Is Angelman syndrome an alternate result of del(15)(q11q13)? *American Journal of Medical Genetics, 28,* 829-838.

Mardirossian, S., Rampon, C., Salvert, D., Fort, P., & Sarda, N. (2009). Impaired hippocampal plasticity and altered neurogenesis in adult Ube3a maternal deficient mouse model for Angelman syndrome. *Experimental Neurology, 220,* 341-348.

Mertz, L.G.B., Chistensen, R., Vogel, I., Hertz, J.M., Nielsen K.B., Gronskov, K., & Ostegaard, J.R. (2013). Angelman syndrome in Denmark. Birth incidence, genetic findings, and at diagnosis. *American Journal of Medical Genetics,* 161A, 2197-2203.

Mertz, L.G.B., Christensen, R., Vogel, I., Hertz, J.M., & Ostergaard, J.R. (2014). Eating behaviour, prenatal and postnatal growth in Angelman syndrome. *Research in Developmental Disabilities*, 35, 2681-2690.

Mertz, L.G.B., Thaulov, P., Trillingsgaard, A., Christensen, R., Vogel, I., Hertz, J.M., & Ostergaard, J.R. (2014). Neurodevelopmental outcome in Angelman syndrome: Genotype-phenotype correlations. *Research in Developmental Disabilities*, 35, 1742-1747.

Moncla, A., Malzac, P., Livet, M. O., Voelckel, M. A., Mancini, J., Delaroziere, J. C., ... Mattei, J.F. (1999). Angelman syndrome resulting from UBE3A mutations in 14 patients from eight families: Clinical manifestations and genetic counselling. *Journal of Medical Genetics*, 36, 554-560.

Moncla, A., Malzac, P., Voelckel, M. A., Auquier, P., Girardot, L., Mattei, M. G.,... Livet, M.O. (1999). Phenotype-genotype correlation in 20 deletion and 20 non-deletion Angelman syndrome patients. *European Journal of Human Genetics*, 7, 131-139.

Mount, R., Oliver, C., Berg, K., & Horsler, K. (2011). Effects of adult familiarity on social behaviours in Angelman syndrome. *Journal of Intellectual Disability Research*, 55, 339-350.

Oliver, C., Demetriades, L., & Hall, S. (2002). Effects of environmental events on smiling and laughing behavior in Angelman syndrome. *American Journal on Mental Retardation*, 107, 194-200.

Oliver, C., Horsler, K., Berg, K., Bellamy, G., Dick, K., & Griffiths, E. (2007). Genomic imprinting and the expression of affect in Angelman syndrome: What's in the smile? *Journal of Child Psychology and Psychiatry*, 48(6), 571-579.

Pelc, K., Cheron, G., & Dan, B. (2008). Behavior and neuropsychiatric manifestations in Angelman syndrome. *Neuropsychiatric Disease and Treatment*, 4, 577-584.

Penner, K. A., Johnston, J., Faircloth, B. H., Irish, P., & Williams, C. A. (1993). Communication, cognition and social interaction in the Angelman syndrome. *American Journal of Medical Genetics*, 46, 34-39.

Peters, S. (2010). *A survey of conventional and complementary and alternative treatments in Angelman syndrome*. Final report of pilot study to the Angelman Syndrome Foundation.

Peters, S. U., Beaudet, A. L., Madduri, N., & Bacino, C. (2004). Autism in Angelman syndrome: implications for autism research. *Clinical Genetics*, 66, 530-536.

Peters, S. U., Goddard-Finegold, J., Beaudet, A.L., Madduri, N., Turcich, M., & Bacino, C. A. (2004). Cognitive and adaptive behavior profiles of children with Angelman syndrome. *American Journal of Medical Genetics*, 128, 110-113.

Peters, S. U., Horowitz, L., Barbieri-Welge, R., Lounds Taylor, J., & Hundley, R. J. (2012). Longitudinal follow-up of autism spectrum features and sensory behaviors in Angelman syndrome by deletion class. *Journal of Child Psychology and Psychiatry*, 53, 152-159.

Peters, S.U., Kaufmann, W.E., Bacino, C.A., Anderson, A.W., Adapa, P., Chu, Z.,… Wilde, E.A. (2011). Alterations in white matter pathways in Angelman syndrome. *Developmental Medicine and Child Neurology, 53*, 361-367.

Petersen, M. B., Brondum-Nielsen, K., Hansen, L. K., & Wulff, K. (1995). Clinical, cytogenetic, and molecular diagnosis of Angelman syndrome: estimated prevalence rate in a Danish county. *American Journal of Medical Genetics, 60*, 261-262.

Philpot, B.D., Thompson, C.E., Franco, L., & Williams, C.A. (2011). Angelman syndrome: advancing the research frontier of neurodevelopmental disorders. *Journal of Neurodevelopmental Disorders, 3*, 50-56.

Radstaake, M., Didden, R., Oliver, C., Allen, D., & Curfs, L. M. G. (2012). Functional analysis and functional communication training in individuals with Angelman syndrome. *Developmental Neurorehabilitation, 15*, 91-104.

Radstaake, M., Didden, R., Lang, R., O'Reilly, M., Sigafoos, J., Lancioni, G.E.,… Curfs, L.M.G. (2013). Functional analysis and functional communication training in the classroom for three children with Angelman syndrome. *Journal of Developmental and Physical Disabilities, 25*, 49-63.

Radstaake, M., Didden, R., Peters-Scheffers, N., Moore, D.W., Anderson, A., & Curfs, L.M.G. (2014). Toilet training in individuals with Angelman syndrome: A case series. *Developmental Neurorehabilitation, 17*(4), 243-250.

Radstaake, M., Didden, R., Peters-Scheffers, N., Sigafoos, J., Korzilius, H., Curfs, L.M.G. (2014). Educational priorities for individuals with Angelman syndrome: a study of parents' perspectives. *Journal of Developmental and Physical Disabilities, 26*, 299-316.

Ramsden, S.C., Clayton-Smith, J., Birch, R., & Buiting, K. (2010). Practice guidelines for the molecular analysis of Prader-Willi and Angelman syndromes. BMC Medical Genetics, 11(70), 1-11.

Rougelle, C., Glatt, H., & Lalande, M. (1997). The Angelman syndrome candidate gene, UBE3A/E6-AP, is imprinted in brain. *Nature Genetics, 17*, 14-15.

Rusinska, A., Dzwonek, A., & Chlebna-Sokol, D. (2013). Recurrent fractures as a new skeletal problem in the course of Angelman syndrome. *Bone, 55*, 461-464.

Sahoo, T., Peters, S. U., Madduri, N. S., Glaze, D. G., German, J. R., Bird, L. M., … Bacino, C. A. (2006). Microarray based comparative genomic hybridization testing in deletion bearing patients with Angelman syndrome: Genotype-phenotype correlations. Journal of Medical Genetics, 43, 512-516.

Sandanam, T., Beange, H., Robson, L., Woolnough, H., Buchholz, T., & Smith, A. (1997). Manifestations in institutionalized adults with Angelman syndrome due to deletion. *American Journal of Medical Genetics, 70*, 415-420.

Smith, A., Wiles, A., Haan, E., McGill, J., Wallace, G., Dixon, J.,…Trent, R.J. (1996). Clinical features in 27 patients with Angelman syndrome resulting from DNA deletion. *Journal of Medical Genetics, 33*, 107-112.

Steffenburg, S., Gillberg, C., Steffenburg, U., & Kyllerman, M. (1996). Autism in Angelman syndrome: A population-based study. *Pediatric Neurology, 14*, 131-136.

Strachan, R., Shaw, R., Burrow, C., Horsler, K., Allen, D., & Oliver, C. (2009). Experimental functional analysis of aggression in children with Angelman syndrome. *Research in Developmental Disabilities, 30*, 1095-1106.

Summers, J. (in press). Application of principles of applied behavior analysis in addressing challenging behaviors in individuals with Angelman syndrome. In S.N. Calculator (Ed.), *Angelman Syndrome: Communication, Education and Related Considerations*. Bentham Books.

Summers, J. (2012a). Neurodevelopmental outcomes in children with Angelman syndrome after 1 year of behavioural intervention. *Developmental Neurorehabilitation, 15*, 239-252.

Summers, J. (2012b). Social and environmental influences on aggressive behavior in individuals with Angelman syndrome. Informational Series on Angelman Syndrome Behaviors developed by the *Canadian Angelman Syndrome Society and Angelman Syndrome Foundation*. Retrieved from www.angelmanbehaviors.org

Summers, J. A., Allison, D. B., Lynch, P. S., & Sandler, L. (1995). Behaviour problems in Angelman syndrome. *Journal of Intellectual Disability Research, 39*, 97-106.

Summers, J. A., & Feldman, M. A. (1999). Distinctive pattern of behavioral functioning in Angelman syndrome. *American Journal on Mental Retardation, 104*, 376-384.

Summers, J., & Hall, E. (2008). Impact of an instructional manual on the implementation of ABA teaching procedures by parents of children with Angelman syndrome. *Journal on Developmental Disabilities, 14*, 26-34.

Summers, J., & Impey, J. (2011). Evaluating joint attention initiation and responding in children with Angelman syndrome. *Journal of Applied Research in Intellectual Disabilities, 24*, 450-458.

Summers, J. A., Lynch, P. S., Harris, J. C., Burke, J. C., Allison, D. B., & Sandler, L. (1992). A combined behavioral/pharmacological treatment of sleep-wake schedule disorder in Angelman syndrome. *Journal of Developmental and Behavioral Pediatrics, 13*, 284-287.

Summers, J., & Szatmari, P. (2009). Using discrete trial instruction toteach children with Angelman syndrome. *Focus on Autism and Other Developmental Disabilities, 24*, 216-226.

Summers, J., Taylor-Weir, D., & Kako, M. (2014). Angelman syndrome. Implications for applied behaviour analysis. In D. Griffiths, R.A. Condillac & M. Legree (Eds.), *Genetic Syndromes and Applied Behaviour Analysis* (pp. 197-223). London: Jessica Kingsley.

Tan, W-H., Bacino, C. A., Skinner, S. A., Anselm, I., Barbieri-Welge, R., Bauer-Carlin, A., ... Bird, L. M. (2011). Angelman Syndrome: Mutations influence features in early childhood. *American Journal of Medical Genetics, Part A., 155*, 81-90.

Tan, W-H., Bird, L.M., Thibert, R.L., & Williams, C.A. (2014). If not Angelman, what is it? A review of Angelman-like syndromes. *American Journal of Medical Genetics Part A, 164A,* 975-992.

Thibert, R.L., Conant, K.D., Braun, E.K., Bruno, P., Said, R.R., Nespeca, M.P., & Thiele, E.A. (2009). Epilepsy in Angelman syndrome: A questionnaire-based assessment of the natural history and current treatment options. *Epilepsia, 50*(11), 2369-2376.

Thibert, R., Pfeifer, H.H., Larson, A.M., Raby, A.R., Reynolds, A.A., Morgan, A.K., & Thiele, E.A. (2012). Low glycemic index treatment for seizures in Angelman syndrome. *Epilepsia, 53*(9), 1498-1502.

Thibert, R.L., Larson, A.M., Hsieh, D.T., Raby, A.R., & Thiele, E.A. (2013). Neurologic manifestations of Angelman syndrome. *Pediatric Neurology, 48*(4), 271-279.

Thomson, A. K., Glasson, E. J., & Bittles, A. H. (2006). A long-term population-based clinical and morbidity profile of Angelman syndrome in Western Australia: 1953-2003. *Disability and Rehabilitation, 28,* 299-305.

Trillingsgaard, A., & Ostergaard, J. R. (2004). Autism in Angelman syndrome: An exploration of comorbidity. *Autism, 8*(2), 163-174.

Van Lierde, A., Atza, M. G., Giardino, D., & Viani, F. (1990). Angelman's syndrome in the first year of life. *Developmental Medicine and Child Neurology, 32,* 1011-1016.

Varela, M. C., Kok, F., Otto, P. A., & Koiffmann, C. P. (2004). Phenotypic variability in Angelman syndrome: Comparison among different deletion classes and between deletion and UPD subjects. *European Journal of Human Genetics, 12,* 987-992.

Walz, N. C. (2007). Parent report of stereotyped behaviors, social interaction, and developmental disturbances in individuals with Angelman syndrome. *Journal of Autism and Developmental Disorders, 37,* 940-947.

Walz, N. C., & Baranek, G. T. (2006). Sensory processing patterns in persons with Angelman syndrome. *American Journal of Occupational Therapy, 60,* 472- 479.

Walz, N.C., & Benson, B.A. (2002). Behavioral phenotypes in children with Down syndrome, Prader-Willi syndrome, Angelman syndrome or non-specific mental retardation. *Journal of Developmental and Physical Disabilities, 14,* 307-321.

Willems, P. J., Dijkstra, I., Brouwer, O. F., & Smit, G. P. A. (1987). Recurrence risk in the Angelman ("happy puppet") syndrome. *American Journal of Medical Genetics, 27,* 773-780.

Williams, C. A. (2010). The behavioral phenotype of the Angelman syndrome. *American Journal of Medical Genetics, 154C:* 432-437.

Williams, C. A., Angelman, H., Clayton-Smith, J., Driscoll, D. J., Hendrickson, J. E., Knoll, J. H. M., ... Zori, R. T. (1995). Angelman syndrome: Consensus for diagnostic criteria. *American Journal of Medical Genetics, 56,* 237-238.

Williams, C. A., Beaudet, A. L., Clayton-Smith, J., Knoll, J. H., Kyllerman, M., Laan, L. A., ... Wagstaff, J. (2006). Angelman Syndrome 2005: Updated Consensus for Diagnostic Criteria. *American Journal of Medical Genetics*, 140A, 413-418.

Williams, C.A., Driscoll, D.J., & Dagli, A. (2010). Clinical and genetic aspects of Angelman syndrome. *Genetic Medicine*, 12(7), 385-395.

Williams, C. A., Zori, R. T., Hendrickson, J., Stalker, H., Marum, T., Whidden, E., ... Driscoll, D.J. (1995). Angelman syndrome. *Current Problems in Pediatrics*, 25, 216-231.

Williams, C. A., Zori, R. T., Stone, J. W., Gray, B. A., Cantu, E. S., & Ostrer, H. (1990). Maternal origin of 15q11-13 deletions in Angelman syndrome suggests a role for genetic imprinting. *American Journal of Medical Genetics*, 35, 350-353.

Wilson, B.J., Sundaram, S.K., Huq, A.H.M., Jeong, J-W., Halverson, S.R., Behen, M.E....Chugani, H.T. (2011). Abnormal language pathway in children with Angelman syndrome. *Pediatric Neurology*, 44(5), 350-356.

Wink, L. (2012). Mental health influences on aggressive behaviour in individuals with Angelman syndrome. Informational Series on Angelman Syndrome Behaviors developed by the *Canadian Angelman Syndrome Society and Angelman Syndrome Foundation*. Retrieved from www.angelmanbehaviors.org

Wulffaert, J., Scholte, E.M., & Van Bercklaer-Onnes, I.A. (2010). Maternal parenting stress in families with a child with Angelman syndrome or Prader-Willi syndrome. *Journal of Intellectual and Developmental Disability*, 35(3), 165-174.

Yamada, K. A., & Volpe, J. J. (1990). Angelman's syndrome in infancy. *Developmental Medicine and Child Neurology*, 32, 1005-1010.

Zingale, M., Zuccarello, R., Buono, S., Elia, M., Alberti, A., Failla, P., & Romano, C. (2012). Communicative and cognitive functioning in Angelman syndrome with UBE3A mutation: A case report. *Life Span and Disability*, 1, 55-67.

Zori, R. T., Hendrickson, J., Woolven, S., Whidden, E. M., Gray, B. & Williams, C. A. (1992). Angelman syndrome: Clinical profile. *Journal of Child Neurology*, 7, 270- 278.

Demysifying Syndromes II

CHAPTER 9

Smith-Lemli-Opitz Syndrome

Malgorzata J. M. Nowaczyk & Elaine Tierney

Introduction

Smith-Lemli-Opitz Syndrome (SLOS) is an *inherited* disorder caused by a defect in the body's *synthesis of cholesterol*. It presents with a characteristic pattern of birth defects associated with mental impairment of variable degree and behavioral abnormalities. SLOS arises as a result of an inherited deficiency of an enzyme called DHCR7 that catalyzes the last step of cholesterol synthesis and causes a generalized cholesterol deficiency. The discovery of the underlying defect has led to an explosion of knowledge of this biochemical pathway. Until this discovery, there were no known biochemical disorders that caused syndromes with multiple birth defects. The gene responsible for SLOS, *DHCR7*, was identified in 1998 by three independent laboratories and specific mutations in individuals with SLOS have been identified. Thus SLOS is the first *metabolic malformation syndrome* known to man with profound effects on the body plan. A number of other defects of the cholesterol synthetic pathway have been found, and a new understanding of the role cholesterol plays in human and vertebrate development and in human behavior has been reached.

Historical Note

SLOS is named after the three physicians who first described this condition: the late Dr. David W. Smith was the father of North American clinical genetics and dysmorphology; Dr. John M. Opitz is the founding editor of *American Journal of Medical Genetics,* the most widely read and quoted clinical genetics journal. They reported three unrelated boys with distinctive facial features, microcephaly, genital anomalies, severe feeding disorder, and global developmental delay (Smith,

Lemli, & Opitz, 1964). These boys were so similar in their appearance that the mother of one of them, when shown the baby picture of one of the others, was certain that it was her son's photograph. All three had an engaging personality and loved to be hugged; however, they also had difficult behaviors characterized by hyperactivity, self-injury, and autistic features. Subsequently, in his innate modesty, Dr. Opitz had suggested an alternative name derived from the first letters of the last names of the original individuals, the RHS syndrome.

For the thirty years since its initial description, this syndrome was one of many esoteric syndromes hidden away in dysmorphology journals and atlases, known only to clinical geneticists and dysmorphologists. However, throughout the years there were clinical clues that suggested an underlying defect of cholesterol metabolism. As early as 1963, there were reports that mouse and rat pups prevented from synthesizing cholesterol during pregnancy had birth defects similar to those observed in individuals with SLOS. Individuals with SLOS who died in infancy or as newborns had large adrenal glands with no lipid (specialized form of fat and cholesterol). Estriol, a pregnancy-related hormone, was suppressed in pregnancies affected with SLOS. These clinical observations have a common denominator — deficiency of the basic building block of steroid hormones, cholesterol. But it was not until 1993 that two individuals with SLOS had their cholesterol level measured. A special laboratory test performed at that time determined that they not only had low plasma cholesterol, but an elevated level of another chemical as well. That compound, 7-dehydrocholesterol (7DHC), was cholesterol's immediate precursor. And so it became clear that this syndrome was caused by a simple biochemical defect in the conversion of 7DHC to cholesterol (Tint et al., 1994).

Another interesting facet of SLOS is its behavioral peculiarities. Individuals with SLOS have a characteristic pattern of behaviors many of which abate or improve when cholesterol therapy starts. How does low cholesterol or elevated 7DHC affect these changes? Is there a relationship between cholesterol, 7DHC, and behavior, personality and psychiatric disorders? Again, evidence mounts that indeed cholesterol plays an important role in normal and abnormal behaviors. Such is the fascinating story of the discovery and the study of SLOS.

Biochemical *Précis*

SLOS is caused by a deficiency of an enzyme involved in formation of cholesterol in the body. This enzyme, called 7-dehydrocholesterol reductase (DHCR7), converts a precursor chemical 7-dehydrocholesterol (7DHC) to cholesterol. In people with SLOS this enzyme is either absent or functions abnormally (Tint et al., 1994). As a result, there is not enough cholesterol produced in the body and 7DHC accumulates, as demonstrated in Figure 1. Cholesterol is an important building block for the body's cell membranes, the myelination of the central nervous system, the formation of all steroid hormones (e.g., cortisol, testosterone, estrogen), and the formation of the bile acids necessary for digestion of fats. Cholesterol deficiency, and possibly elevated 7DHC levels, cause birth defects during prenatal life and poor growth and developmental delays in infancy and childhood. The severity of the physical findings of SLOS is related to the level of cholesterol in the plasma: the lower the cholesterol level the more severe the condition.

Figure 1:

The pivotal role of cholesterol

Figure 1. The pivotal role of cholesterol.

7 dehydrocholesterol

DHCR7 enzyme: deficient in SLOS

cholesterol

Liver: **bile acids** and digestion of fats

Brain, spinal cord and nerves: **myelination**

Bone: **Vitamin D**

Adrenal gland: **steroid hormones**

Testes/Ovaries: **sex hormones**

Nowaczyk, 2001

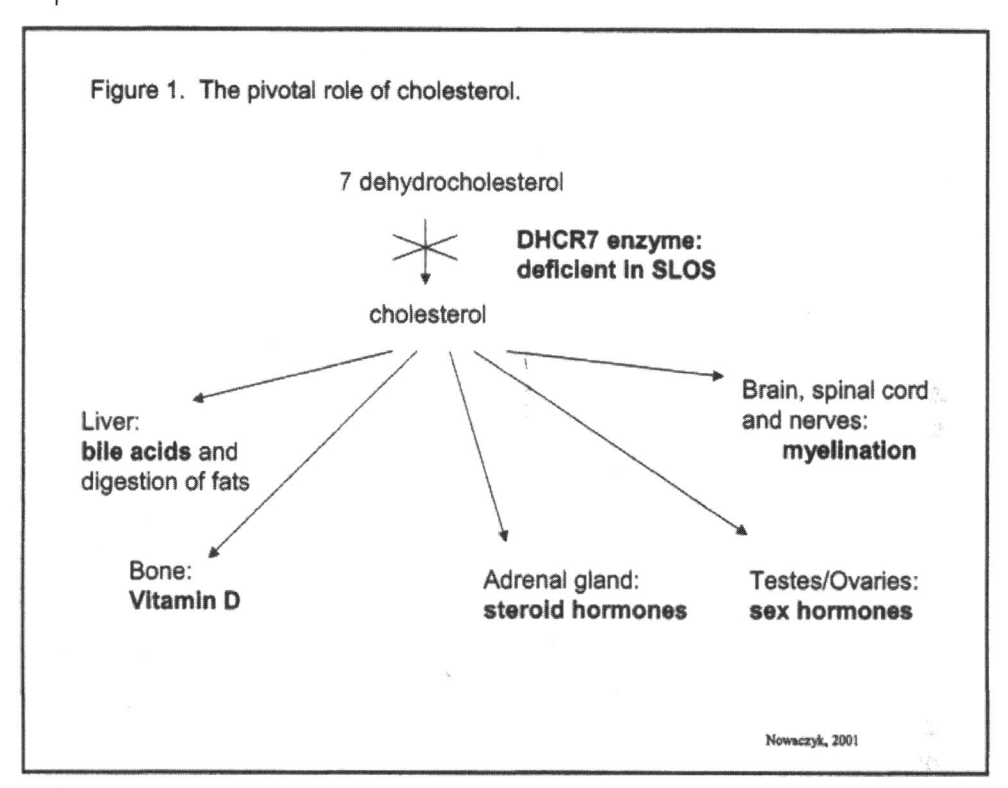

Genetics and Genetic Counselling

SLOS is considered an *autosomal recessive* condition, which means that it is inherited from parents who are both carriers of an abnormally functioning gene (Nowaczyk 2013). Only children inheriting two copies of the SLOS gene, i.e., one copy from each parent, develop the disease (See Figure 2 for an explanation of autosomal recessive inheritance). Parents of children with SLOS are obligate *carriers*, but the presence of a normal gene compensates for the presence of the SLOS gene, which explains why apparently healthy parents can have a child with this type of hereditary condition. When a child with SLOS is conceived, she or he inherits the SLOS gene from both parents. Since both parents also carry a normal gene, any future children they might have could inherit either the SLOS or normal gene from either of them, resulting in a 25% risk of any future child inheriting two copies of the gene from their parents. In other words, there is a 1:4 chance that any child of a carrier couple would have the same condition. There is a 50% chance that any child would inherit one copy of the SLOS gene from either parents and be a carrier. Finally, there is a 25% chance that a child will inherit the normal gene from both parents and therefore not carry the SLOS gene at all. The 25% risk of occurrence is the same for each pregnancy, and does not change with the birth of normal or affected child. Therefore, having one affected child neither increases nor decreases the risk of recurrence of the disease in the future children.

Figure 2.

Autosomal recessive inheritance

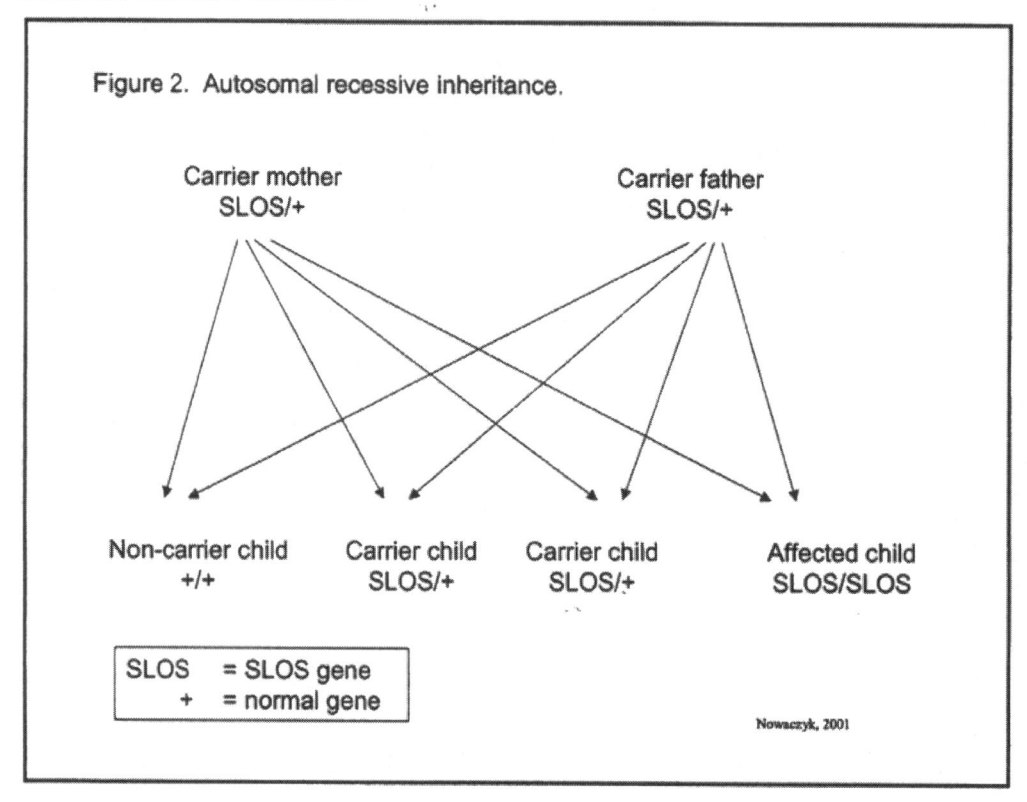

Incidence and Carrier Frequency

SLOS is most common among populations of western and central European origin (Nowaczyk & Waye, 2001). From studies of SLOS it has been estimated that approximately 1:50 Caucasians in North America are carriers. Estimates of the incidence of SLOS vary considerably depending on the diagnostic criteria used and the population being studied. The incidence of severe SLOS in the former Czechoslovakia is estimated to be between 1 in 10,000 and 1 in 20,000, while SLOS occurs less frequently in the more mixed populations of the United Kingdom and North America. SLOS is estimated at 1 in 30,000 for New England (Holmes, 1996), 1 in 20,000 for British Columbia (Lowry & Yong, 1980), and 1 in 26,500 for Ontario (Nowaczyk, McCaughey, Whelan, & Porter, 2001). However, incidence information may be influenced by the fact that in mildly affected individuals the diagnosis of SLOS may be missed. In addition, these estimates may not include the most severe cases, which result in prenatal losses or death in the newborn period. Table 1 provides a summary of SLOS incidence and etiology.

Table 1:
SLOS incidence and etiology

SLOS Genetics in Numbers:	
Incidence	1 in 20,000 – 1 in 50,000
Carrier frequency	1 in 30 – 1 in 50
Risk of recurrence	1 in 4
Number of known mutations	>150
Number of SLOS genes	1

The biochemical abnormalities of SLOS allow an accurate and rapid *prenatal diagnosis*, which is available for families *at increased risk*. SLOS can be diagnosed on material obtained either by amniocentesis at 15 to 20 weeks of pregnancy or by chorionic villus sampling, as early as 11-12 weeks of the pregnancy. Prenatal diagnosis is also available by molecular methods, by determining whether the fetus has inherited two mutated copies of the DHCR7 gene.

SLOS Gene and Its Mutations

The gene involved in SLOS, called *DHCR7*, was identified and mapped to the long arm of chromosome 11 in 1998 (Fitzky et al., 1998; Wassif et al., 1998; Waterham et al., 1998). Currently, more than 150 mutations have been found in individuals with SLOS (Waterham & Hennekam, 2012). The most common mutation, called IVS8-1G>C, causes a complete loss of function and is found in the most severely affected individuals. However, it can also be found in less affected individuals if it is combined with a mutation that preserves some of the enzyme's activity. Most of the surviving individuals with SLOS have at least one mild mutation, while individuals with the lethal forms of SLOS often have enzymes with no residual activity (Waterham & Hennakam, 2012). However, because there are so many different mutations, it is not possible to predict the severity of the condition accurately based on the mutations only.

Physical Features and Natural History

The physical features of SLOS present a *spectrum of variable severity* ranging from severely affected individuals with lethal defects (e.g., holoprosencephaly, renal agenesis) to individuals with minor physical findings who have minimal intellectual impairment or behavioral abnormalities (Kelley & Hennekam, 2000; Nowaczyk & Irons, 2013). The latter individuals may be *misdiagnosed* as having idiopathic intellectual disability, attention deficit-hyperactivity disorder, or autism spectrum disorder (Diaz-Stransky & Tierney, 2012). On the other extreme, individuals with SLOS may have birth defects that may involve all body systems. It is the number and severity of the birth defects that determine the life expectancy and level of functioning. See Table 2 for a summary of common physical effects of SLOS.

Table 2.
Birth Defects Observed in SLOS

Mouth	Cleft palate, cleft lip, excessive sublingual tissue, broad and ridged gums
Face	Epicanthal folds, narrow forehead, short nose, small chin, low set ears, forehead birthmarks, droopy eyelids
Central nervous	Small head, internal brain anomalies
Eyes	Cataracts
Cardiovascular	Complex heart defects of various kinds
Gastrointestinal	Pyloric stenosis, Hirschsprung disease
Liver	Absent gallbladder
Genitalia	Male: hypospadias, undescended testicles, female-appearing
	Female: vaginal or uterine anomalies, hypoplastic labia
Lung	Lung cysts, other major malformations, floppy windpipe
Skeleton	Webbing of 2nd and 3rd toe, club foot, extra fingers or toes

The characteristic facial features of SLOS are microcephaly (small head size), narrow forehead, epicanthal folds, ptosis (droopy eyelids), short nose with anteverted nostrils, micrognathia (small chin), and a hemangioma (reddish birth mark) over the nasal bridge extending onto the forehead. The ears appear low-set, and are posteriorly rotated, but are otherwise normal. The classic, characteristic "SLOS face" may be very subtle in some individuals (Nowaczyk, Tan, Hamid, & Allanson, 2012). In cases with cleft lip, the facial features may be difficult to detect. Oral findings include cleft palate or a high arched and narrow palate, as well as broad and ridged gums. In mildly affected children, the facial features may be subtle and not obvious to the untrained eye.

Although many different forms of CNS anomalies have been reported, individuals with SLOS most commonly have normal appearing brains. About 5% of individuals have various forms of holoprosencephaly (a severe brain abnormality). Extra digits can be found on the hands or feet, or both. The thumb is short and placed close to the wrist; the index finger often has a subtle "zigzag" alignment. The most characteristic finding is the Y-shaped webbing of the 2nd and 3rd toes. Genital anomalies are common in the most severely affected children. The external genitalia in boys range from normal male to female appearing or ambiguous. Girls with SLOS usually have normal genitalia. Congenital heart defects are seen in about fifty percent of individuals with SLOS. About one quarter of individuals have kidney anomalies, such as a small kidney or its absence, kidney cysts, renal swelling, and structural abnormalities of the ureters and bladder. Laryngomalacia and tracheomalacia (floppy larynx and windpipe) may result in breathing difficulties during sleep and in sleep apnea. Abnormalities of intestinal motility (vomiting, gastroesophageal reflux, feeding intolerance, gastrointestinal irritability, and allergies) as well as pyloric stenosis are frequent and contribute significantly to the morbidity. In more severely affected newborns, abnormal lungs, lung hypoplasia, and Hirschsprung disease, involving variable lengths of the gut are common. Eye abnormalities include congenital cataracts and optic nerve hypoplasia.

The severe failure to thrive often overshadows other problems in *surviving* children with SLOS. Newborns and infants may require tube feeding, which in many cases may be permanent. Gastroesophageal reflux with vomiting, gagging, and failure to thrive are frequent. A hypermetabolic state requiring caloric intake significantly in excess of the calculated need based on weight and level of activity is seen in many individuals with SLOS. Syndrome specific growth charts are available (Lee et al., 2012) and allow for appropriate following of the growth of children with SLOS. Low muscle tone is universal in infancy, but it improves with age. Hypertonia, contractures, and orthopedic complications may develop in non-ambulatory children. Recurrent infections (ear infections, pneumonia) are common, as is significant photosensitivity. Other complications that may occur in individuals with SLOS are adrenal insufficiency, liver disease in severely affected newborns, and difficulties with anesthesia (Choi & Nowaczyk, 2000). The type and number of medical specialists and allied health professionals involved with these individuals attests to the complexity of the continuing care of even the least severely affected individuals with SLOS.

Table 3:
Medical and Health Care Specialists
Medical Specialists:
- Gastroenterologist
- Allergist
- Surgeon Neurologist ENT specialist
- Geneticist
- Infectious disease specialist
- Cardiologist
- Nephrologist Urologist
- Developmental specialist
- Anaesthetist
- Psychiatrist (for child and parents)

Health Care Professionals:
- Speech therapist
- Physiotherapist
- Occupational therapist
- Genetic counselor
- Dietician Pharmacist
- Psychologist (for child and parents)
- Behavioral psychologist (for child and parents)
- Educational specialists

Diagnosis

SLOS should be considered in **all** children presenting with the characteristic pattern of malformations and facial features. However, recent evidence shows that SLOS should also be ruled out in children without the severe or characteristic features but who present with autistism spectrum disorder, idiopathic intellectual disability with/without hyperactivity, and idiopathic attention deficit disorder-hyperactivity.

The clinical diagnosis of SLOS requires **biochemical confirmation** by demonstrating elevated serum levels of 7DHC (Tint et al., 1994). Biochemical diagnosis may also be possible on preserved samples from autopsy, neonatal screening blood spots, or stored amniotic fluid or plasma, if no blood samples are available after the death of a child. Approximately 10% of individuals with SLOS have normal levels of cholesterol, and therefore measurement of cholesterol level is not a reliable screening test for SLOS (Nowaczyk, 2013). The levels of 7DHC can also be minimally increased in individuals who are being treated with haloperidol and can lead to false positive results. In these cases the 7DHC levels are directly proportional to the dose of haloperidol and decrease to normal upon discontinuation of haloperidol. 7DHC can also be elevated with tradozone and aripiprazole, (Hall et al., 2012), clozapine, chlorpromazine, and imipramine (Lauth et al., 2010).

The diagnosis of SLOS can also be confirmed using molecular genetics techniques by showing that the patient inherited two copies of the SLOS gene. This method is also used for determining if other members of the family are carriers. Molecular DNA testing is also available for prenatal diagnosis.

Table 4:
Difficulties in Surviving Children
Medical problems
- Failure to thrive
- Feeding intolerance
- Food allergies
- Seizures (uncommon)
- Severe photosensitivity
- Sleep problems; sleep fragmentation; decreased sleep duration

Behavioral problems
- Hypersexuality
- Self-injury
- Autistic spectrum behaviors
- Developmental delays

Behavioral Presentation

Many individuals with SLOS who survive the newborn period have mild to minimal physical problems; however, it is these individuals that have the most severe behavioral problems because of their increased strength and ability to move.

The behavioral presentation of SLOS may include sensory hypersensitivity, anxiety, self-injury, stereotypies (unusual movements), and sometimes aggression. Sensory hyperactivity/sensory hypersensitivity may present with intolerance of various senses such as tactile hypersensitivity and auditory hypersensitivity (Nwokoro & Mulvihill, 1997; Ryan et al., 1998). These individuals tend not to walk on grass or sand barefooted. Certain noises tend to bother them disproportionately. These include sounds that are bothersome to the general population, such as the sound of fingernails on a chalkboard, but also include other sounds. Individuals with SLOS may be bothered by sirens, bells, and vacuum cleaners and can be bothered by any sound they hear. Oral sensitivity may also be present. The individuals tend to refuse oral feedings, which may be due to various causes including gastroesophageal reflux and possibly swallowing difficulties. When they do eat, they may be very food selective in choosing to eat few foods or choosing only foods of a certain texture. Individuals may like to smell objects as well. Visual stimulation is sometimes avoided, and individuals may be overly sensitive to light or the flickering of light.

Individuals who are oversensitive to certain stimuli often are fascinated by other stimuli associated with that same sense. For example, a person who would not walk on grass or would avoid sticky items may like to rub soft and silky textures. Individuals who will not take oral feeding may place many non-edible items in their mouths and may swallow the items (pica). Individuals who dislike certain noises, such as that from a vacuum cleaner, may be fascinated by the sounds of paper being crinkled or the noise a toy makes.

Individuals often show anxiety and distress out of keeping with various situations. New social situations may be distressing, as are changes in daily routines and physical changes at home (e.g., furniture being moved).

Table 5:
Characteristic Behaviors of SLOS
Sensory hypersensitivity
- tactile
- auditory
- visual
- oral tactile

Autistic spectrum behaviors
- gaze avoidance
- stereotypies

Anxiety

Self-injury

Hyperactivity/attention deficits

Backward arching

Fifty percent of individuals with SLOS have a characteristic movement (*opisthokinesis*) in which they throw themselves backward in an arching motion that is usually very sudden in nature (Tierney, Nwokoro, & Kelly, 2000). Thirty-five to 50% of individuals have been self-injurious at some time (Ryan et al., 1998;

Tierney et al., 2001), most commonly taking the form of biting of the forearms. The bites can leave bruises or break the skin. Chronic biting can lead to persistent skin discoloration, coarsening, and secondary infections.

Sleep disturbance can be a severe impairment to parental and family functioning. Some individuals with SLOS require numerous sleep-aid medications, often with limited success. It is not uncommon for parents of children with SLOS to have disrupted sleep for many years (M. Nowaczyk & E. Tierney, personal observations). Please see Table 6 for more information about how SLOS can affect families.

Table 6:
Factors Affecting Parents/Siblings
- Severe sleep deprivation
- Guilt ("I gave it to my child" and survivor guilt in siblings)
- Family planning
- Worry over child's future/death
- Safety
- Socialization
- Presence of depressive disorders
- Lost time from work/Financial issues

Psychiatric Risk

SLOS has been found to be associated with autism spectrum disorder in 50-70% of individuals (Sikora, Petit-Kekel, Penfield, Merkens, & Steiner, 2006; Tierney et al., 2001). Tierney et al.'s findings suggested that early supplementation with cholesterol could improve outcome of autism spectrum symptoms. In a group of 9 subjects who started cholesterol before the age of 5.0 years, the parents were asked questions: 1) regarding the child's present state if the child was less than 5.0 years at the time of the interview, or 2) regarding the child's abilities at age 4.0 - 5.0 years if the individual was older than 5.0 years at the time of the interview. Of these 9 individuals, 22% who started cholesterol before the age of 5 years met autism disorder criteria. But, in a group of 8 participants who started cholesterol after the age of 5.0 years, the parents were asked questions regarding the child's abilities at age 4.0 - 5.0 years prior to cholesterol being started, and 88% met the autism criteria (Tierney et al., 2001).

Psychological Features and Vulnerabilities

Communication

Individuals with SLOS usually have difficulties in understanding spoken language. They have difficulty in understanding spoken words and engaging in reciprocal conversation (dialogue), which are referred to as receptive (understanding/hearing) and expressive (speaking) language difficulties. Because these individuals can understand so much more than they can communicate verbally, pictures can be used (as detailed below) to allow the persons to express their needs. These pictures can be placed on electronic devices such as iPads and are described below. Educational aids are listed below under "Education opportunities." (Kelley, 1997; Nwokoro & Mulvihill, 1997; Tint et al., 1994).

Similar types of difficulties are often seen in individuals with autism and various other genetic disorders. Because of the difficulties with spoken language, pictures or photographs can be used to communicate effectively. The use of pictures in this manner has been called Functional Communication Training (FCT) and is also often referred to as the Picture Exchange Communication Training (PECT). The pictures can be attached to an object physically or digitally on which the child can touch the physical pictures or the digital image. The object can be a device that plays a voice recording when touched. The individual's parent or guardian can record her/his voice message that says something such as "doll." Thus, when the child touches the picture of a doll, the device will state "doll" and will reinforce the child's understanding of the object and the spoken word. Devices that hold the pictures can be a round base holding 1 picture, a small board that can hold a few pictures, iPads, or boards and computers that can hold many pictures and voice recordings. For individuals who have good motor ability, pictures can be backed with Velcro™, and the individual can pick up the picture and hand it to the person who can help to obtain the object or action desired. The pictures can also be placed on a ring on a belt that allows the individual to move the pictures around to find the ones he or she wants to show someone. Alternative keyboards can be used with computers to assist communication.

Social Skills

Individuals with SLOS tend to have difficulties with social interactions. It appears that after cholesterol supplementation is begun, individuals seek out interaction to a greater degree. The individuals may be affectionate and seek social interaction, but still have fewer interactions than most people and have difficulties in creating and maintaining friendships. One of the changes that may be seen with adolescents and adults is the desire for romantic relationships.

Because of the social difficulties that individuals display, social skills training can help them to learn the social aspects of behavior. This training can be performed throughout the day including at school. For example, when it is snacktime at school, the children can take turns acting as the "host" in which they offer the snack and the roles of the "host" and the "guests" can be practiced. Prior to social events, the socially expected interactions can be rehearsed so that the individual will have better social skills and experiences to draw upon.

Treatment and Interventions

Pharmacological Interventions

During an open label trial of cholesterol supplementation (Kelley & Hennekam, 2000), it was found that cholesterol therapy is associated with a decrease in the number of infections, with increased weight gain and growth, with an improved sleep, and with a statistically significant decrease in autistic behaviors. Treatment with cholesterol has been reported to decrease irritability and hyperactivity and to lead to a happier affect and an improved attention span (Irons et al., 1997; Nwokoro & Mulvihill, 1997; Opitz, 1999). Self-injury also decreased with supplementation (Irons et al., 1997). Other behaviors that decreased with supplementation were aggressive behaviors (Nwokoro & Mulvihill, 1997; Ryan et al., 1998), temper outbursts, trichotillomania (compulsive hair pulling), and tactile defensiveness (Nwokoro & Mulvihill, 1997). The sensory hypersensitivity tends to decrease as individuals became older. Individuals with SLOS treated with cholesterol have also been reported to be more sociable, including initiating hugs, and more active after having had been passive (Irons et al., 1997; Ryan et al., 1998). But, in a longitudinal study of 14 individuals with SLOS who receive continuous cholesterol supplementation, it was found the developmental quotients did not improve over time (Sikora et al., 2004)

No side effects of cholesterol therapy have been reported to date. Although the effect of cholesterol supplementation on developmental outcome is disappointing (Kelley & Hennekam, 2000; Nowaczyk & Irons, 2013), it is possible that early administration of cholesterol therapy in infancy or in childhood may improve developmental outcomes in some individuals with SLOS.

The starting dose of cholesterol is 40 to 50 mg/kg/day, increasing as needed for growth. Cholesterol is supplied either in a natural form (eggs, cream, liver) or as purified cholesterol. Because of the feeding difficulties in infants and younger children and because a cholesterol-rich diet is unpalatable, tube feeding is often required. Medical and surgical management of gastroesophageal reflux is required in many cases.

When necessary, fresh frozen plasma is used as a source of cholesterol for rapid management of infections or surgical procedures. Occasionally, when acutely ill, individuals with SLOS might develop overt adrenal insufficiency requiring treatment. There is limited evidence that statins (a group of medications used to lower cholesterol in adults with abnormally high levels), may improve residual DHCR7 enzyme activity in some select individuals leading to the increase in plasma cholesterol levels. Surgical treatment is required for birth defects such as congenital heart defects, Hirschsprung disease, pyloric stenosis, and skeletal anomalies.

Some of the medications that are used to treat behavioral and psychiatric disorders (haloperidol, tradozone, aripiprazole, and possibly other antidepressants and antipsychotics) lower the production of cholesterol by interfering with DHCR7. But, despite the potential lowering of cholesterol production, positive benefits of the medicines may help the individual.

Physical Needs and Assistive Devices

Because of muscle weakness and orthopedic abnormalities, individuals may require the assistance of physical and occupational therapists. Various devices are required to assist in mobility and strength building and to correct orthopedic problems. These apparatuses may include splints and braces for feet, standing boards, walkers, and wheelchairs or scooters for individuals more affected. Individuals who have a gastric tube will often have an automated device referred to as a "feeding pump" that delivers nutrition to the stomach via the gastric tube at the rate at which it is programmed.

Educational Opportunities

The receptive and expressive language difficulties experienced by individuals with SLOS need to be taken into account by school curricula. In addition to the communication difficulties, the behavioral features such as auditory hyperactivity, difficulty with change in routine, and the presence of repetitive behaviors need also be addressed. It is essential that the school provide speech and language therapy with a speech pathologist who is trained in augmentative techniques such as picture exchange as described above. Augmentative communication technology is required for most individuals, and it is essential that the various means of communication are used across the day at school in all classes.

Individuals usually require occupational therapy intervention to evaluate for and teach means of better hand usage. Individuals gain skills through toy use. Younger children and individuals who are more severely affected may benefit from toys that are touch- or switch-activated. Devices such as computers and adapted pencil grips may be used. For children who ride on buses, seat-belt restraints may be required.

School curriculum and other programs for child development and learning should also emphasize visual aids. These visual aids can be used in both school assignments and communication in the classrooms or vocational settings. An example is the use of a board on the wall displaying cards that show the sequence of activities for that day. Because individuals with autism have the similar language difficulties and features to these individuals with SLOS also have, children with SLOS may benefit from an autism school curriculum.

Vocational

Adults with SLOS have been reported to have profound intellectual disability to normal IQ (Kelley, 1997; Lowry & Yong, 1980; Opitz, 1999). Some adults with SLOS may present with behavioral characteristics of autism spectrum disorders. It may be helpful to have the parents/guardians share information regarding SLOS and autism symptoms so that the day programs or vocational programs can better serve the individuals' needs. There is limited research in this domain, and further research is warranted.

Socio-Sexual

Individuals with severe forms of SLOS often have delayed puberty (M. Nowaczyk & E. Tierney, personal observations). Cholesterol supplementation has resulted in pubertal changes in a number of older individuals with the appearance of facial and body hair, body odor, and acne. There are no reports of menstrual changes upon starting cholesterol. Individuals with SLOS may have normal desires for relationships.

In working with individuals who have SLOS, parents and guardians have experienced fears of behavior worsening during the teen years after puberty begins. It is unclear if behaviors are worsening during puberty more than at other ages. But, the increasing size of an individual can make the individual harder to physically control. This is another area that is not well researched and more empirical research is required.

Summary

SLOS is an inherited genetic disorder of cholesterol production. It presents with a characteristic pattern of facial features, birth defects, intellectual disability, and behavior.

Treatment with cholesterol improves the general health and behavior of individuals with SLOS, but not the intellectual outcome. Because of the complexity of medical, emotional, behavioral, and developmental problems with which these individuals present and their families experience, a multidisciplinary and coordinated care is required. Resources are available and an active and dedicated parent support group exists.

Resources

SLOS Official Foundation
http://www.smithlemliopitz.org

GeneReviews: Smith-Lemli-Opitz Syndrome http://www.ncbi.nlm.nih.gov/books/NBK1143/

US National Library of Medicine
http://www4.ncbi.nlm.nih.gov/PubMed/

Autism Society of America
http://www.autism-society.org

Autism/Pervasive Developmental Disorders resources network http://www.autism-pdd.net/

The Association for Behavior Analysis (*An International Organization*). http://www.aba.wmich.edu/memberdirectory/index.asp
This site will help you locate a behavioral psychologist who might be able to treat difficult behaviors.

Americans with Disabilities Act Document Center: http://janweb.icdi.wvu.edu/kinder/

Car and bus seatbelts/restraints information
http://www.easywayproducts.com/ schoolbus.html

Biochemical and Genetic Testing for SLOS is available in Canada though the Regional Genetic Services of Southwestern Ontario at McMaster University, Hamilton, Ontario, Canada.
National Information Center for Children and Youth with Disabilities NICHCY

http://www.nichcy.org

Information specialists are available to speak with you about your area of interest or concern. Call NICHCY at 1-800-695-0285 (Voice/TTY), phones answered "live" 9:30 a.m. to 6:30 p.m. EST; voice-mail all other times or E-mail nichcy@aed.org.

NICHCY makes available a wide variety of publications, including fact sheets on specific disabilities, state resource sheets, parent guides, bibliographies, and our issue papers, "News Digest" and "Transition Summary." Most publications can be printed off the Internet. Documents may also be requested in print. Publications are also available in alternative formats upon request.

NICHCY can put you in touch with disability organizations, parent groups, and professional associations at the state and national level (USA).

References

Choi, P.T., & Nowaczyk, M.J. (2000). Anesthetic considerations in Smith-Lemli-Opitz syndrome. *Canadian Journal of Anaesthesia, 47*(6), 556-61.

Diaz-Stransky, A. & Tierney, E. (2012). Cognitive and behavioral aspects of Smith-Lemli-Opitz syndrome. *American Journal of Medical Genetics, 160C*, 295–300.

Fitzky, B.U., Witsch-Baumarter, M., Erdel, M., Lee, J.N., Paik, Y.K., Glossman, H. ... Moebius, F.F. (1998). Mutation in the 7-sterol reductase gene in individuals with the Smith-Lemli-Opitz syndrome. *Proceedings of the National Academy of Science, 95*, 8181-8186.

Hall, P., Michels, V., Gavrilov, D., Matern, D., Oglesbee, D., Raymond, K., ... Tortorelli, S. (2013). Aripiprazole and trazodone cause elevations of 7-dehydrocholesterol in the absence of Smith-Lemli-Opitz Syndrome. *Molecular Genetics and Metabolism, 110*(1-2),176-8.

Holmes, L.B. (1996). Prevalence of Smith-Lemli-Opitz (SLO). *American Journal of Medical Genetics, 50*, 334.

Irons, M., Elias, E.R., Abuelo, D., Bull, M.J., Greene, C.L., Johnson, V.P., ... Salen, G. (1997) Treatment of Smith-Lemli-Opitz syndrome: Results of a multicenter trial. *American Journal of Medical Genetics, 68*(3), 311-314.

Kelley, R. (1997). A new face for an old syndrome. *American Journal of Medical Genetics, 68*, 251-256.

Kelley R. I. & Hennekam, R.C. (2000). The Smith-Lemli-Opitz syndrome. *Journal of Medical Genetics, 37*, 321-335.

Lauth, M., Rohnalter, V., Bergström, A., Kooshesh, M., Svenningsson, P., & Toftgård, R. (2010). Antipsychotic drugs regulate hedgehog signaling by modulation of 7-dehydrocholesterol reductase levels. *Molecular Pharmacology, 78*(3), 486-96.

Lee, R.W., McGready J, Conley S.K, Yanjanin N.M., Nowaczyk M.J., & Porter F.D. (2012). Growth charts for individuals with Smith-Lemli-Opitz syndrome. *American Journal of Medical Genetics A., 158A*(11), 2707-2713.

Lowry, R. B. & Yong, S. L. (1980). Borderline normal intelligence in the Smith-Lemli-Opitz (RSH) syndrome. *American Journal of Medical Genetics, 5,* 137-143.

Nowaczyk, M.J.M. (2013). Smith-Lemli-Opitz syndrome. In R.A. Pagon, M.P. Adam, H. H. Ardinge, T.D. Bird , C.R. Dolan, C.T. Fong… K. Stephens (Eds.), *GeneReviews®* [Internet]. Seattle (WA): University of Washington, Seattle; 1993-2014. 1998 Nov 13 [updated 2013 Jun 20].

Nowaczyk, M.J.M. & Irons M.B. (2013). Smith-Lemli-Opitz syndrome: Phenotype, natural history and epidemiology. *American Journal of Medical Genetics, 160C,* 250–262.

Nowaczyk, M.J., McCaughey, D., Whelan, D.T., & Porter, F.D. (2001). Incidence of Smith-Lemli-Opitz syndrome in Ontario, Canada. *American Journal of Medical Genetics, 102*(1),18-20.

Nowaczyk, M. J. M., Nakamura, L. M., Eng, B., Porter, F. D., & Waye, J. S. (2001). Frequency and ethnic distribution of the common *DHCR7* mutation in the Smith-Lemli-Opitz syndrome. *American Journal of Medical Genetics, 102,* 383-386.

Nowaczyk, M.J.M., Tan, M., Hamid, J.S., & Allanson, J.E. (2012). Smith-Lemli-Opitz syndrome: Objective assessment of facial phenotype. *American Journal of Medical Genetics, 158A,* 1020–1028.

Nowaczyk, M.J. & Waye, J.S. (2001). The Smith-Lemli-Opitz syndrome: A novel metabolic way of understanding developmental biology, embryogenesis, and dysmorphology. *Clinical Genetics, 59 (6),* 375-386.

Nwokoro, N.A. & Mulvihill, J.J. (1997). Children and bile acid replacement therapy in children and adults with Smith-Lemli-Opitz (SLO/RSH) syndrome. *American Journal of Medical Genetics 68,* 315-321.

Opitz, J. M. (1999). RSH (so called Smith-Lemli-Opitz) syndrome. *Current Opinions in Pediatrics, 11,* 353-362.

Ryan, A. K., Bartlett, K., Clayton, P., Eaton, S., Mills, L., Donnai, D.,…Burn, J., (1998). Smith-Lemli-Opitz syndrome: A variable clinical and biochemical phenotype. *Journal of Medical Genetics, 35,* 558-565.

Sikora D.M., Ruggiero M., Petit-Kekel K., Merkens L.S., Connor W.E., & Steiner R.D. (2004). Cholesterol supplementation does not improve developmental progress in Smith-Lemli-Opitz syndrome. *Journal of Pediatrics, 144*(6), 783-91.

Sikora, D.M., Pettit-Kekel, K., Penfield, J., Merkens, L.S., & Steiner, R.D. (2006). The near universal presence of autism spectrum disorders in children with Smith-Lemli-Opitz syndrome. *American Journal of Medical Genetics, 140*(14), 1511-1518.

Smith, D. W., Lemli, L., & Opitz , J. M. (1964). A newly recognized syndrome of multiple congenital anomalies. *Journal of Pediatrics, 64,* 210-217.

Tierney, E., Nwokoro, N.A., & Kelly, R. I. (2000). Behavioral phenotype of RSH/Smith-Lemli-Opitz syndrome. *Intellectual disability and Developmental Disabilities Research Reviews, 6(2),* 131-134.

Tierney, E., Nwokoro, N., Porter, F.D., Freund, L.S., Ghuman, J. K., & Kelly, R. I. (2001). Behavior phenotype in the RSH/ Smith-Lemli-Opitz syndrome. *American Journal of Medical Genetics, 98(1)*, 191-200.

Tint, G.S., Irons, M., Elias, E.R., Batta, A.K., Frieden, R., Chen, T.S., & Salen, G. (1994). Defective cholesterol biosynthesis associated with the Smith-Lemli-Opitz syndrome. *New England Journal of Medicine, 330*, 107-113.

Wassif, C.A., Maslen, C., Kachilele-Linjeile, S., Lin, D., Linck, L.M., Connor, W.W.,... Porter, F.D. (1998). Mutations in the human sterol Δ7-reductase gene at 11q12-13 cause Smith-Lemli-Opitz syndrome. *American Journal of Human Genetics, 63*, 55-62.

Waterham, H.R., Wijburg, F.A., Hennekam, R.C.M., Vreken, P., Poll-The, B.R., Dorland, L., ...Wanders, R.J. (1998). Smith-Lemli-Opitz syndrome is caused by mutations in the 7-dehydrocholesterol reductase gene. *American Journal of Human Genetics, 63*, 329-338.

Waterham, H. R. & Hennekam, R.C. (2012). Mutational spectrum of Smith-Lemli-Opitz syndrome. *American Journal of Medical Genetics, 160C(4)*, 263-84.

Demysifying Syndromes II

CHAPTER 10

When Syndromes Demystify: Family and Professional Perspectives

Kerry Boyd, Deborah Richards, Courtney Bishop, and Shelley L. Watson

As a parent, I often find myself doing detective work about health implications of Down Syndrome. Oftentimes, healthcare professionals tell parents that low muscle tone, elevated Thyroid Stimulating Hormone, slower growth... are "just part of Down Syndrome" (and therefore no reasons for worry; nothing can be done). Some parents learn to accept that. To what degree though is it right that we all (healthcare professionals and families) become so complacent? Which drivers for complacency or acceptance are legitimate and which ones need to be demystified?

(Mother of a three year old daughter with Down syndrome)

As parents and professionals caring for people with complex needs, we do not want to be mystified. We want to have clear cut answers and solutions to challenges. Most professionals would admit that, despite training or expertise, there are situations that are mystifying because of lack of clarity. In most helping professions, we seek clarity through language-based interactions. Clinicians and educators are typically trained in language-based practices. We become dependent on verbal interchanges or written descriptions to understand problems and generate solutions. We are comfortable when we can ask questions and get answers. When we encounter significant communication barriers we can feel ill-equipped and even de-skilled. This perceived lack of competence has been the experience of many professionals at some point in our careers when faced with people-in-need who are affected by intellectual and other developmental disabilities. Fortunately, communication barriers do not need to eclipse clinical clarity. Perplexing and complex situations can be demystified.

Demysifying Syndromes II

An appreciation of genetic syndromes can help us to "get the picture" of someone who has an intellectual/developmental disability with a complex presentation. When we work to "get a clear picture," we are seeking relevant information that leads to understanding and focused help. We can use the analogy of getting a clear picture with digital photography. Digital photographs are made up of pixels – tiny colored dots, that when brought together with sufficient density, form a picture. The more pixels (points of information), the better the resolution, and the clearer the picture. As we gather information about the person's biological makeup (much of which is based on a genetic "blueprint"), we learn about physical attributes, vulnerabilities, and cognitive or behavioral characteristics. With that information, we are better able to improve health and devise plans of care to monitor, manage, or treat problems. With the rapid developments in the field of clinical genetics, benefits are not only emerging for those affected by the more common, recognizable syndromes, but also for those who have rare conditions or small genetic mutations (fewer pixels, but nonetheless, important information).

The biopsychosocial model is based on understanding the complexity of human beings and the multiplex of influences, all the way from the microscopic to the macro-systemic: molecules, cells, organs, physiological dynamics, psychological experience, environmental influences, and social determinants of health (Borrell-Carrio, Suchman, & Epstein, 2004; Engels, 1981). At any level, there can be problems that contribute to ill health and dysfunction. Information about a clinically significant genetic anomaly can point to potential problems at any of the other levels. Although there is recognition of tremendous (and mysterious) variability among individuals, there are also known phenotypic expressions of genetic anomalies (something this book aims, in part, to demystify). When a person is identified with a well described genetic syndrome, we have a potentially rich source of information—a more densely pixilated picture of the possible and probable phenotypic features.

The accumulated information pixelates the phenotypic picture, contributing clarity to our understanding of the lifespan issues of the affected person and allowing for more informed care. Beyond the digital snapshot, the field's progress may currently be more along the lines of a digital storyboard. In our present reality, we take the best information we have and apply it to the real-life challenges people face. This is where the pixilated photograph or digital storyboard analogies fall short. What follows are family perspectives and clinician stories aimed at bringing "Demystifying Syndromes" to real life.

In my daughter's first days of life, specialists investigated and performed various tests on her to discover the cause of her unique symptoms and abnormalities. My husband and I ached for knowledge, for knowing what lay ahead and how to support our sweet baby. 5 months later the genetic testing gave us our diagnosis although as a rare disorder it failed to provide us with the glimpse into the future that we so desperately wanted. However, the diagnosis did give us and our medical team an outline of issues to be proactively looking at. It also gave us a global network of families to connect and share information with. More so, it gave us a basis to allow other support systems and community resources to partner with us. My daughter's diagnosis does not change who she is; it does not define her or limit her. Rather it is a window into her that helps us understand and support her more effectively, so that she can and does thrive.

(Mother of a 4 year old with a rare genetic syndrome)

Healthcare Perspective

Healthcare professionals have repeatedly acknowledged insufficient training to equip them for work with people affected by intellectual/developmental disabilities. Without appropriate knowledge and skills, health practitioners naturally tend to shy away or default to perfunctory examinations and inadequate treatments. In the absence of the tools of a "clear history" and "comprehensive physical exam," clinicians often feel "in the dark" without necessary information to guide management. It is well-known that even common medical and mental health problems can be overshadowed by the presence of intellectual/developmental disability. That is how my story began. Two decades ago, with apprehension, I joined an interdisciplinary team that specialized in working with adults who presented with dual diagnosis (intellectual/developmental disabilities and mental health needs). As a physician with very little prior experience, I could not picture how I would get beyond the disability-related barriers to provide competent care. Before I knew it, I found the people I met extremely compelling and the benefits of teamwork incredibly rewarding. I learned from the encounters and became confident that a biopsychosocial approach works!

Many of the children and adults seen in clinical settings have been identified with a known genetic etiology; the majority, however, do not. Appreciation of the value of genetic syndrome information for biopsychosocial understanding and care has grown over the course of my clinical career, as illustrated by a series of encounters I had with "Sandy." Sandy was one of my first patients in psychiatry specialty training. She was 15 years old at the time. Previous psychiatric consultations referred to unspecified intellectual and speech/language deficits. When I met her, I was admittedly mystified. I couldn't fully understand her communication or why she had such a dramatic cluster of problems: medical (vomiting), psychiatric (anxiety, apparent psychosis), and social (distressed interactions). Although the parents understood her speech, they were at a loss to explain why she had experienced a rapid deterioration in her thinking processes, mood, and behavior, resulting in a series of hospitalizations. In 1989, the genetic test capabilities were not sophisticated enough to pick up on her genetic condition. Services, supports, and treatments were based on fewer data points, and we had to make inferences about the reasons for her behaviors. The family continued to search for answers and relief for their daughter's mental and physical struggles.

In 1995, I met the family again, when I began to work with the adult dual diagnosis specialty service. This time a referral for genetic testing resulted in the diagnosis of 22q11.2 Deletion Syndrome (DS). This information brought clarity regarding the medical, psychiatric, and psychological struggles of this young lady. Additionally, parents and the broader team of caregivers had an emerging clinical literature to provide added direction. The family also participated in research, adding their data to clarify the 22q11.2 DS phenotypic picture for others. The genetic finding clearly did not define her, but it did lead to clearer definition to her clinical picture. 22q11.2 DS literature emphasizes the diverse presentations of individuals but also potential challenges in physical, medical, cognitive, and mental health realms. The clarity that resulted from the biopsychosocial information led to focused interventions and improved quality of life.

Since that time, I have seen many similar situations where, after learning about submicroscopic genetic influences, the affected individuals and the people around them were able to use the clearer picture to create a better reality.

> Our youngest sister, when she was 51 years old, was diagnosed with 22q11.2 DS. The diagnosis was an answer to prayer, explaining the challenges our sister faced daily and provided access to other knowledgeable specialists. The diagnosis provided us with an understanding of what we might encounter going forward, enabling us to help. Knowing the diagnosis gave our sister an answer to the "why," and it also removed some of the mystery for her. Our sister has become more comfortable living with the syndrome, knowing that she shares similar manifestations with others. We are optimistic that our sister and others, of all ages, will benefit from the worldwide work and specialized services that are now available. Living with 22q11.2DS is a learning and growing experience, for all of us together.
>
> (Sisters of a woman living with 22q11.2 Deletion Syndrome)

Family Consultant and Researcher Perspective

Fifteen years ago, I took a course on genetic syndromes through the Dual Diagnosis Certificate Program offered by NADD and Brock University. Through this course I learned about a variety of genetic diagnoses, presenting characteristics, and associated behavioral phenotypes. I was fortunate to be able to take two courses that summer, and the previous week I had learned about family-centered supports. As I sat in the genetics course, I kept thinking about the families that I had learned about in the previous week and how their experiences must be so different, depending on their child's diagnosis-specific issues. This thought is what prompted me to complete my Ph.D. in Educational Psychology and start researching families of children with developmental disabilities.

Through my research, I have been honored to meet so many amazing parents and other family members of individuals with various developmental disabilities. I am continually struck with amazement at the resilience and strength of family members who have had to advocate for the steps needed to get a diagnosis for their loved one, recognizing that something was "going on" with their child and seeking to find answers. Some parents were able to find relief and clarity with a diagnosis, others were faced with rare disorders for which little is known, and many are still looking for answers.

Families of loved ones with disabilities often seek a diagnosis with the hope of an improved quality of life, treatment, intervention, and social support (Gillman, Heyman, & Swain, 2000; Watson, 2008). In the absence of an understandable cause for a disability, some parents have expressed distress and even guilt, but discovering the cause of a child's disability can help to reduce such feelings (Watson, 2008). Trute (2005) has suggested that "not knowing" is the greatest stressor for parents, contributing to family members' anxieties and fears, but a diagnosis provides family members with clarity and a greater sense of control (Knox, Parmenter, Atkinson, & Yazbeck, 2000).

Parents who have not yet received a diagnosis are often worried about an uncertain future prognosis or the lack of specific strategies to help their child. Families without a clear diagnosis have been found to experience greater emotional burden (Lenhard, Breitenbach, Ebert, Schindelhauer-Deutscher, & Henn, 2005). As one mother of a child with an unidentified developmental disorder explained, "It's the unknown that's very difficult... Without definite knowledge of what she has, you're flying day by day" (Watson, 2008, p. 174).

As a researcher and consultant who has worked with family members of individuals with disabilities for years, I continually see the benefits of syndrome identification, whether genetic or another etiology. The information allows families to plan for supports, explain the special needs of their loved one to others, and ultimately have greater control over their lives.

> The "correct" diagnosis was important to our family in order to plan management of Stephanie's treatment team. We wanted the right combination of physio and occupational therapy, speech, seizure clinic, meds, specialists, and personal support... We also wanted to understand the natural history of Stephanie's disability and future implications—what would home life be like, what is to be expected from the disability... it really helped to know that there was nothing I could have done differently during pregnancy to prevent Stephanie's disability; that it was out of my control...
>
> (Mother of a daughter with Rett syndrome)

Behavior Consultant Perspective

Behavior consultants are often among the first professionals called in when there is confusion or concern about the behavior of a person with a developmental disability. We do our work in schools, homes, agency based residences, day programs, work environments, clinical/therapy/hospital, and other community settings. Generally speaking, our role is to clarify the purpose or function of a problem behavior

Demysifying Syndromes II

and work toward solutions. Behavior consultants can develop strategies to mitigate stressful circumstances as well as teach alternative and more adaptive behaviors. We also provide education and individualized training to caregivers. These responsibilities cannot be accomplished without a well-rounded and comprehensive assessment. Due to the risk of implementing strategies that could positively or negatively impact an individual and those around him or her, decisions must be informed. A blurry behavioral picture comes into focus by examining the contributions of biological, psychological, and social variables. One of the most useful pieces of information a behavior consultant can have is a genetic syndrome diagnosis. Knowledge of a genetic disorder is like having an outline of the picture you are trying to put in focus. Where the phenotype is recognized and well-described, we start to see more of how the syndrome features affect the person. Genetic disorder literature can provide descriptions of biological, psychological, and socially influential features that contribute to a behavioral phenotype. These variables need to be acknowledged in order to guide our assessment and aid in development of individualized intervention.

Take Carol for instance, a 54 year old women with a history of "complex, challenging behaviors." Those who know her describe her as "charismatic," "expressive," and "overly friendly." She loves puzzles and word searches. When she gets excited, she makes "a high-pitched squeal" and engages in "self-hugging." She was referred for property destruction, self-injurious behavior (skin/nail picking, biting, head banging), and physical aggression (grabbing, forcefully hitting housemates and staff). Carol has a number of medical issues along with hearing and vision impairments. Her staff members note she appears "high functioning," in that she can do a number of tasks independently (general hygiene, make meals), play advanced games (solitaire, free cell), and read books. She was employed but lost her job, not because she lacked skill, but because she had difficulty respecting interpersonal boundaries. She also kept falling asleep at work. She has "never" slept well at night. Social as she was, her opportunities were few because she could escalate to physical aggression and property destruction without warning and for no apparent reason.

A deeper examination into her history revealed that she had engaged in other high risk behaviors such as injuring herself and eloping without regard for safety. When Carol was younger, she was referred to a residential treatment program for "inappropriate sexual advances towards men" and for inserting objects into her vagina. The patterns of high-risk behaviors resulted in environmental safeguards and restrictive access to her community.

If you have not guessed already, Carol had undiagnosed Smith-Magenis syndrome (SMS). Recognizing SMS guided the assessment and support protocols in different directions. Without this diagnosis I would have invested extensive time trying to establish the possible maintaining functions of her multiple, and very challenging, behaviors. Instead, I turned my attention to her social interactions and sleep patterns. Referrals were made for medical review and psychiatric assessment. Education around the phenotypic characteristics of SMS became the foremost intervention. Her regular staff team was enlightened about the syndrome-related influences on her behavior: sleep disturbance and peripheral neuropathy (associated with her skin picking and biting). Information was provided about SMS best practices to address sleep disturbances and healthcare needs. I implemented a number of antecedent strategies (less intrusive and more proactive). The team recognized the necessity for positive adult attention and activities that capitalized on her strengths. They readily recognized her emotional immaturity, especially when stressed (regardless of how "high functioning" she appears). This, of course, is only a brief synopsis to illustrate how being cognizant of genetic disorders and associated behavioral phenotypes is invaluable to the process of getting the clearest possible picture to derive the most suitable supports and interventions.

I cannot stress enough the importance of becoming informed around different genetic disorders, acknowledging the influence on the person, and therefore their behavior, then using the available information to support that person in a comprehensive and holistic manner.

> We received a diagnosis of Smith-Magenis syndrome for my daughter at 6 months of age, which, at the time, was considered very early. It felt like we were stepping into a black hole with so much unknown. Here we had a diagnosis, but now what? We had to move forward without a roadmap. The isolation we felt was paralyzing at times, and the uncertainties were great.
>
> So, we had to surround ourselves with medical professionals who cared enough to want to understand her syndrome. We also found professionals that were willing to work with us in outlining her treatments and therapies by first taking cues from our daughter. We sought out doctors who had seen and treated rare syndrome patients before and who were also open to the challenges of treating a child with so many unknowns. These professionals also had to be partners with us, her parents, as we were the best reporters of our daughter's condition. If we saw a doctor who was not willing to invest the time, we moved on. Luckily, we found doctors and therapists who were committed to pursuing the best care for our daughter and willing to work alongside her parents.
>
> The diagnosis of Smith-Magenis also opened doors to resources and supports that may not have been available to us if this specific diagnosis was not discovered. The rarity of the syndrome gave us access to years of therapies and interventions, especially in the public school system. We were very grateful for that "advantage," and it helped tremendously in the school setting. Though the first days after the diagnosis were crushing and sad, it gave us a springboard towards advocacy for our daughter and then eventually for other families who have a child with Smith-Magenis syndrome.
>
> (Mother of an adult daughter with Smith-Magenis syndrome)

Developmental Support Team Perspective

"Perplexing," "challenging," and "difficult" are only a few words that describe the front line support staff experience when faced with working with adults who have acquired the label of "behavioral problem." More often than not, direct support professionals are left with countless questions and very few answers about a resident who is labeled as "difficult." Typically, we have to rely on personal files that have been following the person for years filled with descriptive behavior reports, psychological assessments with multiple recommendations and medical reports of "behavioral problem/developmental delay/intellectual disability," as if these findings were cause and effect.

This may be an all too common scenario for those who in fact have an undiagnosed genetic syndrome. Could the "challenging behaviors" cited in files actually be patterns related to a behavioral phenotype seen with a particular genetic syndrome? Could the behaviors be signaling a co-morbid physical condition associated with a genetic syndrome? Early reports of older adults rarely indicate these possibilities. This raises the question of whether it is beneficial for someone historically labeled as having "bad behavior" to be labeled again, this time with a genetic disorder. We struggle with the idea of adding to the litany of diagnoses if it means just another behavior plan or psychotropic medication will be added to the daily "cocktail". The bottom line question becomes: *Would another diagnosis improve the person's quality of life?* If the answer is yes, then the front line staff advocacy role begins. Support staff must decide what steps to follow in cases where the challenging behavior is unexplained. The first step is to recognize the tendency to accept the status quo (accept the "bad behavior" designation). Rather than just accept the language of past files that negatively labels the person because of his or her behavior, consider what may be driving this behavior, with due consideration to a genetic syndrome. My experience has been that it only takes one staff member to influence the attitudes and beliefs others have toward the most "challenging" individuals.

One of my best lessons about no longer accepting the "bad behavior diagnosis" was learned when I came to know a wonderful man who had these very labels documented in a thick and persuasive personal file. By 16 years old he had lived in a number of foster homes throughout his short life. His file indicated that he had "autistic like" behaviors such as hand flapping and repetitive movements. He had difficulty interacting socially and making eye contact. His impulsive and aggressive behaviors were typical occurrences. His file also went on to say that he required intensive behavioral programs to address his ongoing violence. His behaviors were unimproved by years of token economy programs, isolating him from others, and denying him activities (common practice in the 1970s and 1980s). He was moved from setting to setting in the hope that it would make a difference, again to no avail.

Then in 1990, I attended a 2 day presentation on dual diagnosis that included genetic syndromes, and medical or mental health conditions linked to these syndromes. The information sparked the thought that this man, who was labeled as having "bad behavior," may in fact have a genetic syndrome and co-morbid conditions.

Unfortunately, in the 1990s it was not easy to find a doctor who understood dual diagnosis, but after much advocacy we were able to find a psychiatrist and arranged for tests that verified this man had lived his life with fragile X syndrome (FXS). He also was experiencing temporal lobe seizures (more common with FXS). Anticonvulsant medication reduced some of the aggressive episodes that staff described as "like black-outs" and "coming out of the blue." Yet, it did not explain his impulsivity or the aggressiveness he displayed when he was refusing to go to an activity, or take a bath, or change his routine, or if someone entered his personal space. Through further advocating and probing with professionals, the psychiatrist was able to treat him for anxiety and attention deficit hyperactivity disorder (also commonly co-morbid with FXS). They realized his difficulty with eye contact and other "autistic like" tendencies described in that initial report were related to FXS. The staff team became experts on FXS, and the story changed dramatically.

> She was extremely sociable with adults. I naturally assumed that this was because I was older when she was born so that my friends didn't have little friends running around... She didn't have brothers and sisters, so I assumed this was because she just didn't have experience with children her age. And that turned out to be one of the characteristics of some children with Williams syndrome, which blew me away – you wouldn't think that that would be genetic in any way. It actually took a lot of guilt from me because I was blaming myself.
>
> (Father of a daughter with Williams syndrome)

Conclusion

Genetic syndrome knowledge integrated into a biopsychosocial approach provides a clearer picture that informs care. The relevance comes when we are face-to-face with real people and those who care for them. The benefits are experienced in various ways. When syndromes demystify, the picture can improve and change realities.

> There are some people who never know what's wrong with their child, and I think that knowing what's wrong at least gives us a hint that they are OK and some typical problems that Angelman children run into. We should be aware of that so we can be proactive in dealing with those problems. I think that's really important, and I am glad we got the diagnosis.
>
> (Father of a daughter with Angelman syndrome)

References

Borrell-Carrio, F., Suchman, A., & Epstein, R. (2004). The biopsychosocial model 25 years later: Principles, practice, and scientific inquiry. *Annals of Family Medicine*, 2(6), 576-582.

Engels, G. (1981). The clinical application of the biopsychosocial model. *The Journal of Medicine & Philosophy* 6(2), 101-124.

Gillman, M., Heyman, B., & Swain, J. (2000). What's in a name? The implications of diagnosis for people with learning difficulties and their family careers. *Disability and Society*, 15, 389–409.

Knox, M., Parmenter, T. R., Atkinson, N., & Yazbeck, M. (2000). Family control: The views of families who have a child with an intellectual disability. *Journal of Applied Research in Intellectual Disabilities*, 13, 17–28.

Lenhard, W., Breitenbach, E., Ebert, H., Schindelhauer-Deutscher, H. J., & Henn, W. (2005). Psychological benefit of diagnostic certainty for mothers of children with disabilities: Lessons from Down syndrome. *American Journal of Medical Genetics, 133A,* 170–175.

Trute, B. (2005). *Family-centred care in childhood disability services: Understanding the steps in the dance.* Paper presented at the Family Supports for Children with Disabilities Research Symposium, Edmonton, AB.

Watson, S. L. (2008). "Something you have to do": Why do parents of children with developmental disabilities seek a differential diagnosis? *Developmental Disabilities Bulletin, 36,* 168–198.

Appendix

22q11.2 Deletion Syndrome

Formerly known as DiGeorge Syndrome (DGS), Velocardiofacial syndrome (VCFS)
Incidence: 1 in 2,000-4,000 live births
Etiology: Microdeletion on the long arm of one of the two chromosomes 22
How to test: Microarray (FISH test with a standard probe will detect most, but not all, 22q11.2 deletions)

Physical Characteristics (highly variable)	Behavioural/Neurologic Characteristics	Common Medical Vulnerabilities	Cognitive Implications
Long, narrow face	***Psychiatric***	Congenital heart defects	***Strengths***
Small mouth	Autism spectrum disorder	Velopharyngeal insufficiency	Rote verbal memory
Prominent nasal root	Attention deficit hyperactivity disorder (mostly inattentive type) in childhood	Hypocalcemia	Verbal IQ
Prominent nasal tip		Hypothyroidism and hyperthyroidism	Verbal recognition
Narrow eye opening			Initial auditory attention and simple focused attention
Small ears with thick, overfolded helices	Anxiety disorders	Autoimmune conditions	
	Schizophrenia	Recurrent respiratory and/or ear infections	Word reading and word decoding
Small hands	***Neurological***	Scoliosis	***Weaknesses***
Tapered fingers	Epilepsy, seizures	Sensory problems	Arithmetic
Obesity as adults	Parkinson's Disease	Anemia	Non-verbal processing
Dental problems	Other movement disorders	Gastroesophageal reflux disease	Visual-spatial skills
			Complex verbal memory
			Facial processing and recall
			Language processing
			Reading comprehension

This knowledge can also assist in appropriate differential diagnosis (i.e., identify-

Demysifying Syndromes II

Angelman Syndrome

Formerly known as *Happy Puppet Syndrome*
Incidence: 1 in 25,000 live births
Etiology: Maternal deficiency of UBE3A gene on chromosome 15q11-q13; underlying mechanisms consist of genetic deletion, paternal uniparental disomy, mutation of UBE3A gene or imprinting centre defect
How to test: Methylation analysis followed by cytogenetic and molecular testing, if positive; mutation analysis of UBE3A

Physical Characteristics

Movement or balance disorder
Jerky, unsteady gait
Tremors (shakiness)
Characteristic facial appearance:
Long face/prominent jaw
Wide mouth
Protruding tongue
Microcephaly- small head, with flat back
Deep-set eyes

Behavioral Characteristics

Happy disposition Lack of speech Short attention span
Frequent laughter- unprovoked smiling and laughter (unknown if mood-based)
Hyperactivity
Grabbing others
Frequent smiling
Hand flapping (excited/ when walking)
Inappropriate laughter
Mouthing objects
Sleep disorder
Affinity for water, shiny objects, and musical toys

Common Medical Vulnerabilities

Seizures- 90%
Seizures become less severe with age and are the only common medical problem; appear between 1 and 3 years of age
Sleep disorders
Scoliosis and joint contractures
Constipation

Strategies

Keep active and mobile for as long as possible
Encourage physical activity
Use adaptive devices to maintain mobility
Encourage fluid and fiibre intake
Establish good sleep routine

Cognitive and Language

Strengths

Receptive language higher than expressive language
Able to use nonverbal forms of communication
Requesting skills
Better ability for concrete tasks that require less language
Adaptive skills for socialization

Weaknesses

Severe intellectual disability
Production of sounds and words
Imitation of actions
Adaptive motor skills

Strategies

Provide alternative and augmentative communication strategies (i.e., picture exchange/ picture boards, speech generating devices)

# Appendix

Down Syndrome
Incidence: 1 out of every 700-1,000 live births
Etiology: Extra copy of chromosome 21
How to test: Amniocentesis, chromosome studies

Physical Characteristics

Characteristic facial appearance:
- Small head with flat-looking face
- Small ears and mouth Protruding tongue
- Upward slant to eyes, with epicanthal folds at inner corners
- Broad neck

Short stature Hypotonia

Increased mobility of joints

Small or undeveloped middle bone of the 5th finger

Single crease across center of palm

Brushfield spots (white spots in iris)

Lack of Moro reflex

Behavioral Characteristics

Often amiable personality, a facility for imitation

Obstinacy, keen sense of the ridiculous, and excellent memory

Alzheimer's disease

14-40% of people with Down syndrome show behavioral symptoms of Alzheimer's, usually after age 45

Depression (please see Chapter 3 for discussion)

Common Medical Vulnerabilities

Congenital heart defects- 50%

Hearing loss (ear infections)- 66-89%

Ophthalmic conditions (strabismus)- 60%

Gastrointestinal- 5%

Hypothyroidism- 50-90%

Dental (crowding, periodontitis)- 60-100%

Orthopedic (atlantoaxial subluxation)- 15%

Obesity- 50-60%

Skin conditions (dry skin, eczema)- 50%

Seizure disorder- 6-13%

Risk of seizures increases with age Males are generally sterile

Fertility rate in females is low

Women with Down syndrome may be at an increased risk for post- menopausal health disorders, such as breast cancer, depression, and osteoporosis

Alzheimer's disease

After age 30, nearly all people with Down syndrome show the plaques and tangles characteristic of Alzheimer neuropathology, although there is not a direct correlation between plaques and tangles and the severity of Alzheimer's

Preventative strategies

Regular cardiac, hearing, vision, and thyroid exams

Neck radiography after 3 years Preventative dental care Weight management

Cognitive Implications

Strengths

Clear developmental trajectory

Visual memory strengths

Sequential processing intact

Can learn sequential tasks well

Weaknesses

Lower IQ scores as develop across childhood/ adolescence

Developmental rate slows throughout childhood

Average IQ is 55

Strategies

Manual signs easier to acquire- bridge to verbal language

Acquisition of communication as early as possible

Break tasks into small steps (traditional tasks analysis works well)

Inclusive setting (sociability)

Demysifying Syndromes II

Fragile X Syndrome

Incidence: 1 in 4000 males and 1 in 8000 females
Most common hereditary cause of intellectual disabilities in all populations Etiology: X-linked inheritance with trinucleotide repeat expansion
How to test: DNA analysis of FMR1 gene

Physical Characteristics
Macrocephaly Large ears
Long, narrow face Macroorchidism Low muscle tone
Hyperextensible joints
Flat feet
Soft skin

Behavioral Characteristics
Speech pattern- short bursts, repetitive phrases
Imitation skills with inflection Delayed emotional reactions Stalling-avoidance Overreaction to minor events Attention deficits
Verbal vs. physical aggression
Gaze aversion (not just poor eye contact)- starts at age 2
Hyperarousal is often the root of anxiety (eye contact, overstimulation); this is demonstrated by self-injury (hand, wrist-biting); mouthing objects and clothes; hand flapping

Strategies
Be aware of anxiety triggers:
Forced eye contact
Personal space
Tactile defensiveness
Emotional tone of peers and staff
Changes in routine
Auditory stimuli
Changes in environment

Common Medical Vulnerabilities
Mitral valve prolapse-
Seizures
Strabismus

Cognitivec Implications
Strengths
Excellent long-term memory
Verbal skills
Repertoire of acquired knowledge
Expressive and receptive vocabularies

Weaknesses
Auditory-verbal short-term memory
Visual-perceptual short-term memory
Sequential processing Sustaining attention Integrating information
Certain visual-spatial and perceptual organization tasks

Strategies
Teach task to another student; child with Fragile X will observe and learn task
Respond well to structure and routine

Rett Syndrome

Incidence: Primarily in females
1 in 10,000 female births
Etiology: Mutations in the MECP2 gene on the X chromosome
How to test: Molecular analysis of the MECP2 gene

Physical Characteristics

Wide-based gait, similar to Angelman syndrome

Poor circulation — cold hands and feet

High metabolic rate

Scoliosis

Very expressive eyes

Normal head size at birth, but slowed growth between 5 months and 4 years

Hypotrophic (underdeveloped) small feet

Behavioral Characteristics

Period of regression, withdrawal (normal progress from 6 to 18 months)

Loss of acquired hand and speech skills by age 1-2 years

Onset of stereotypies — hand wringing or washing, hand mouthing

Lifelong stereotypies — often unable to use hands

Self-injury — 40-50%

Common Medical Vulnerabilities

Seizures

Hyperventilation

Central breathing dysfunction

Sleep disturbance — 70%

Scoliosis

Constipation

Strategies

Pharmacological, especially for seizures

Careful monitoring of scoliosis

Cognitive Implications

Strength

Very expressive eyes

Weaknesses

Severe to profound intellectual disability

Severe, impaired expressive and receptive language develop between 1-4 years

Strategies

Communication board

Demysifying Syndromes II

Smith-Lemli-Opitz Syndrome

Incidence: 1 in 40,000 live births
Etiology: Autosomal recessive disorder of cholesterol metabolism How to test: 7 dehydrocholesterol analysis

Physical Characteristics
Epicanthal folds
Ptosis Microcephaly Small jaw
Small upturned nose
2nd and 3rd toe syndactyly (>95%)
Short thumbs Postaxial polydactyly Cleft palate Hypotonia
Genital malformations from hypospadias to female genitalia in boys

Behavioral Characteristics
Feeding problems as babies
Poor growth, failure to thrive
Behavioral difficulties or Autistic features
Severe sleep disturbance

Common Medical Vulnerabilities
Low blood cholesterol level
Photosensitivity
Cardiac defect
Pyloric stenosis
Constipation
Hearing loss
Frequent ear infections
Gastroesophageal reflux
Food allergies

Strategies
Dietary therapy, aimed at correcting cholesterol deficiency
Surgical treatment of pyloric stenosis
Feeding tube placement
Hearing tests are important due to risk of hearing loss
Dietician consultation
Nutritional support

Common Medical Vulnerabilities

Strengths
Acquisition of good language and adaptive skills is common

Weaknesses
Intellectual disability
Expressive language disorder

Strategies
Speech therapy
Audiology

Appendix

Smith-Magenis Syndrome*
Incidence: 1 in 25,000
Etiology: Deletion of chromosome 17p11.2 region How to test: Chromosomal Microarray Analysis (CMA) and in some cases, FISH

Physical Characteristics

Flat mid-face Flat head shape

Broad nasal bridge

Upper lip shaped like a "cupid's bow"

Fair hair and complexion

Hypotonia

Missing secondary lower bicuspids

Lurching gait

Thin appearance to lower legs

Dry skin on hand and feet

Short in stature

Short fingers Ear anomalies

Deep, hoarse voice Strabismus Nearsightedness

Behavioral Characteristics

Engaging, endearing, full of personality, a sense of humor

Appreciate attention, and appears to crave one-to-one interactions and may often compete with others for attention; eager to please

Perseveration- repeatedly asking the same questions

Onychotillomania (picking at/pulling at fingernails and toenails) and polyembolokoilamania (orifice stuffing) are common. In females there may be vaginal stuffing, which may appear like an indicator of sexual abuse, but actually form of self-injury

Self-injurious behaviors- hand biting (most common); head banging (many outgrow this); skin picking

Sleep disturbances- frequent awakenings at night; deficient REM sleep; early wake-up; narcolepsy- like episodes during day; abnormal melatonin metabolism

Poor impulse control- aggressive hugging, prolonged tantrums, outbursts

Do not adjust well to changes in routine

Hugging- aggressive (rib-crushing; indiscriminate hugging of others)

Self-hugging- almost like a tic "spasmodic upper body squeezing tic thing, with facial grimacing". This is involuntary and appears when excited (less common with age)

Tactile defensiveness

Typically difficult times include transitions from activities and changes in routine; therefore, try to prepare the individual for such changes

Medical Vulnerabilities

Sleep abnormalities- aberrant levels of melatonin, disturbed biological clock and circadian rhythm

Some have poor vision (extreme near-sightedness, detached retina)

Hearing impairments

Teeth large pulp chambers and low levels of enamel; therefore, get lots of cavities

Peripheral neuropathy (numbness/tingles in fingers and toes)

Scoliosis

Chest abnormalities (pes cavus or pes planus)

Chronic ear infections- lead to conductive hearing loss and speech problems

25% have cardiac problems

Heightened risk of hypothyroidism

Seizures

Urinary tract anomalies

Cognitive Implications
Strengths

Long-term memory for places, people, and things

Letter/word recognition

Simultaneous processing skills

Weaknesses

Moderate to mild range of intellectual disability

Weaknesses in sequential processing and visual short-term memory

Strategies

Structured classroom with consistent well defined limits

Close student: staff ratio

Reinforcers and motivators

Care providers need to be:

Emotionally neutral in response to challenges to avoid power struggles

Comfortable with close proximity

Consistent approach among staff; frequent staff meeting

*Characteristics are not in order of prevalence or incidence and may not be present in all individuals at all ages.

Demysifying Syndromes II

Williams Syndrome

Incidence: 1 in 20,000 live births
Etiology: Microdeletion of chromosome 7q11.23
How to test: If diagnosis is clinically suspected, targeted FISH analysis of 7q11.23; chromosomal microarray analysis done for other reasons will also identify 7q11.23 microdeletion

Physical Characteristics

Characteristic face: Short, upturned nose Long philtrum
Broad forehead with bitemporal narrowing
Full cheeks
Puffiness under the eyes
Prominent earlobes
Starburst pattern in iris
Hoarse voice Hyperextensible, joints

Behavioral Characteristics
Sociability

High rates of anxiety/fears/ phobias
Friendly demeanor- no stranger anxiety
Hyperacusis/ hypersensitivity to sound- increased interest in music
Difficulty making or keeping friends
Vulnerable to exploitation

Strategies

Minimize distractions (Ritalin)
Sound sensitivity management
Be attuned to obsessions- set boundaries
Social skills training Anxiety/phobia management Comfort/reassure/move on
Cognitive behavior therapy- systematic desensitization

Common Medical Vulnerabilities

Infantile hypercalcemia
Supravalvular aortic sclerosis
Other cardiac problems Hypertension
Peptic ulcers, diverticulitis
Constipation, abdominal pain
Otitis Media
Premature aging of the skin
Tendency to develop hernias, urinary tract infections, and bladder diverticulae
Strabismus

Strategies

Primary care provider should follow published health care guidelines for people with WS

Cognitive Implications

Strengths Verbal abilities and expressive language
Facial recognition
Weaknesses
Mild to moderate ID
Major impairments in visuospatial tasks

Strategies

Verbally-presented instruction in addition to visual materials
Occupational therapy for visuospatial deficits

Authors

Dr. Anne Bassett is a Professor of Psychiatry at the University of Toronto, Canada Research Chair in Schizophrenia Genetics and Genomics, and an international expert on 22q11.2DS. She holds the Dalglish Chair in 22q11.2 Deletion Syndrome and is the Director of the Dalglish Family Hearts and Minds Clinic at the Toronto General Hospital, the first clinic dedicated to adults with 22q11.2DS. Dr. Bassett is also the Director of the Clinical Genetics Research Program at CAMH.

Courtney Bishop is a recent graduate from the Masters of Arts Program in Applied Disability Studies through Brock University and is currently a behavior consultant with Hamilton Brant Behavior Services. Some of her interests include: research around advocating for the rights of persons with disabilities, the role of genetics in supporting persons with developmental disabilities, organizational change, and the collaborative support of service providers within the developmental sector.

Dr. Erik Boot is a Dutch physician, specializing in intellectual disability medicine. In 2010 he completed his PhD thesis on adults with 22q11.2DS and neurotransmitter systems, and he has been the lead author or co-author of multiple publications related to 22q11.2DS. Currently, he is pursuing a 22q11.2DS clinical and research fellowship training at the Dalglish Hearts and Minds Clinic for adults with 22q11.2DS from September 2014 to August 2016.

Dr. Kerry Boyd is a psychiatrist who has dedicated her career to the field of developmental disabilities across the lifespan. She is an Associate Clinical Professor for the Department of Psychiatry and Behavioural Neurosciences at McMaster University. She is a clinician and Chief Clinical Officer for Bethesda Services in Ontario. She also works at McMaster Children's Hospital. Dr. Boyd is a recipient of an Associated Medical Services Phoenix Project Fellowship (2013-15) with work aimed at advancing compassionate, person-centred care for people affected by developmental disabilities.

Marcia Braden is a licensed psychologist with a practice in Colorado, USA. Her specialty is treating children and adolescents with neurodevelopmental delays. She is an international expert in the treatment of educational and behavioral issues with those who have fragile X syndrome. She has developed a number of educational treatment tools, published various articles and has made book contributions related to fragile X syndrome. Her own book, *Fragile, Handle with Care* is considered to be one of the best handbook for parents and professionals.

Brenda Finucane, MS, LGC, is a licensed genetic counselor and the Associate Director of the Autism and Developmental Medicine Institute of Geisinger Health System in Lewisburg, PA. Her clinical and research activities have focused on genetic causes of neurodevelopmental disorders. Ms. Finucane has particular expertise in the behavioral and cognitive manifestations of fragile X, Smith-Magenis, 15q duplication, and other syndromes that result in complex intellectual and neuropsychological symptoms.

Dr. Sandra Fisman is Professor and Chair of the Division of Child and Adolescent Psychiatry at the Schulich School of Medicine and Dentistry, Western University, London, Ontario. She has Founder Status with the Royal College of Physicians and Surgeons of Canada in Child and Adolescent Psychiatry Subspecialty. Her interest in the autism spectrum disorders derives from her clinical work and research in families with developmentally challenged children and their families.

Dorothy Griffiths is a professor in the Child and Youth Studies Department and the Centre for Applied Disabilities Studies at Brock University, St. Catharines, Ontario. She is the co-Director of the International Dual Diagnosis Programme. Dr. Griffiths is a an author and editor of numerous books, chapters, and authors, including a recent book on Genetic Syndromes and Applied Behaviour Analysis. She has lectured throughout North America and in Europe. Dr. Griffiths has been appointed a member of the Order of Ontario and Order of Canada for her seminal work and advocacy for persons with intellectual disabilities.

Barbara Haas-Givler, MEd, BCBA is a board certified behavior analyst and educational consultant with extensive experience in special education. Ms. Haas-Givler frequently presents at local and national conferences and provides consultations and trainings. She has co-authored several publications on topics related to genetic syndromes, including frequently cited articles on the educational and behavioral manifestations of Smith-Magenis syndrome.

Chelsea Lowther is a PhD candidate in the University of Toronto Institute of Medical Science. In 2012, she graduated with first class standing from the University of Prince Edward Island with a Bachelor of Science majoring in Psychology. Her current graduate studies have focused on identifying the underlying genetic causes of comorbid intellectual disability and schizophrenia. She has won numerous academic awards and presented her research findings at several international meetings.

Dr. Margaret Nowaczyk is a pediatrician and a clinical geneticist at McMaster University and an associate professor of Pediatrics and Pathology & Molecular Medicine.

Robert J. Pary, M.D. Professor Emeritus, Department of Psychiatry, Southern Illinois University School of Medicine. Currently working on the Consultation-Liaison Service for Department of Interment Medicine, Medicine-Psychiatry Division, Southern Illinois University School of Medicine, Springfield, Illinois.

Authors

Deborah Richards, M.A., C.H.M.H. is a clinical consultant and therapist working with people who have dual and multiple diagnoses including those individuals who have genetic disorders. Her primary focus is working with those who have problematic sexual behaviors as well as victims of sexual abuse. She has a wide range of publications and has presented both nationally and internationally.

Dr. Marcy Schuster is a recent graduate of Immaculata University with a Psy.D. in Clinical Psychology who is completing her Post-Doctoral work at Elwyn. Dr. Schuster has extensive experience in behavior analytic approaches to problem behaviors particularly in children with intellectual disability and children with autistic spectrum disorder. Her post-doctoral work has focused on children in foster care and children with fragile X syndrome.

Dr. Elliott Simon is a licensed psychologist with over 30 years as a clinician, researcher and administrator in the field of intellectual disability. He is currently the Executive Director of Research and Quality Improvement at Elwyn. Clinically, Dr. Simon specializes in individuals with intellectual disability and co-occurring behavioral health disorders. His research interests include developmental disabilities and psychiatric disorders, behavioral and cognitive profiles of genetic syndromes, the conceptualization of intellectual disability as it relates to the death penalty, and the history of intellectual disability with numerous publications in these areas.

Jane Summers, Ph.D., C.Psych. is a registered psychologist. She is the Director of Interprofessional Practice for the Underserved Populations Program at the Centre for Addiction and Mental Health in Toronto, Ontario. She is also a member of the Scientific Advisory Committee of the Angelman Syndrome Foundation.

Elaine Tierney, M.D. is Director of Psychiatry of the Kennedy Krieger Institute and Associate Professor of Psychiatry and Behavioral Sciences of the Johns Hopkins University School of Medicine. She specializes in treating individuals with genetic disorders and researching the behavioural phenotype of genetic disorders.

Shelley Watson, Ph.D. is an Associate Professor in Psychology and Rural and Northern Health at Laurentian University in Sudbury, Ontario. Her research focuses on families of individuals with disabilities, as well as the sexuality challenges associated with specific disabilities.

Demysifying Syndromes II